Human Relations and
Other Difficulties

Human Relations and Other Difficulties

[ESSAYS]

Mary-Kay Wilmers

FARRAR, STRAUS AND GIROUX | NEW YORK

Farrar, Straus and Giroux
120 Broadway, New York 10271

Library of Congress Cataloging-in-Publication Data
Names: Wilmers, Mary-Kay, author. | Lanchester, John, author of
  introduction.
Title: Human relations and other difficulties : essays /
  Mary-Kay Wilmers.
Description: First American edition. | New York : Farrar, Straus and
  Giroux, 2019.
Identifiers: LCCN 2019012401 | ISBN 9780374173494 (hardcover)
Classification: LCC PN5123.W55 A25 2019 | DDC 824/.92—dc23
LC record available at https://lccn.loc.gov/2019012401

Our books may be purchased in bulk for promotional, educational,
or business use. Please contact your local bookseller or the Macmillan Corporate
and Premium Sales Department at 1-800-221-7945, extension 5442,
or by e-mail at MacmillanSpecialMarkets@macmillan.com.

www.fsgbooks.com
www.twitter.com/fsgbooks · www.facebook.com/fsgbooks

1 3 5 7 9 10 8 6 4 2

To Andrew O'Hagan who had the idea and
John Lanchester who made it happen

CONTENTS

Human Relations and
Other Difficulties

Introduction

by John Lanchester

In the 1956 edition of the Badminton School magazine, the Literary Club's end of year report describes a focus on Irish drama, concentrating on the work of Synge, Shaw, and O'Casey. Unfortunately, 'exams of all sorts have prevented us from having as many meetings as we would have liked,' but things picked up when they were over. 'At the end of the Summer Term we organised a literary competition,' reports the head of the club, 'ostensibly in aid of refugees (there was an entry fee) but with the surreptitious motive of extracting literary works for the Magazine.'

That is the first surviving piece of writing by Mary-Kay Wilmers, and the activity with which it ends—extracting literary works from reluctant writers—has been the central focus of her working life for more than 50 years. She began doing it at Faber, in the days when the dominant presence at the company was T. S. Eliot. (There was a hierarchy to the way his colleagues referred to him: seniors called him 'Tom'; underlings 'the GLP', for 'Greatest Living Poet'.) She left Faber to go and work with Karl Miller at the *Listener*, went to the *Times Literary Supplement*, then co-founded the *London Review of Books* in 1979. She has been sole editor of 'the paper'—as it is always known in *LRB*-speak—ever since 1992. That is a lot of not-so-surreptitious extracting of pieces. ('Pieces', incidentally, is another example of *LRB*-speak: the things it publishes are always known not as reviews, essays, or articles, but pieces.)

Alongside all this, though, there has always been another version of Mary-Kay, and that is Mary-Kay as writer. When I first met her, after I started out as the *LRB*'s editorial assistant at the beginning of 1987, writing was more central to her work and indeed to her identity than it is now. 'I don't go on about it,' she once said, waving away a cloud of smoke from her cigarette, 'but that's my main thing.' She meant writing. Both parts of that were true: she didn't go on about it, but it was. She put a lot of effort and energy into her writing, and always had a piece on the go to the side of her editorial work. She had written for Ian Hamilton's *New Review* (her piece on obituaries is collected here) and had had a personal thank-you note from William Shawn after he published her piece on encyclopedias in the *New Yorker* (that piece is here too). She would certainly have written more for Shawn if editing her own magazine hadn't got in the way.

Everybody who reads the *LRB* is deeply in her debt for the heroic contribution she has made to the culture as an editor. Some of us have a small accompanying regret, though, and that is that she hasn't done more writing along with it. We get the reasons: the main one is to do with time. But we miss those unwritten pieces nonetheless. She is one of the *LRB*'s most distinctive contributors, with a tone and affect that isn't quite like anyone else's. A few of the pieces I read over and again, back when I first knew Mary-Kay, trying to work out what it was about them that was different. It was a long time later that I found the key, in a remark that Janet Malcolm made about Joseph Mitchell: she used to marvel, she said, at how he managed to get 'the marks of writing' off his work. Mary-Kay's pieces are like that: they don't smell of writing.

The pieces in this book don't read as effortful, but that's misleading. Mary-Kay works as hard at her writing as anyone I know. She is not the kind of writer who does things off the top of her head: I don't think I've ever seen anyone who takes more notes. She once reported her son Will, then about 14, saying she was 'copying out the book'—it was funny because he didn't mean it as a joke, and also because, as she put it, 'that about sums it up.' The end product is clear as vodka, a clarity which is all the more striking since Mary-Kay is often in two minds about things. In her pieces she specialises in seeing both sides of a question; for instance in 'Narcissism and Its Discontents', she sees both the ways in which it must be quite nice to be a committed narcissist, as Jean Rhys was, and also the ways in which a lifelong focus on your own looks is certain to end in misery. Freud's greatness comes through in her essay on Janet Malcolm, and so does his pettiness; the interestingness of psychoanalysis as a world, and the cultish limitations of its world-view. Other pieces show us both sides of the question on subjects as diverse as novel-reviewing, Patty Hearst, and Ann Fleming. She is never more translucent than when she is ambivalent. It's an unusual talent.

The Fleming review also shows off one of Mary-Kay's great gifts, which is for apt quotation. That is one of the reasons she 'copies out the book', to home in on the most relevantly quotable part of it. In the case of Fleming's letters, the whole piece (indeed the whole book) can be boiled down to one single incident during a rowdy party. Various aristocrats were swearing uncontrollably and, as Fleming recounted in a letter to Evelyn Waugh, Deborah Devonshire turned to Roy Jenkins to intervene:

'Debo said to Roy Jenkins: "Can't you stop them by saying something Labour?"'—'but this,' she says to Waugh, 'is something Roy has never been able to do.'

That's not just a book summed up, it's a whole world.

Rereading these pieces, there were many things I remembered and one big thing I didn't. It is great fun to bask in the aphoristic asperity that is one of the big pleasures of her writing. On Jean Rhys: 'Reluctant to make any move unassisted by fate, she simply waited for men to arrive and then to depart.' On Henry James senior: 'He was ambitious in his expectations of his children, but what he required of them was intangible: neither achievement nor success but "just" that they should "*be* something"—something unspecifiably general, which could loosely be translated as "interesting".' 'Heroines endear themselves by their difficulties and until the SLA kidnapped her Patricia Hearst's only difficulty was that she was a bit short.' On Marianne Moore and her mother: 'They lived as if they didn't quite know how to do it.'

The thing I hadn't noticed, though, and which came as a surprise reading *Human Relations and Other Difficulties* in one go rather than as a series of pieces over many years, was that there is a secret thread to the collection. After the first four pieces, all the essays are from the *LRB*, and almost all of them are about women. Mary-Kay's great concern is not so much gender as the relation between the genders, and especially the effect on women of men's expectations, men's gaze, and men's power. 'It's a matter of expectations and how they can be met,' she says in discussing Jean Rhys, and that is true for all the lives she discusses. Women's reality is framed by men; it is men who have all the important agency in the world; women's agency is limited by men, is determined principally by the way they want to be perceived and defined by men. The world of her pieces is about women's lives in a man's world. As she says in a piece from the early 1990s:

I didn't do consciousness-raising with my sisters in the late 1960s. I was married at the time and it seemed to me that if my consciousness were raised another millimetre I would go out of my mind. I used to think then that had I had the chance to marry Charles Darwin (or Einstein or Metternich) I might have been able to accept the arrangements that marriage entails a little more gracefully.

Of course, it wouldn't be a collection of pieces by Mary-Kay if there wasn't evidence that she was in two minds about things. The warmest piece in *Human Relations and Other Difficulties* is about a man, Peter Campbell, the *LRB*'s longstanding designer, artist, and a presence who was 'always at the heart of the *LRB*' from its founding until his death in 2011. In 1992 Mary-Kay remarked to Peter, 'Why is it always men painting naked women? Why is it never women painting naked men?' The image on the front of this book, which was used as an *LRB* cover, is Peter's response to the question, and is also a sly opportunity to slip in a portrait of Mary-Kay. It's a picture which captures not just Mary-Kay's remark about art but also Peter's vision of Mary-Kay as an artist with her back turned, watching, judging, and covertly telling her side of the story.

I Was Dilapidated

'What did you have?'

'A boy.'

'Congratulations.'

If your first child is a girl I'm told people say: 'How nice.' How nice. My child is of course wonderful but I am also—embarrassingly—slightly proud that he's a boy. Childbirth is full of such pitfalls, where the wish to be congratulated overrules common sense. I don't find the standard notion of the good wife very compelling. But the pressure to be 'a good mother' according to the prevailing definitions is practically irresistible. I can keep my head when David Holbrook, in his most recent outburst against 'art, thought and life in our time', warns that it is a failure in mothering that produces intellectuals and other pornographers: it's less easy to steer a clear course through all the varied strictures of the psychoanalysts themselves.* Worse still, it's by no means adequate to try to behave like a good mother, because that involves an act of will: goodness itself is supposed to emerge. Before Bowlby, you only had to keep your children clean and set a decent moral example. Now ordinary self-ishness is thought somehow to be expelled in the moment of delivery, or sooner: it's selfish, you're told by the masked figures gathered expectantly around you, if you can't manage without forceps. Better mothers don't need them.

It's logical enough. Since having children is a matter of choice, or, some might say, a deliberate self-indulgence, there is an obvious obligation to do the best one can by them. What worries me is that logic is so seldom invoked: naturalness, spontaneity are the *mots d'ordre*. Which hardly takes into account the fury one may oneself feel at an infant who rages when he should be feeding, and indeed would like to be feeding if only he could stop raging. On the other hand, I find little consolation in the knowledge that if on these occasions I were to act on what I take to be my 'natural' inclination and batter my baby, the law would return a verdict of diminished responsibility and I wouldn't go to prison: I'd rather go to prison. But why is 'natural' taken to be a synonym for 'good'?

I accept that much of what I'm saying could be ascribed to puerperal paranoia, with the proviso that the form the paranoia takes derives from current attitudes. According to *New Society* it's a rare father who can change his child's nappy. Until children reach an age where they can be reasoned with, the only notices fathers get are good ones. I like changing my son's nappy—foolish of Freud not to pay more attention to Jocasta's part in the relationship. But sometimes I wonder why I'm thought to have a special scatological aptitude. People ask me eagerly if I enjoyed feeding him myself: I didn't. The first weeks of feeding were often very humiliating (I've never felt so sympathetic to men's fears of impotence), particularly when the humiliation was repeated every three hours. Now I'm proud of being a self-sufficient life-support system—farmer, wholesaler, restaurant and waiter—but initially I felt as if I'd been pinned to a conveyor belt serving a remote and self-obsessed baby. Eager to cram something into my own mouth, I took up smoking; a friend in the same situation started biting her nails.

I'd read plenty of articles about mothers getting upset when their children grow up and leave home, but it seemed a bit much to resent his leaving the womb. Still, he'd been mine before and now I was his. I couldn't sleep without his permission, I ate for his sake rather than mine, I felt guilty if I took an aspirin, and if I was late home it was as if I was capriciously denying him his means of existence. If I got upset his provisions were threatened, and if the provisions were threatened I got upset. In addition, he was admired and I was dilapidated. Childrearing manuals have a section on the importance of the mother making the father feel that he too has a relationship with the new child—but it was six weeks before I felt I had a relationship with the child myself. My husband was the supervisor, a position which left him free to enjoy the child. 'For Dockery a son,' I thought, with uncharitable memories of Larkin's poem.

In short, I didn't get depressed because I couldn't cope, as the books said I might: unless things are really bad you can always grit your teeth and make yourself cope. I got depressed because instead of maternal goodness welling up inside me, the situation seemed to open up new areas of badness in my character. Perhaps paediatricians believe in the power of positive thinking: I've always found it harmful. There's nothing magical about a mother's relationship with her baby: like most others, it takes two to get it going. Once the baby begins to enjoy feeding, once it starts responding to situations in a way that you can understand and smiling huge smiles and playing and 'talking' and watching, then you begin to feel the famous warm glow. Before that you're on your own, and the least 'natural' thing in the world is suddenly to change your character.

Sex and Dehumanisation by David Holbrook.

Civis Britannicus Fuit

If the *Times* is still in any sense the institution it once was, it's because of its letters page and its obituary column: the voice of the people (some of them) and the voice of God, a benign, very English God, or school-master, not much interested in foreign fiddle-faddle but ingenious in drawing up the end-of-term reports:

> Hugessen's career was a successful one and he was fortunate in never
> having had to meet a situation demanding more of him than he
> had to offer; for he had his limitations, of which he was charmingly
> conscious and which he openly admitted. He had not, for instance,
> the kind of compelling personality which can influence men or
> events. Indeed, there was something boyish, almost ungrown-up
> about him: not for nothing did the nickname 'Snatch', conferred on
> him at school, stick to him all his life.

Sir Hughe Knatchbull-Hugessen was British ambassador to Tur-key from 1939 to 1944. The book *Operation Cicero* described how his

Albanian valet regularly photographed secret documents sent to him by the Foreign Office and passed them on to the German Embassy. 'It is proof of the high regard felt in the Foreign Office for Hugessen,' his obituarist noted, 'that this strange affair did not affect his career.' And it is proof of the high regard God was once thought to feel for Englishmen that on Hugessen's death his many limitations were celebrated over three columns. But then Hugessen belonged to an era when heaven smiled on Englishmen, especially Englishmen of average ability; and Hugessen had 'a mind which instinctively eschewed complexities and so saved him from the pitfalls which, especially in dealings with clever foreigners, beset the path of the over-ingenious intellectual'.

Hugessen died in 1971 at the age of 84, but his obituary would have been written years earlier, possibly by someone who died long before him. If one compares current obituaries with those that were published 20 years ago what one notices first is that the notion of a state of grace—civis Britannicus fuit—has yielded to the more stringent doctrine of justification by works. In part the difference is the consequence of a policy decision. When William Haley became editor of the *Times* in 1952 he decided that inclusion in *Debrett*, or even *Who's Who*, was no longer in itself sufficient grounds for an obituary: people were to be selected on the basis of their achievement. And although inclusion in *Who's Who* is still sometimes considered an adequate reason, it too has changed.

Before Haley's decree took effect members of the aristocracy who had done nothing much beyond providing fellowship in the hunting field and conviviality at the dinner table, unmemorable members of the armed services and the Church ('he found a congenial task in looking after the Guardsmen stationed in the castle'), as well as anyone who was thought to be charming in charmed circles—friends of friends, public schoolmasters, an archbishop's wife's secretary—could all count on making some kind of splash when they died. Now they stop a hole at the bottom of a column.

Lord Shuttleworth (fourth baron and MC), who died recently, got two inches; Lord Greenway (third baron) scarcely more than one: no more than was needed to list his school and university, his regiment, his marriage and his heir—how, one wonders, did he occupy the spaces in between? When the miners' leader Will Lawther died two months ago his life was reckoned to have been some 25 times more important to the nation and his death was reported as a news item on the front page (a gauge of real fame comparable only to the fame of those, like Brigitte Bardot, whose parents' deaths are noted). Or, to take a more humdrum example, the obituary of John Bonfield, general secretary of the NGA—admittedly, a newspaper union, and perhaps a special case—ran for 15 inches, taking precedence over 'one of the most notable and learned figures of the legal and academic world in England and the Continent'. (John Bonfield was listed in *Who's Who*, Professor Cohn, the notable and learned figure, was not.)

The gain in democracy has been achieved at the customary cost in style and idiosyncrasy; these largely disappeared with the shared feelings and values that had once made it possible to spell out the shortcomings, say, of the British ambassador to Turkey, without fear of hostile readers wishing to know how he'd got the job in the first place. When Florence Nightingale died the *Times* mourned her death *in propria persona*. And readers of Mrs. Humphry Ward's obituary were told how to get to her funeral: 'The funeral will be at Aldbury, Tring, on Saturday at 3.15; the train for Tring leaves Euston at 1.40.' The obituary of Arthur Nikisch, a Hungarian conductor who died in 1922, enjoins on its readers the memory of the concerts he gave in this country, as if going to his concerts had been a national habit: 'For some his first performance of Tchaikovsky's Fifth Symphony remains a thing never to be forgotten; others can say that they never felt the thrill of Brahms's Fourth till Nikisch played it . . .' It's the tone—though the language may be too fulsome—of a school magazine paying tribute to a former master.

Yet his fulsomeness didn't prevent the obituary writer from concluding with some frosty (schoolmasterish) remarks: 'It has been said by some who knew him and admired him'—the obituarist himself on another occasion?—'that his perfect economy of the art of the stick was due to the fact that he was temperamentally lazy and hated any unnecessary physical exertion.' It's this sort of kindly blow below the belt that makes idle obituary reading an enjoyable pastime, though now that many obituarists consider themselves obliged to justify their subject's claims on our attention these jabs occur less frequently. And when they do, may exceed the proper bounds of malice—but there is more to be said about that.

The most assured obituaries were (probably always are) written within a closed circle: maybe even the circle of those whose forthcoming marriages and social engagements are announced, deaths are commemorated, on the court page of the *Times*. In November 1955 Admiral Sir William James paid tribute to his friend Buddy Needham (a major and an Hon): 'With his natural dignity, quiet courtesy'—noisy courtesy?—'and integrity he sometimes seemed to belong to an age that has passed. His type has become rarer since the impact of the last war on our standards and values and may fade out in this new age of scramble.' Whatever of the new age of scramble, dignity and courtesy and integrity are still the regular coinage of obituaries and like most of the common virtues that feature in such listings (humility is the incongruous favourite) they give little idea of what the deceased was like: but are instead attributes no one, especially not someone with a sense of being beleaguered in an age of scramble, would like to think himself unresponsive to. On the other hand, many of the pre-scramble values, confidence in which gave obituary writers their assurance, would now come under a heading of unacceptable snobbery.

Take money. Onassis got a very tart obituary, dwelling more on the fortunes he lost than on the fortunes he made and generally sneering at his character. 'From refugee to great riches', the subheading read: as a description of what followed it might just as well have said 'From refugee to stinking riches'. Even now, it seems, making money is not quite the same as inheriting it; besides, Onassis was foreign, disreputable, and notorious. A less notorious, though far more disreputable Spaniard of stinking wealth, who underwrote all Franco's endeavours both during and after the Civil War, got by fairly recently with a very bland account of his doings. 'He bequeaths his name like Croesus as a household word for riches' was the one flourish the obituary of Onassis allowed him. Lord Rosebery's wealth, however—and not all of it English—was most ceremoniously described (again in an obituary written many years before its subject's death at the age of 92):

> Albert Edward Harry Meyer Archibald Primrose, sixth Earl of
> Rosebery . . . was the heir to truly vast possessions. His parents'
> marriage had brought together the considerable Rosebery estates
> in Scotland and the wealth and properties of Baron Meyer de
> Rothschild, whose only daughter was perhaps the greatest heiress
> of her time.

The Rosebery family's five houses were then listed and the tribute continued: 'None of these imposing establishments was administered with undue regard to economy, and the splendour of the Rosebery *grande tenue* was legendary and even intimidating.'

Lord Rosebery's wealth, in other words, was celebrated with a perfectly easy conscience. Money-making is seldom mentioned in contemporary obituaries. Tributes to men who have spent their life in the City rarely refer to their success in that area: it is more likely to be discussed in cases where the subject has disposed of his money in such a way that he can be described as a philanthropist, and then the discussion is naturally influenced by the charitable context. Obituaries of City men, and personal tributes to them even more, show a pervasive uneasiness about the City's reputation. Sometimes they are concerned to defend its institutions: the Stock Exchange under Lord Ritchie of Dundee's chairmanship 'resented unfair criticism which contributed'—'attributed' I hope is the word that was meant, but it may not be—'financial scandals to the City and the Stock Exchange'; sometimes to defend their man or to single him out from the dishonest ruck: Frederick Althaus's influence, a friend or colleague wrote, 'was invariably used in the course'—cause?—'of justice and tolerance. These qualities are not so universal in the world of finance . . . that they do not occasion sincere admiration when found'; and sometimes an obituary will seek, as Sir Denys Lowson's did, to protect the City from the man's own reputation: 'In the quarter century since the war, however, the ethics of the City generally advanced in a way which placed Sir Denys increasingly out of tune with the City establishment.' Not if some of the other obituaries are to be believed.

Taste, style, tenue indeed, is another area that has become more difficult to handle. Sir Ronald Storrs, 'Middle Eastern Proconsul', was a contemporary of Buddy Needham's:

Although entirely English, he had a cosmopolitan outlook, to which were added a discriminating taste, a Voltairian cynicism, a lucidity of thought (which recalled Anatole France) and a zest for the good things in art, literature, music, cooking, conversation and, it may be added, the company of those who were doing important things in the world of affairs and of society.

This cultural/culinary scrambled egg doesn't elicit a warm response in the now ageing age of scramble; but it has to be said that allusions to writers—even writers as familiar as Voltaire, let alone Anatole France—or indeed to the habit of reading are not often found in the obituaries of anyone who dies today under the age of 75 and who was not a writer. Michael Dawson, son of Geoffrey Dawson, the former editor of the *Times*, was described in a tribute as evoking 'for his many friends the kind of memories which William Cory immortalised for Heraclitus'—but I remember this because in many months of careful reading I didn't notice any other allusions of that kind beyond a nod to Lowes Dickinson in a tribute from the 90-year-old Sir Charles Tennyson to his contemporary Colin Agnew.

Even hobbies, heart-sinkers though they are, seem to have been cast aside, possibly in favour of scrambling. Hugessen, again, had many—none of which he was very good at:

> He played the piano more than adequately, though without any strong feeling for music, and could make pleasant sketches in pencil, pen and watercolours. He had a ready pen (an aunt on his mother's side was the author of that Victorian bestseller *Little Lord Fauntleroy*) and was fond of writing light humorous verse, less unamusing to the uninitiated than such productions usually are.

The only places where the traditional accomplishments of the drawing room are not only still practised but, unlike Hugessen's talents, applauded by obituarists are the 'Circuit mess' and the 'Chambers dinner party' where, for instance, Judge Wingate-Saul, 'the wit of the Northern Circuit', could be depended on to enliven a soirée with his 'brilliant poems, done usually in heroic couplets and off the cuff'. And if not him, then perhaps Mr. Justice Brabin, 'a fountain of laughter and gaiety'. Or Michael Albery QC, who 'had something of the theatre in his make up' and 'could turn out elegant verses in Latin, Greek, French and English'. Lawyers, it seems from their obituaries, derive a lot of pleasure from their own and each other's company (judges and barristers, that is: solicitors don't often get obituaries in the *Times*).

The family is another casualty of the age of scramble. 'Stock', which used to matter such a lot, has now, understandably, vanished from the obituarist's vocabulary. But where families are of little account, so very often is the subject's early life and the influences on it. When Lord De La Warr died at the beginning of this year, the account of his political career began:

> He had been a youthful enthusiast of Labour ideals and although
> he later forsook the political party and background of his wonderful
> mother, Muriel, Countess De La Warr, to whom, as he always said,
> he owed so much, he remained essentially a democrat . . .

Current obituaries seldom give mothers their due, but Lord De La Warr was 75 when he died, so one can assume that the obituary had been commissioned in readiness for his death at least 25 years ago. Besides, it was probably written by a fellow member of the aristocracy to whom mothers are less of an embarrassment: the only thing that was said about D. H. Lawrence's mother in his obituary was that some of his work was 'at least so far biographical as to tell the world that his father was a coalminer and his mother a woman of finer grain'.

Lord De La Warr defied his mother despite an 'almost boyish bonhomie'. Lord Rosebery, though 'spirited and strong-willed', was an obedient son to a seemingly very bossy father:

> After leaving Eton, Rosebery went to the Royal Military Academy
> and was commissioned in the Grenadier Guards. But in 1903, at his

father's insistence, he very reluctantly resigned his commission to stand as Liberal candidate for Midlothian.

Later, when Campbell-Bannerman 'invited him to second the address at the opening of the new Parliament . . . his father peremptorily forbade him to accept the offer'. This apparently 'quenched what little political aspirations he had'. Generally speaking, the grander the family the more familiar the manner of the obituary and the richer it is in plot and characterisation. Rosebery's obituary seems to have been written by a family friend: the character who in a novel tells the story after its more active participants have died or dispersed. For him it is obviously an important factor that Rosebery's father preferred his younger son, Neil Primrose:

> Although Rosebery's relationship with his father was always close, that between Neil and the fifth Earl was, as Lord Birkenhead has written, more like that between brothers, and 'was among the most touching in a life full of idealised love'. Neil Primrose's death in action in 1917 . . . was a blow from which the father never recovered.

Perhaps Lord Birkenhead wrote this too.

An obituary like Lord Rosebery's is written as if in answer to the question: what became of the fifth Earl of Rosebery's eldest son? The majority of contemporary tributes, perhaps because they are mostly written by admiring colleagues rather than doubtful friends (Hugessen's was written by a very doubtful friend), look at people's lives from the end—the summit of their achievement—backwards. At their dullest they chart in a plodding, plotless way a steady progression from a degree at University College to a knighthood and several honorary doctorates 60 years later; or celebrate the achievement for which the person was best known and treat the rest of his life as if it had no bearing on it. The commemoration of the journalist and broadcaster William Hardcastle consisted almost entirely of a commendation of *The World at One*—'a programme concerned with the hard commodity of what has just happened'. And most sportsmen—like winners of the MC—seem only to have existed for one mad magenta moment.

Still, more competent obituary writers haven't altogether lost interest in the early steps of a career (Fred Streeter, 'a talisman of horticultural rectitude in the average home', began his broadcasting life with a talk on runner beans that elicited some 200 letters), and some also take the trouble to explain the particular nature of their subject's expertise. Plot is introduced when there is some doubt about the person's achievement or a conflict between his character and the requirements of whatever job he did ('unhappily tact was not his longest suit'). But some of the most vivid 'professional' obituaries are those that narrowly concentrate on telling a story: the precise combination of luck and ability that made Sir George Dowty pre-eminent in the field of industrial hydraulics; how the boxer Georges Carpentier (an exception among sportsmen) won fame and lost it and won it and lost it again. Army careers are particularly fruitful in this respect; and the obituary column is a good source of Second World War escape stories and tales of how the ramshackle British overcame the mighty foreigner. (General Sir William Platt was praised for giving 'competent leadership': did his fellow generals not even do that?)

Most of these obituaries were written to the greater glory of a profession, at least wherever possible. Lord Rosebery's commemorated a class and with it an old-fashioned Englishness that has now disappeared. Lord De La Warr's much married sister, Lady Idina Sackville, died 20 years before he did. A brief obituary notice was followed by two tributes which evoke a romantic Englishwoman admired for her glamour and resilience, whose life seems to typify the life once led by upper-class women of means—if only in novels:

In all parts of the world people who had known and loved her . . .
will remember her as she was in the days between the wars—not
beautiful in the narrow sense of the word, but enchanting . . .
She had a fund of courage which nothing could shake—physical
courage in the hunting field and big-game hunting; moral courage
in meeting the great grief of her life, the death in action of her two
sons . . . It was her health and not the Mau Mau outbreak which
forced her to leave her beloved home in the Kenya Highlands. She
would have scorned to run away from danger.

The tribute, from 'V.S.–W.', quoted a Chinese poem translated by
Arthur Waley: 'The sound of her silk skirt has stopped.' Christabel
Lady Ampthill, who died the other day, was 'a great beauty' whose
'skill and bravery in the hunting field were a byword in almost every
pack in England and Ireland'.

It would be hard now (and it was never altogether easy) to say
exactly what kind of people get obituaries in the *Times* and whether
there are unfair exclusions to match the sometimes surprising inclu-
sions. If a conspiracy exists in the selection of candidates, it is haphazard and unspoken. Some posts and positions (as it were, senior prefect,
head of house, major scholar, captain of hockey) carry an obituary in
the way that some posts carry a knighthood. Otherwise what matters
is to know someone who knows someone (usually a *Times* correspondent) who knows the obituaries editor, since he depends on a network
of connections to tell him who is doing well (and will one day rate an
obituary) and who is doing badly (and will shortly be requiring one).
It helps to have lunch in the places where people who have connections with the *Times* have lunch: 'I saw so-and-so at the Travellers and
he wasn't looking well.' And it helps to have your death announced
in the *Times* because early proofs of the announcements are seen by
the obituaries department—which might indicate that people who

take the *Times* are more likely to end up in it. Signed appreciations from friends give an idea of the kind of person the paper considers too marginal: figures of intense local interest, the sort of whom it is said that 'South Devon suffered a sad loss through his death'; scholars in obscure fields; the very old who may have lapsed from public attention; society figures; and Christopher Booker's old schoolmaster among whose 'devoted pupils at Shrewsbury were the three founding editors of *Private Eye*'.

The obituaries of foreigners, when they occur, which is erratically and with no sense of the relative importance, say, of Hannah Arendt and 'Mrs. Viola Townsend Winmill of Warrenton, Virginia, United States, horse lover and coach woman', are usually written by members of the *Times* staff and reflect their interests. Americans, particularly those connected with the cinema, do better than real foreigners, among whom the most consistently noticed seem to be German opera producers and designers—probably for the same reason that German opera productions are often reviewed in the *Times*: because it's an area the arts editor is especially interested in. Presumably no one on the staff cares as much about German musicology; Friedrich Blume, the Berenson, so it's said, of musicologists, got a note five inches long and three weeks late. Hannah Arendt was thought to deserve four inches, considerably less than Jimmy Nervo and an obscure American oilman commemorated on the same day. Even then the obituarist was scarcely lavish: 'Her published work,' he said, 'earned her respect if not always approval.' A few days later, in a tribute from Bernard Crick, she was described as 'perhaps the most original and important political philosopher of our times'. Professor Crick remarked that she 'had little impact in this country'—but the *Times* had already made that perfectly clear. God, it seems, has not lost his mistrust of clever foreigners.

In tributes to politicians the voice that is heard is not God's but his viceroy's, the *Times* leader writer. (It can also be detected, under the present editor, William Rees-Mogg, in long and thoughtful commemorations of English Catholic dignitaries.) In the case of minor politicians odd remarks give away the identity of God's view and that of the *Times*. Maurice Edelman, for instance, 'had long ceased to be enamoured of the left or Russia'—'enamoured' would not have been the word used had the attachment been thought suitable. But when statesmen (English or foreign) die their obituaries are as much a political statement as a tribute to their achievement. De Valera, though praised for his patriotism, was scarcely praised at all: 'There was a bleak integrity and refusal to count the cost about many of his actions that was in apparent contradiction to the transparent opportunism of others.' Franco, on the other hand, got off lightly in an obituary anxious to let bygones be bygones, to honour him for making Spain a respectable member of the Western alliance and to defend him from attacks made by less moderate opponents of the regime. The presence on the page of four photographs of the great 'dictator who gave Spain a period of law and order' indicated a fairly unambivalent celebration.

Even less ambivalent was the commendation of Ross McWhirter, 'champion of individual freedom'. Had he died in his bed, he might have been commemorated as a 'controversial' figure who edited *The Guinness Book of Records*. As it was, murdered by the IRA, he was portrayed, by someone with views not unlike those the *Times* columnist Ronald Butt sometimes expresses, as a hero in an unheroic time: 'He was, and it is curious that it has to be said, a man of unfashionable cut and cast of mind . . . He was not just a talker content to grumble and rail, he was a doer; he acted.' (The same could be said of the 'vociferous and intimidating minority' against whom his doing was done.) It was incongruously left to the *Times* sports correspondent, who at any other time might have written the obituary, to add that his 'political views sometimes seemed extreme'. There is nothing new in this editorial interest. In the past people have failed altogether to get a notice because the *Times* didn't like their opinions; while Chamberlain's obituary was written, probably by Geoffrey Dawson himself, with striking political bias. He was said, for instance, to have been bitterly attacked by the Labour Party for 'appearing to condone the Italian military action against what they chose to call "democracy" in Spain'. As for appeasement, it had 'failed with honour': 'By exhausting every possibility of peace before entering upon war Chamberlain had at least brought Britain into the conflict with clean hands.' An air force would have been more useful.

The tribute to Chamberlain was exceptional in saying nothing about his character: perhaps the conflict between the time and the *Times* made it difficult for the writer to find a form of words acceptable to both sides. Not that obituarists are discouraged by problems of that kind: only Oscar Wilde himself (for whom 'death soon ended what must have been a life of wretchedness and unavailing regret') was more fond of paradox than the common or garden obituary writer. Poor Mrs. Humphry Ward: 'As inspiration declined, her technique improved, and as her special message grew less her output grew greater.' Sir Kenneth Pickthorn, we're told, had a 'talent for repartee and a capacity for sustained logic which made him invincible even when he was unpersuasive'. In less artful hands, antitheses—in fact, excuses—are set up that even Sir Kenneth's logic could not have sustained. 'He was inclined to see the issues in terms of black and white but this in no way detracted from his kind and helpful nature'—why should it? 'The experts might not always agree with him but his clear expression and often entertaining manner was a valuable contribution to our understanding of human evolution': his writing was worthless but readable. On the one hand a vice, on the other a virtue, but rarely the virtue of vices or vices of virtue: 'Laconic, penetrating—at times acid in his comments he never gave offence.' Nor even the vices of vices: 'His often disconcertingly blunt manner sometimes gave a false impression of rudeness and insensitiveness.'

Similarly, the deceased is never what he seemed to be if what he seemed to be was unattractive: 'Although he cultivated a somewhat grandiose exterior and formidable manner, he was at heart a complex, sensitive man.' If so-and-so's manner is pompous, he is in fact very jolly; if his manner is light-hearted, he is in fact very serious. The historian J. E. Neale seems to have taken in both sets of contradictions: 'Behind the warm genial personality was a tough conscientious scholar' and 'beneath his Lancastrian bluntness and moments of supreme tactlessness . . . was a profound humility in the presence of historical scholarship and the mellow generosity of a great scholar.' In this way all qualities are neutered and nothing really bad has been said about anyone. If a man is widely disliked, he has 'no concealment, no dissimulation, no artifice, no humbug'; if a man is eager to get on, it is for the sake of something wider, for he is 'without personal ambition'; a 'large and influential landowner' is 'a very humble man'; a man renowned for the bizarreness of his dress is said to be 'devoid of interest in personal appearance'.

It's all a ruse, of course, a way of slipping unkind things which are also sometimes called the truth into the context of an encomium. How important is this truth-telling function where it concerns people's character, and how often does it become a liberty? Very often, would be the stern answer; and although the taking of liberties is a large part of what makes obituaries a pleasure to read it could more easily be justified when the values of the people who read them were less disparate. Besides, the truth about people's characters and private lives isn't told in all sorts of ways, the most obvious of which is that homosexuality is never mentioned. Or is told of some but not of others. In Constance Malleson's obituary there was no reference to her relationship with Bertrand Russell: Utrillo's devoted seven inches to the irregularities of his life and three to his work. Or is darkly hinted at but never revealed: the nature of Oscar Wilde's offence; or 'the emotional wound, so long unhealed' but for which Eliot's 'poetry might well have been more genial, less ascetic'. Sometimes what might appear to be the truth turns out not to have been the truth at all: L. S. Lowry's obituary portrayed him as an inarticulate recluse—a few days later someone who seemed to know him well described him as 'one of the most fluent conversationalists one has been privileged to encounter'. And sometimes the truth seems to be a flimsy disguise for malice. One doesn't have to be Alastair Forbes or a fan of Cyril Connolly's at all to feel some unease on reading that he was 'a notable victim in the lists of love'.

Writers are particularly liable to malicious obituaries. Perhaps because they are not protected by a professional *parti pris*; perhaps because they are considered, as Cyril Connolly probably was, to have placed their lives in the public domain. A more likely reason, however, is that their obituaries are the work of other writers who review their lives as they would their books and have little inhibition in passing judgment on either, or in using their lives in evidence against their books. Ezra Pound's obituary, described by Janet Adam Smith in an angry letter to the *Times* as a 'mishmash of literary opinion and personal speculation', launched into an opaquely detailed account of his private life from which it soon followed that he was a 'major craftsman and an extraordinary energy but not a major human poet'. The truly remarkable aspect of the piece, however, was its opening attack on Eliot. Pound died not long after the publication of the draft manuscript of *The Waste Land* and someone evidently thought his obituary the right occasion to settle some old scores. The draft of *The Waste Land*, this person said:

> reveals that Pound, whom one tends to think of as coarse and boisterous where Eliot was refined and reticent, had a kind of

essential innocence and fastidiousness that was denied to his friend . . . From Louis Zukofsky to Alfred Alvarez, many of Pound's best friends (to use the horrible old joke-cliché) were Jews. The young Eliot of *The Waste Land* period seems, about Jews, to have had an almost insane physical nausea. If *The Waste Land* had been published in its first draft, it would have been a document of, not exactly madness, but very distressing psychological instability. Pound was the main instrument in turning it into an enigmatic near-masterpiece. His own anti-Jewishness was simplistic and ideological, based on ideas about usury. Jews tend to be open-minded and intelligent, and Pound tended to like individual Jews. Eliot was right to salute him as 'il miglior fabbro' and might also have saluted him as a less obsessed and tormented soul.

Still, it was nice of the writer to put in a good word for the Jews.

Rex Stout got an enthusiastic obituary recently and Agatha Christie's, though coolish ('she was not, in fact, a particularly good writer'), was not unpleasant. Thornton Wilder's obituarist wouldn't quite say whether he agreed with the public (who liked him) or the critics (who didn't), but gave the public the benefit of the doubt. D. H. Lawrence, however, queered his pitch:

There was that in his intelligence which might have made him the writer of some things worthy of the best of English literature. But as time went on . . . he confused decency with hypocrisy, and honesty with the free and public use of vulgar words.

And so he 'missed the place among the very best which his genius might have won'. Eliot, 'OM and Nobel Prizeman' (*sic*), did all right in his own obituary: given the OM it could hardly be otherwise. And if there was 'that' in his work which did not please the school matron who sits at the right hand of God, it turns out that it was only an affectation of the kind that intellectuals are easily taken in by: *The Waste Land*'s

> presentation of disillusionment and the disintegration of values, catching the mood of the time, made it the poetic gospel of the post-war intelligentsia; at the time, however, few either of its detractors or its admirers saw through the surface innovations and the language of despair to the deep respect for tradition and the keen moral sense which underlay them.

When Joyce died—'an Irishman whose book *Ulysses* gave rise to much controversy'—Eliot wrote to the *Times* complaining that the obituary had been written by someone quite unsuited to the task. Not that whoever it was had not tried to be fair: 'In person Joyce was gentle and kindly, living a laborious life in his Paris flat, tended by his devoted, humorous wife'; a pity, though, that 'the appreciation of the eternal and serene beauty of nature and the higher sides of human character was not granted to Joyce.'

The *Times* declined to print Eliot's letter, which was published in *Horizon*. 'The first business of an obituary writer,' Eliot said:

> is to give the important facts about the life of the deceased, and to give some notion of the position which he enjoyed. He is not called upon to pronounce summary judgment (especially when his notice is unsigned), though it is part of his proper function, when his subject is a writer, to give some notion of what was thought of him by the best qualified critics of his time.

Traditionally *Times* obituaries have not confined themselves to the important facts nor refrained from delivering summary judgments—that is part of their interest and their charm. And however numinous anonymity makes them seem, they often deliver the wrong summary judgments—but that too is part of their eccentric, English charm. At their very best they are short biographical essays, offering something more than the facts—an account of the life that was led, of what it meant to be that person as well as to do what he did.

It has been customary for *Times* obituaries of the very eminent to be reprinted in the *DNB*. And in 1975 for the first time a selection of obituaries was published in volume form; 'a contemporary dictionary and reference book of international biography' was how Philip Howard described it in the *Times*.* But the average obituary is quite different from an entry in a dictionary of biography, its function being not just to assess achievement and assign merit but to honour someone who may well receive no further honour. The inhabitants of a perfect world, Lionel Trilling said in a reference to Morris's *News from Nowhere*, might feel that 'being a person is not interesting in the way that novelists had shown it to be in the old unregenerate time.' Hugessen wasn't a great man and wouldn't rate a place in a biographical dictionary, but his obituary was mindful of the interestingness of being that person, with those limitations, in the old unregenerate pre-scrambling time.

*Obituaries from the *Times*, 1961–1970.

Next to Godliness

Pears' soap is a venerable English soap: the first to proclaim itself gentler than any other and the subject of one of Britain's first and most celebrated advertising campaigns. It is oval, the colour of candied orange peel, and translucent. 'Delicately perfumed with the flowers of an English garden', according to the company publicity handout; but what it brings to mind is not the flowers of the garden so much as the old domestic institutions—shallow baths in icy boarding-school bathrooms, and coal fires in the nursery. The advertising campaign began some 100 years ago, when Mary Pears married a young man named Thomas Barratt, whom she had met at an academy of dancing and deportment. Barratt joined the Pears family business, and turned out to be an advertising genius.

In 1897, Pears, under Barratt's direction, published a one-volume encyclopedia—*Pears' Shilling Cyclopædia*. It was the noonday of the British Empire, the year of Queen Victoria's Diamond Jubilee. The encyclopedia quickly earned its place in Victorian households between the family Bible and the works of Dickens. Thousands of copies were sold in British possessions overseas. The *Times* of London said, 'It is neither inadequate nor inaccurate,' which wasn't altogether accurate; an Irish convict said that it was 'the most popular book in the prison library'. Pears claimed in their advertisements that nothing had 'ever before been issued equal to it at twenty times its price'. It is now in its 88th edition and still flourishing.

The business was started by Andrew Pears, Mary's great-grand-father, who set up shop in London in the year of the French Revolution and soon became a prosperous manufacturer of good soap for the better classes. But by the time Thomas Barratt joined A. & F. Pears, Ltd., in 1865, the Industrial Revolution had taken place and the better classes had ceased to matter so much, commercially speaking: wide promotion could achieve wide sales among all sorts of people. No one saw this more clearly than Barratt, who boasted that he would adver-tise as no soapmaker had advertised before. There aren't many tricks of advertising as it is now practised that Barratt didn't think of. He persuaded the president of the Royal College of Surgeons to tell the world that his soap was uncommonly safe and healthy, and the beau-tiful Lillie Langtry to say that Pears' soap was the only soap she used. On a trip to New York, he stuck his foot in Henry Ward Beecher's door and got him to write the following encomium:

If Cleanliness is next to Godliness, soap must be considered as a 'means of Grace'—and a clergyman who recommends moral things should be willing to recommend soap. I am told that my commendation of Pears' Soap some dozen years ago has assured for it a large sale in the US. I am willing to stand by any word in favour of it that I ever uttered. A man must be fastidious indeed who is not satisfied with it.

In order to spread the good man's word, Barratt bought the entire front page of the *New York Herald*—something that had never been done before. In the first 80 years of Pears' existence, a total of 500 pounds sterling was spent on advertising its soap; within a few years of Barratt's joining the firm, the annual advertising budget was in the order of 125,000 pounds. He imported a quarter of a million French ten-centime pieces—which at the time were accepted as the equivalent of an English penny—and put them into circulation with the name 'Pears' stamped on each one. An Act of Parliament had to be passed to get them out of circulation.

In his own way, Barratt became a patron of the arts, going to art exhibitions to buy up potential advertising material. One of his most successful ads derived from a painting he saw at an exhibition in Paris. In one corner of the picture, a squalling baby was leaning out of a tin bath trying to grab a rubber toy just out of its reach. Barratt bought the right to reproduce the baby and the bath, substituting for the toy a bar of Pears' soap. His caption—'He won't be happy till he gets it'—straightaway became part of the stock-in-trade of music-hall comedians, cartoonists, and politicians. Another, more sweetly English painting brought Barratt's advertisements their greatest fame—and, thanks to the ad, there was for a time no more popular English work of art. The painting was *Bubbles*, an 1886 portrait by Sir John Millais of his grandson watching a soap bubble he had just blown through a clay pipe. The *Illustrated London News* owned the copyright, and for 2,200 pounds Barratt acquired the right to use it. After Millais's death, in 1896, it was said that he had not liked the way Barratt exploited his work, and the issue was heatedly argued in a series of letters to the *Times*. Millais's son, in a biography of his father published in 1899, said that Millais was 'furious' when Barratt showed him the ad. Barratt did not agree; according to him, Millais had called it 'magnificent':

Encouraged by his generous words [Barratt wrote to the *Times*], I spoke of the advantage which it was possible for the large advertiser to lend to art—he could give a very much greater publicity to a good picture than it could receive by being hung on the walls of the Royal Academy. Sir John Millais, with alacrity, appreciated that idea, and when I stated the extreme difficulty experienced by those desirous of advertising by means of the graphic art, to induce good men to paint pictures, Sir John, taking his pipe from his mouth, said, 'What . . . nonsense! I will paint as many pictures for advertising as you like to give me commissions for.'

The subject of the painting, Millais's grandson, who later became Admiral Sir William James, did not die until 1973—and he was always known to his friends as Bubbles.

Like all good advertisers, Barratt was quick to see ways in which the interests of his soap might be made to coincide with those of his country. He believed, and had told the public, that its health, its looks, and its soul stood to gain by the use of Pears' soap; he had not yet found a way of saying that it improved the mind. By the end of the 19th century, there was a large, newly literate section of the British working class eager for self-improvement. There were also, among the wealthier classes, many shrewd philanthropists eager to assist them. When Barratt got the idea of publishing his *Shilling Cyclopædia*, Pears became the first soap manufacturer to join their ranks. At least, Barratt is said to have had the idea himself, but it is possible that the *Cyclopædia* was as much the inspiration of its printer—David Bryce, of Glasgow. There was no mention in the book of the editor's name, and the records of the two firms, Bryce and Pears, have been destroyed, but the present editor has researched the matter, and it seems likely that Bryce compiled the *Cyclopædia* himself. The work was so consistent in its beliefs and its prejudices, its enthusiasms and its waywardness that it is hard to believe that the anonymous compiler was acting on someone else's instructions. Many of the ideas that it put forward would scarcely have met with the approval of the directors of A. & F. Pears.

It opened with a short 'Dictionary', 'comprising'—so the title page boasted—'Besides the Ordinary and Newest Words in the Language, Short Explanations of a large number of Scientific, Philosophical, Literary, & Technical Terms'. Among these 'terms' one finds the noun 'deipnosophists', defined as 'those who discussed learned subjects at table'. The *Cyclopædia* was intended at one level as the aspiring deipnosophist's vade mecum. After the 'Dictionary' came a 'Compendium of General Knowledge Containing a Mass of Curious and Useful Information about Things that every one Ought to Know'. There was plenty to fill an awkward gap at the dinner table: the reason that telegraph wires apparently rise and fall; the origin of flags; the eating methods of barnacles (they are said to kick their food into their mouths). If the conversation turned to bees, a deipnosophist anxious to impress his fellow diners might mention that 'this was probably the first insect which gained any attention from humanity'; and if the talk was of ancient Egypt he might allude to the curious fact that 'a cargo of mummy cats was brought to Liverpool from Egypt in 1890, and included 180,000 mummies weighing about 20 tons.' (Even more curious, these mummified cats 'sold very briskly. "Heads" went for 4s. 6d. each, and "bodies"—without heads—for 5s. 6d.') In another section, deipnosophists could acquaint themselves with the meaning of familiar Latin phrases; and if they wished to vary their discourse they could pick up a few tricks from the 'Dictionary of Synonyms and Antonyms'. A young man eager to say something meaningful to a person of the opposite sex could consult the chapter on the 'Language of Flowers': a simple reference to peaches would apparently convey to his interlocutor that her qualities, like her charms, were unequalled. The *Cyclopædia* contained a 'Gazetteer of the World' and, for the wives and families of deipnosophists, cooking instructions with suggested menus for large dinner parties in every month of the year, and a 'Dictionary of Medical Information for the Household'.

In 1914, A. & F. Pears, Ltd., became a part of Lever Brothers (now Unilever), but Pears' soap is still known by its old name. Similarly, the *Cyclopædia*, though it has been published for some years by an independent publisher, is still called *Pears' Cyclopædia*. A facsimile of the first edition has recently been issued by Pelham Books. It costs five pounds—100 times what it cost in 1897—but it has become a best-seller all over again. No section of it is without interest.

In the 'Dictionary', one sees how certain words, particularly those involving morals and manners, have hardened with age and constant usage. The 'egoists' of the 1890s were guilty only in an epistemological sense: in the definition of the 'Dictionary', they were certain of nothing but their own existence; 'genteel' manners still meant 'polished' manners, and not, as now, an excess of manners; and an 'uncouth' person was only 'unusual'—not today's lout. People weren't 'nice' in the sense of being amiable, but some exercised 'tact', which was a 'nice perception', or were 'nice'—that is, 'scrupulous'—'in their actions'. A 'cartel' in the halcyon days of free enterprise meant no more than an 'agreement in relation to exchange of prisoners'; the term 'quarantine' applied only to ships, not to children with mumps; and 'empiricism' implied not an open mind but a wilful disregard for science.

A chapter headed 'Desk Information on Subjects of Daily Reference' offers rules for spelling, the proportion of Anglo-Saxon—as opposed to foreign—words used by 'our chief English authors', guidance on how to guess a person's age, a table of heights and weights for women (but not for men), and a great deal more practical and statistical information assembled in a friendly, avuncular way, the aim being to assist the upwardly mobile in their dealings with the world at large. For the autodidact, for instance, there were 'hints as to using books'—'Never handle books unless with clean hands . . . never drop a book upon the floor,' and so on. (It's good to be reminded that books were once so well thought of.) Cads were informed that 'a mutual promise of marriage is binding in English law,' so they could not go back on their arrangements with the girl next door, however attractive the mill-owner's daughter had suddenly become. And readers who happened to catch sight of a passing businessman were warned not to open the window and give him a shout, for 'except in a case of necessity' it was a breach of etiquette to 'stop a businessman in the street'. For hypochondriacs, there was a list of 'Cautions in Visiting the Sick'. Do not visit the sick, it said, 'when you are fatigued, or when in a state of perspiration, or with the stomach empty, for in such conditions you are very liable to take the infection'. In other words, you don't have to visit your ailing aunt if you want to go out to lunch.

From the 'Dictionary of Cookery and Pastry' one learns how timidly we cook and eat today. For instance, these are the instructions for making mock turtle soup: 'Put a well-fed calf's head on in a large pot . . . boil . . . scrape the hair clean off . . . remove the flesh on both sides from the bone, divide the head; take out the tongue.' For Albert soup: 'Take the two points of the hind houghs of an ox.' And to make a dish of lamb's head you washed the head, plucked it thoroughly, then put it in a large pot, 'leaving the windpipe hanging over the outside'. What was offered here was 'the practice of cookery and pastry adapted to the business of everyday life', so one has to assume that these were recipes for dishes eaten not at Windsor Castle but in quite ordinary houses. The quantities and variety are stunning. Ten to 12 pounds of the middle part of a brisket was the quantity of meat advised for a beef stew, and for roast beef a 16-pound joint. Soups might be made with anything from strawberries to macaroni, duck might be stewed, turkey boiled, ox cheeks made into cutlets, oysters into soufflés (or fried or scalloped or creamed), chicken into custards, fish into sausages, and brown bread into ice cream. There are recipes for nine kinds of scone; for gingerbread, gingerbread (superior), plain gingerbread and very plain gingerbread; and for cakes and puddings whose names now read like an elegy for the England of country-house luncheons and nursery teas.

The 'Medical Dictionary' is a salutary reminder of what it was like to live in those days when TB was 'probably the greatest scourge that ever visited mankind' and when the suggested treatment for almost every illness, because it was the only available line of action, was 'free evacuation of the bowels'. 'The treatment of asthma should in every instance commence by clearing the bowels': after reading entry upon entry giving the same advice, one begins to see Freud's discussion of anality in a new light. For the ordinary British doctor, 'that commonest of all evils and predisposer of disease' was constipation; Freud called it anal retention. Hysteria was another condition ripe for a Freudian takeover, because the *Cyclopædia* makes it abundantly clear that in late Victorian Britain, as in pre-Freudian Vienna, women's disquiets and discontents were still attributed to indefinable disorders of the womb.

A great many Victorian publications were launched with the purpose of disseminating useful knowledge—a characteristically Victorian concept. What distinguished *Pears' Cyclopædia* from the rest was, first, its price—it was a marvellous shilling's worth—and second, its 'Compendium of General Knowledge', which in its two hundred pages exemplified almost every form of Victorian popular literature, with the exception of fiction (though many of its biographies of famous men and women read like tiny novels, some as lurid as any popular melodrama). It is highly entertaining and surprisingly subversive. Although intended to elevate and improve the minds of its readers, its message is not orthodox; there is, to take one example, no evidence of support for the Church of England—a bias that must have endeared it to many working-class readers who distrusted the established church. It is weak on the pure sciences, compared with other improving volumes, but rich in information of a technological kind, and it offers 'a meal of healthful, useful and agreeable mental instruction' (the phrase comes from William Chambers, who edited the first venture in high-minded popular journalism, *Chambers's Edinburgh Journal*). It also offers, in the manner of more vulgar enterprises, a wide stock of amusing anecdotes, amazing facts, and generally useless knowledge.

Take the first page. After 'Abbas Pasha', 'Abolitionists', 'Absinthe', 'Achilles' and 'Acoustics' comes this sequence:

ACTORS AS SWORDSMEN. Sir Henry Irving is said to be the most expert . . .

ACTORS, LONG-LIVED. Mr. Underhill, the famous comedian of the Stuart period, performed in the reigns of Charles II, James II, William III, and Queen Anne . . .

ACTORS PLAYING EVERY MALE PART IN A PLAY. The veteran actor, Mr. Henry Howe, played every male part in *The Lady of Lyons*.

ACTORS' STATURE. Mr. Fritz Reinma, Sergeant Caramel in *The Old Guard*, stands about 6 ft. 4 in. . . .

ACTORS WITH OFFICIAL ROBES . . .

ACTRESS WHO HAS PERFORMED MOST OFTEN BEFORE THE QUEEN . . .

ACTRESS WHO HAS PLAYED GREATEST NUMBER OF PARTS . . .

The compiler, it seems, was eager to assure his readers that they would find in the 'Compendium' answers not only to questions they had long been asking but to questions they would never have thought to ask.

There is enough bizarre material to satisfy the most idle curiosity.

Catastrophe and misfortune are particularly well covered. An entry on banking commemorates history's most spectacular bankruptcies. ('The worst bankruptcy on record was that of Overend, Gurney & Co. . . . whose failure entailed the failure of other firms to the awful amount of £100,000,000.') Other entries catalogue the most devastating shipwrecks, the biggest fires, the worst famines, the most ghastly earthquakes. Statistics of every sort abound. The author with the longest index; the novel with the shortest title ('A novel has been published in the USA under the title "?"'); the theatre with the largest seating capacity; the cost of building Solomon's Temple; the physical dimensions of heaven:

> A cube of 12,000 furlongs is 496,793,088,000,000,000,000 cubic feet. [The initial figure derives from the Book of Revelation.] If half of that is reserved for the Throne of God and the Court of Heaven, and a quarter of it for the streets of the city, there is still left enough space to provide 30,321,843,750,000,000 ordinary-sized rooms. That would give one room apiece to all the inhabitants of a million worlds as thickly peopled as the earth is now.

Meanwhile, Sarah Bernhardt's is the largest bed in the world; and the most expensive feathers are those that form the tuft in the Prince of Wales's crown—they 'took twenty years to collect, are valued at £10,000, and are known to have caused the death of least twenty hunters'.

The number of pins manufactured each day ('50 to 60 *million* . . . in England alone'), the occupations of suicides (soldiers head the list, followed by butchers), the odds against a woman's getting married after the age of 60—there is no limit to the diversity of topics. Some of the entries under the letter 'T' are 'Trades Injurious to Teeth', 'Tourists Killed in the Alps' (24 a year), 'Tight Rope across Niagara', 'Tea

Drinkers, the Greatest' (Australians), 'Tree's Height from Its Shadow', 'Tips in Country Houses' and 'Thirteen at Table':

> If the average age of the company is 72½ years, then there is a scientific probability that one of them will die within a year; if the average age is less than 72½ years, there is no scientific probability at all. If the average age is 20 years, there must be 129 people at dinner before there is any scientific probability of one of them dying within a year. At 30 years there must be 119, at 40 years 103, at 50 years 73, at 60 years 35, and at 70 years 17.

The compiler introduces the 'Compendium' with a prefatory note that makes no mention of these odd facts. The subjects treated, he says, are those to which he has had his attention drawn in the ordinary course of conversation or reading. He doesn't say that in discussing them he has expressed his own opinions with the boldness of Dr. Johnson compiling his famous dictionary 150 years earlier. Like Dr. Johnson, he clearly relished his task. His enjoyment is everywhere apparent. In facetious distortions: Darwin's book is called 'Origin of Species by Natural Solution', and Keats's most famous ode is 'Ode to a Grecian Inn'. In joky asides: describing the fashionable belief in Theosophy, he observes that 'the chief agents in founding the present "boom" were Madame H.P. Blavatsky, Colonel H.S. Olcott and Mr W.Q. Judge' and adds, 'With such initials it was impossible to fail!' In provocative fabrications: judges, he says, 'were not allowed to wear gloves on the English bench for fear of bribes being dropped into them'. In whimsical formulations: 'Monkeys are dear little things, and so like men.' In artful paradoxes: *Dieu et mon droit* 'was first adopted on the arms of England by Richard I; but Elizabeth, the most notorious flirt of her century—which also saw Mary Stuart—displaced it for *Semper eadem*, "Always the same".' In extravagant denunciations: 'the one danger' of Froebel's system of education was a 'tendency to teach by implication, that the maximum results can be obtained with the minimum effort—a most pestilential heresy'. In heartfelt commendations: Simon de Montfort was 'the best swordsman in Europe and a really good man', Pericles 'the finest of the ancient Greeks'. And in heartless dismissals:

> Werner Friedrich, the German poet . . . was the founder of the branch of the Romantic School of Poets that dealt with the extravagant mysteries of 'fate-tragedies'. His own fate was tragic enough, as he married three times, and was three times divorced, and then entered the Romish Church as a priest.

Poor Werner: remembered for three inauspicious marriages that drove him to celibacy.

Modern encyclopedias are uniform and poker-faced. The compiler of the 'Compendium of General Knowledge' praised as he pleased, jeered as he pleased, condemned as he pleased. Take contemporary British writers. Elizabeth Barrett Browning was 'one of the greatest poetesses that have ever lived'; Kipling 'is probably the most brilliant writer of short stories that the world has ever seen', Carlyle 'one of the Greatest English writers of this century', Thackeray 'one of the most lovable of English writers'. Tennyson 'had a morbid dislike to adverse criticism' but 'never failed to profit by it when revising his work'; Dickens 'strained far too much after "effect"'; George Meredith's 'difficult style is unnecessarily irritating, and has deservedly prevented him from ever becoming popular'; while Mrs. Henry Wood's work is 'rather vulgar'. The compiler could also, of course, ignore as he pleased: Tolstoy is 'the Russian novelist', but Dostoevsky has no entry at all. In modern Italian literature, incidentally, 'there is no name of outstanding importance.' Yet there is nothing eccentric or perverse in these observations; the compiler was telling his readers which books he thought they would benefit from reading. Not Mrs. Henry Wood's 'essentially commonplace melodrama'. Nor, on the other hand, Meredith's rebarbative novels. Dickens was to be approached with care, because, although a 'great artist', he was sometimes—it's inferred— more interested in 'effect' than in telling the truth, whereas Thackeray, a less popular writer, had a more acute sense of the dangers of social aspiration. The compiler writes about Thackeray with personal affection:

> Widely as he was and is read and admired, the superficial stricture upon him, that he was 'a cynic', is often repeated. So far as it rests on any basis, the criticism is due to his intense and even morbid sensitiveness to 'snobbishness', against which he is always raising his protest. But he did not really think meanly of human nature, and he was himself a man of most tender heart.

None of these were necessarily fashionable opinions, and those writers who read what the *Cyclopædia* had to say about them would not have attached much importance to it. But the compiler was unsympathetic to fashion, and favoured writers such as Carlyle and Tolstoy ('the only real prophet of the present age'), who denounced it from a great height.

Like most of his contemporaries (though not Carlyle), the compiler of the *Cyclopædia* earnestly believed in the possibility of progress. All that was needed were improvements in knowledge. Not simply more knowledge but the right sort of knowledge, which would lead inevitably to the right sort of society. He called this knowledge 'scientific', meaning that it could be fitted into a rational system, and the subjects that interested him were those, like education, moral philosophy, and politics, that pertained to deep issues of social organisation. A few great men had done well and many had done badly, but this was largely a matter of accident or whim and therefore relatively unimportant. Hence his nonchalant treatment of kings and queens and politicians.

Explanations of individual behaviour—the mitigations of psychology—were not for him: a villain was simply a villain. Nero was 'the bestial Emperor of Rome', who 'murdered . . . his vile mother'. Tiberius 'fell under the execrable influence of the incarnate fiend Sejanus' and 'spent his last years in gluttony and solitude on the island of Capreoe'. Judge Jeffreys, the notorious hanging judge of Devon and Cornwall, 'died—where he ought to have lived—in the Tower of London'. The compiler's position, broadly speaking, was on the side of the people against their rulers. When the Marquise de Pompadour, 'the millionaire mistress of Louis XV', died, it was 'amidst the rejoicings of a downtrodden nation at a deliverance which anticipated their most ardent hopes'. He had a reluctant admiration for Napoleon, 'the Man of Destiny', but had little to say for the French kings, their wives, or their mistresses. His entry under 'Louis' reads: 'Louis is the name of many of the French kings, of whom the most important are Louis IX ("the saint"), Louis XIV (by no means a saint) and Louis XVI.' Louis XVI 'was far too weak . . . and the queen gave herself up to gaiety, so that it is not surprising to find him arrested . . . tried . . . and guillotined.'

The English kings were scarcely more deserving of respect. Here is the entry for George III:

> George III had the distinction of reigning for sixty years, of losing the American Colonies in 1775–83, of being a contemporary of the French Revolution and the Napoleonic Wars, and of going mad several times during his long reign.

Richard III 'was *not* hunch-backed, but he was a liar and a murderer'. Charles II was 'indolent, extravagant and licentious'. Henry VII, however, did well: 'His policy of depressing the feudal nobility and exalting the middle ranks was excellent.' And Henry VIII 'was very popular as a musician and an athlete, in spite of his tyranny'. The most he could say for Queen Victoria was that 'Her Majesty is an authoress,' and he didn't think much of her ministers; he criticised Gladstone, for instance, for failing 'from cowardice or procrastination' to relieve General Gordon at Khartoum, for splitting the Liberal Party, and for opposing women's suffrage—'in itself a logical and just arrangement in any country where men have suffrage but . . . thwarted persistently in Britain by Mr. and Mrs. Gladstone'.

There were many other logical and just arrangements that were being thwarted, either by the obstinacy of individuals or by the self-interest of a class. The compiler felt this strongly. The distribution of land and the distribution of wealth are two obvious instances. In 1897, according to his figures, half of the land belonged to 7,400 individuals and the other half to 312,500 individuals. The computation is curious, but the moral was simple: land, being 'a source of natural wealth . . . ought not to be in the hands of a chosen few'. On the subject of wealth he preaches a small sermon:

> It seems curious that so many people should make material wealth their ideal and goal in life, when they must know that it is limited in supply, and that, if they get it to excess, someone else must go without it. On the other hand, all the wealth which is 'not made with hands', is not limited; and the more each of us has—e.g. of knowledge, leisure, health etc—the more we can give to or share with our neighbours.

The cure was not revolution. In France, the disciples of Rousseau 'began their "return to nature" by destroying everything—creeds, institutions, customs, lives; and on their ruins Napoleon constructed his own positive ambition.' As for Bakunin and his disciples, what they proposed was simply rubbish—'illegitimate and absurd extravagances and inanities'. Nor was the goal, as he saw it, a dictatorship of the proletariat. 'An educated democracy,' he said, 'is probably the most righteous form of government' (and an uneducated democracy, he added, 'one of the most pernicious forms'). The compiler's sympathies are with the 'Scientific Socialists':

> Scientific Socialists seem to really know what their ideal is, how they got it, and how they want to carry it out. They define it as a state of things in which every soul in the nation shall have an equal chance of realising such perfection as it is naturally capable of realising—as a pot-boy or a premier—without any reference to the lot into which, by fortune or by misfortune, it has been born; and they assert, often with too little regard for the feelings of the rich middle class, that at present society does not give the mass of men the 'chance' of realising such perfection; education does not give them the 'will', and natural inheritance of brain and body—due mainly to bad food—does not give them the power. Further, they consider that this feverish scramble for material wealth is both unseemly and unscientific, because what one man gets another has to go without.

Their proposals, he says, 'may be inexpedient but they are perfectly legitimate'. Speaking of the Co-operative Movement, he is more confident: 'It embodies a right principle, which must win eventually.' Barratt and his fellow directors—if they ever read the *Cyclopædia*—showed surprising tolerance in allowing these opinions to go out under their name.

Neither the interests of A. & F. Pears, Ltd., nor anonymity nor the encyclopedia format acted as constraints on the compiler. He is most emphatic on behalf of trade unions, berating the 'numerous rash ignoramuses who babble across dinner tables about strikes and Trade Unions' when the unions have paid out very much more in 'PROVIDENT BENEFIT' than in 'STRIKE PAY' and have 'secured and maintained the highest rate of wages, the shortest hours, and the best conditions of work'. He returns again and again to these issues. An entry on Worth, 'the great ladies' tailor', is not about clothes but about working conditions: 'His business . . . employs nearly a thousand workwomen, more than half of them on the premises—the only sanitary and economic system—for outside work lends itself to sweating and to the spread of disease.' He begins an entry on machinery in a characteristically angry mood: 'A good deal of plausible nonsense has been written and spoken in the attempt to prove that Machinery does not displace human labour.' But he ends with a Wellsian vision of a better world: 'One bright hope for the future of the race is in the wide development of Machinery . . . which will eventually free human labour from all unhealthy, disagreeable and degrading forms of work.'

Personal morality interested the compiler much less: if society were organised on 'scientific' principles, people could be expected to behave better. Neither secular nor divine models were needed. Christ interests him so little that he gives no information about Him beyond reproducing a 'text' of the sentence passed by Pontius Pilate and allegedly engraved on a brass plate that had been found near Naples. Nothing in the religious cast of mind met with his sympathy; and although there is evidence in the *Cyclopædia* of religious prejudice, there is no suggestion of any kind of religious allegiance. The prejudice was not in any way unusual: like many Englishmen (and even more Scotsmen), the compiler disliked and distrusted the Catholic Church. He describes the Reformation as 'the beginning of modern social life' ('it purified morals, multiplied the centres of spiritual life, and made men think for themselves'), and variously characterises the pre-Reformation Catholic Church as despotic, corrupt, and depraved.

(In an entry on religious architecture, he observes that 'the set horizontal lines of a classical temple' were 'peculiarly appropriate to the depraved Italian Church of the Renaissance'.) Its later practices and ways of thought were no more to his liking. Even the expression 'Roman Catholic' offended him. 'A "Roman Catholic,"' he said, 'is simply a gross contradiction in terms, for a person cannot be both Roman, i.e. a particular sect, and Catholic, i.e. universal.' The epithet he uses is 'Romish', as in 'Romish Church'. When a saint is mentioned, it is often in order to show how gullible or self-regarding religious people can be: the 'mania' for imitating Simeon Stylites was, for example, 'a form of conceited asceticism'. The traffic in relics, an easy target, prompts these reflections:

> Relics were declared, by the Romish Council of Trent in 1563,
> to be worthy of veneration, and the declaration elicited a curious
> phenomenon in Economics—that things of which the supply was
> naturally 'limited' could be increased to meet demand. The number
> of crucifixes made of 'the true Cross' was large enough to have
> paved every street in London.

But Protestants could also go too far: the doctrine of predestination 'has led many men into gross presumption, and more into utter despair'; the Quakers 'neglect the common courtesies of society'; the Boers 'are rigid Calvinists and very cruel'. Only Buddhism, because it encourages a mean in all things, escaped his strictures.

A tradition of freethinking was well established in the Lowlands of Scotland by the late 19th century; and if Bryce was indeed the compiler of the *Cyclopædia*, there is every reason to suppose that he belonged to that tradition. (Conversely, the attitude of the *Cyclopædia* towards religion and religious affairs encourages the view that Bryce put it together.) But whoever the compiler was it seems clear that the ideology that corresponded most closely to his own was secularism, 'a philosophy of life, the gist of which consists in the advocacy of free thought':

> Secularists believe that the best means of arriving at the truth is to place perfect confidence in the operations of human reason. They do not consider that faculty to be infallible, but they think that reason should only be corrected by reason, and that no restraint, penal, moral, or social, should be placed upon holding, expressing, or acting up to an opinion intelligently formed, and sincerely held, however contrary that opinion may be to those generally held.

It doesn't on the face of it seem likely that the management of A. & F. Pears wished to promulgate free thought or any other opinions contrary to those generally held—that, as we know, is not the advertiser's way—but the compiler had presumably not been told to toe a party line. He was, it turns out, an agnostic and a socialist. He had no particular respect for Queen Victoria or for Gladstone, the embodiment of official Victorian morality. Was he at least a patriot?

> One person out of every four that are alive upon the face of the earth is a subject of Queen Victoria. Of every 100 square miles in Europe she rules over 3, of every 100 in Asia 10, of every 100 in Africa 19, of every 100 in America 24, and of every 100 in Australasia 60. The proportion of her subjects is 6 per cent in America, 11 per cent in Europe . . . Compared with other empires of the earth [the British Empire] is 40 times as large as the Italian, 10 times as large as the German . . . The United Kingdom has colonies nearly 100 times its own area, while the French colonies are only a dozen times as large as France, the German only 5 times the size of Germany, the Russian only 3½ times the size of Russia, and the Italian only

2½ times the size of Italy; and during Queen Victoria's reign the increase of empire has been a 'Scotland-Ireland' every year.

It sounds good, but here again the compiler's sentiments are ambiguous, and any Englishman who, reading this, felt disposed to congratulate himself on his native genius would be making a mistake. In the next sentence, the compiler observes, 'For this extraordinary result the geography of the country is mainly responsible.' Geography, being a scientific subject, commanded his respect, and he was inclined to consider under that heading the rise and fall of empires and other events usually thought to belong to history. On the other hand, the British Empire, thus placed on a scientific footing, could simply be accepted as a fact. He did not praise it on patriotic grounds or condemn it on socialist grounds; he just admired its dimensions.

He disapproves of many British institutions for not being 'scientific', by which in that context he means socialist, and others he treats with a proper scepticism (secularists, he said, regard scepticism 'as a moral duty'). Scattered entries reveal a pride in Scottish achievements—one of the longest in the entire 'Compendium' is devoted to 'Scotch Railway Speeds'. But on the whole—and contrary to contemporary fashion—he sets little store by race or nationality, except where he singles out those who for reasons of exoticness had qualified for anthropological attention: the Bedouins, who 'lead solitary, precarious lives, but . . . have violent passions and love robbery'; the Eskimos, who 'are not deficient in intellect, and are kind and hospitable'; the Gypsies, whose 'one merit seems to be their love of and talent for music'. Of the Jews he says that 'in modern times . . . they have produced some of the greatest men in the arts and literature,' and cites Spinoza, Mendelssohn, Heine—and Beethoven and Schubert. In an adjacent entry he specifies the prices for which various Jews sold their relatives and friends: 'Joseph was sold by his brethren for about £2 7s. 0d.; Judas sold his Master for £3 10s. 8d.; Naaman offered Elisha more than £10,000; and the debtor who refused to forgive his fellow servant the 100 pence . . . had himself been forgiven a debt of £3,422,625.'

His assumptions would today be called Eurocentric. Chopsticks, for instance, are 'the Chinese substitute for our knife, fork and spoon'—and soy sauce, no doubt, their substitute for Gentleman's Relish. The Russians are praised for saving Europe from the Asiatic horde: 'It is fairly true to say that there is not a freeman between the Pruth and the Adriatic today who does not owe his freedom mainly to Russia' . . . well, he does only say 'fairly'. 'The laziness of the negroes' has been responsible for the decline in West Indian sugar production. But Europeans and Americans have defects, too. The French have been let down by their 'lust for military glory'; the standards of American political life are not high: James A. Garfield, he says, was 'elected president mainly because of his sterling honesty—an unusual claim to political advancement anywhere, and least of all in America'.

The soap hasn't changed much, either.

The Language of
Novel Reviewing

How do novel reviews begin? Just like novels very often:

> Motherless boys may be pitied by mothers but are not infrequently
> envied by other boys.

> For the friends of the Piontek family, 31 August 1939 was a red-letter day.

> All her life Jean Hawkins was obedient.

It looks as though the writers of these reviews have set out not to
summarise the plot but to tell the story, with the drawback, from the
novelist's point of view, that readers may content themselves with the
reviewer's version. Other reviews begin with a different sort of story—
the reviewer's:

> Halfway through Beryl Bainbridge's new novel I found I was
> laughing until the tears ran down my cheeks.

Some start by characterising the novel:

> An aura of death, despair, madness and futility hangs over the late
> James Jones's posthumous novel.

Others by characterising the reviewer: 'Count me among the Philis-
tines,' says Jerome Charyn, inauspiciously, at the start of a review in
the *New York Times*. Some begin with a paragraph on the novel now;
some begin by addressing the reader:

> You might not think there would be much wit or lyricism to the
> story of a subnormal wall-eyed Balkan peasant who spends 13 years
> masturbating in a pigsty . . .

Some kick off at the end: '*Final Payments* is a well-made, realistic novel
of refined sensibility and moral scruple'; and others at the beginning:
'The five writers under review have been browsing . . .'

Different openings suggest different attitudes, both to the novel and
to the practice of reviewing novels. There are ideologies of the novel
and ideologies of the novel review, fictional conventions and reviewing
conventions. They don't necessarily overlap. A regular reviewer, confident of his own constituency, may describe a novel in terms of his
own responses to it: he wouldn't for that reason applaud a novelist for
writing in a similarly personal vein. What reviews have in common is
that they must all in some degree be re-creations: reshapings of what
the novelist has already shaped. The writer's fortunes depend on the
reviews he gets but the reviewer depends on the book to see that his
account of it—his 'story', to use the language of the newspaper compos-
ing room—is interesting. Dull novels don't elicit interesting reviews:
not unless a reviewer decides to be amusing at the novel's expense or
tactfully confines himself to some incidental aspect of it. A generous

reviewer may also invent for the novel the qualities it might have had but hasn't got.

The most brusque reviews occur in the most marginal newspapers: 'The new novel by Camden author Beryl Bainbridge,' said the *Camden Journal*, 'took just a few hours to read yet cost £3.95 . . . The story is fairly interesting, mildly amusing and a little sad.' A hundred years ago the most brutal things were said about novelists and their works (cf. Henry James on *Our Mutual Friend*: 'It is poor with the poverty not of momentary embarrassment, but of permanent exhaustion'). Today many literary editors, alert to the fact that the novel is under pressure, ask their reviewers to be kind and most of them are. Kind to the old novelist because he is old; kind to the young novelist because he is young; to the English writer because he is English ('all quiet, wry precision about manners and oddities') and not American or German; to others because they are black (or white) or women (or men) or refugees from the Soviet Union. Every liberal and illiberal orthodoxy has its champions. Failings are seen to be bound up with virtues ('there are rough edges to his serious simplicity'); even turned into them ('though inelegant and sometimes blurred, their heaviness and urgency create their own order of precision'); but seldom passionately denounced, and although every novelist has had bad reviews to complain of, it sometimes seems as if novel reviewing were a branch of the welfare state.

The reasons have a lot to do with the economics of publishing. In the 1920s Cyril Connolly described the reviewing of novels as 'the white man's grave of journalism': 'for each scant clearing made wearily among the springing vegetation,' he sighed, 'the jungle overnight encroaches twice as far.'[1] The jungle has now dwindled to something more like a botanic garden ('it is a knockdown miracle that publishers continue to put out first novels,' noted a reviewer in the *Times*),[2] and far from having to hack his way through the springing vegetation, the critic is required to give the kiss of life to each week's precarious flowering. 'SAVE THE NOVEL,' implored the novelist Angus Wolfe Murray addressing reviewers.[3] Only in the case of such writers as Harold Robbins or Sidney Sheldon, whose fortunes or morale he cannot affect, does the reviewer have the freedom to write as he pleases.

Given that the novel is to be saved, what claims do reviewers make for it? John Gardner in his book *On Moral Fiction* (1978) complains of the flimsiness of 'our serious fiction':

> The emphasis, among younger artists, on surface and novelty of effect is merely symptomatic. The sickness goes deeper, to an almost total loss of faith in—or perhaps understanding of—how true art works. True art, by specific technical means now commonly forgotten, clarifies life, establishes models of human action, casts nets towards the future, carefully judges our right and wrong directions, celebrates and mourns.

But it is clear from the exhilarated comments they make that many reviewers regularly find in the novel they have been reading the kind of guidance and instruction Gardner has in mind:

> In the vaunted creative process, he has transcended himself and given us an access to liberty.

> Her book is full of lessons about the art of creative literature, and about life, and how each reflects and enhances and deepens the meaning of the other.

> Its indignation is blazingly imaginative, furiously vital and gives us hope.

> A truer and deeper perception of the world's agony comes from the . . . stories . . . about her native land.

There is no suggestion here that novelists are suffering from diminished responsibility or reviewers from any cramping of their responses. But it depends which reviewers one reads. Hope, agony, the meaning of life and of art, a transcending of the self: for every critic who finds these in the novels sent to him for review—and a critic who finds them once tends to find them once a week—there are more who see confusion, ambivalence, ambiguity, and count themselves well pleased:

> The best English novelists are getting more ambiguous all the time.

> I suppose this is what Iris Murdoch means when she distinguishes between philosophy and fiction—that what the novel does superlatively is mirror our continuing confusion and muddle.

Gardner is not eccentric in detecting among both novelists and critics an active commitment to uncertainty; as a reviewer in the *Times Literary Supplement* observed apropos of a novel involving a mystery and its detection: 'Once upon a time novels and readers and detectives discovered things; now they fail to discover them.'[4] An achieved character is a mixed-up character: 'his grief and obsession lack ambiguity and don't feel real'; he 'is confused but by that token the more convincing'. Gardner finds repugnant the notion that confusion may be the most appropriate response to a confusing world, but on countless occasions novels are praised for making it clear that nothing is clear, that a trouble-free verisimilitude can no longer be expected:

> The book is convincingly comic, and at the same time ambiguous and nervy enough to suggest that nothing is as solid as it seems.

> His theatrical memoir-scribbling existence is the best (i.e. most problematic) metaphor for how most of us function.

The brackets here reinforce the point, assuming as they do a coincidence of meaning between 'best' and 'most problematic'. In another review Frank Tuohy's stories of English life are said to have a 'grim predictability' but when he writes about Englishmen abroad his 'subtle talent emerges':

> The barriers of language and culture give rise to a slightly baffled and tentative querying of reality; perspectives shift and blur, appearances bemuse and all our certainties suddenly lack foundation.

The writer should not merely baffle but himself be baffled: a way perhaps of acknowledging, and absorbing into a naturalistic tradition, the more exigent dubieties of such postmodernist writers as Borges, Sarraute, or Robbe-Grillet, whose ritual dismemberings of plot and character, especially when mimicked by native writers, have not gone down well among either reviewers or the public.

The baffled writer has various ways of disclaiming verisimilitude. In Renata Adler's *Speedboat*, for instance, the narrative is fragmented into a series of discrete events, anecdotes, perceptions. Elizabeth Hardwick, writing about the book in the *New York Review*, showed her respect for it by adopting in her review the novel's own fragmentary procedures. Likening it to some of the work of Barthelme, Pynchon, and Vonnegut, she claimed for all of them an 'honourable' attempt to deploy 'the intelligence that questions the shape of life and wonders what we can really act upon'; but then added:

> It is important to concede the honour, the nerve, the ambition— important even if it is hard to believe anyone in the world could be happier reading *Gravity's Rainbow* than reading *Dead Souls*.

The old, unreconstructed pleasures of reading sometimes slip the reviewer's mind but a conflict between enjoyment and the 'honourable' measures writers take to accommodate doubt and perplexity has to be acknowledged. Take Robert Nye's *Merlin*. Instead of a plot, it offers, as many non-conventional novels now conventionally do, a sprawling of plots, lists, jokes, and retelling of old stories. A prospective reader may be more grateful for a review that tells him what it is like to read such a novel ('In the end, it is just too much . . . rather like finding a hotel that serves you a Christmas dinner three times a day') than for one written in the spirit of the novel itself and dedicated to teasing out its many 'implications about art and reality'.

The most frequent recourse of the baffled writer is to offer himself as part of his fiction, stepping into the novel either in person (Margaret Drabble in *The Realms of Gold*) or in the guise of another novel writer purportedly engaged in writing this novel or another novel contingent on it, so that the novel tells two stories concurrently, its own and the novelist's, thereby foreshadowing, and in some cases forestalling, its own reviews. Two recent instances have been *The World According to Garp* by John Irving and John Wain's *The Pardoner's Tale*. The latter links a conventional account of a novelist's life with the equally conventional novel he is currently writing. Malcolm Bradbury, a critic committed to the notion of the text that doubts itself, praised it as being 'among [Wain's] best novels, realism modestly considering itself'. Reviewers often talk about realism as if it were something tangible (Tim O'Brien's *Going After Cacciato* contained, according to the *New Statesman*, 'a strange and impressive balance of realisms'), the idea being that where intention and meaning are in doubt, literary styles and devices have a life of their own. *The World According to Garp* is a much more complicated book, baroque, labyrinthine, full of internal fictions and comments on those fictions. One reviewer remarked that 'there is little one can say about the book or its author that Irving has not in some way anticipated in his own text.' The baffled writer, it turns out, has this advantage over his critics: he can tell them what is wrong with his novel before they tell him.

Just as some novels supply their own reviews, so many reviews supply their own novels. It isn't so much a matter of different interpretations (which are unavoidable: one reviewer saw in *The Pardoner's Tale* 'the lineaments of gratified desire . . . persuasively drawn . . . an amorous haze spreading delight', another 'a man who has evaded what real love requires') as of giving a novelistic account of the novel. For instance:

> William Trevor's characters . . . seem to live perpetually in an afternoon sun which filters through the Georgian fanlight onto a balding carpet.

Or:

> Whether 'she' is Nell or Julie or Ellen there's always the same tear-stained voice, stuffing old love letters into the mouth to hold back the sob at parting.

That Beryl Bainbridge has a quirky way of doing things may be put straightforwardly:

> She views life from so odd an angle that normal proportions and emphases are disconcertingly altered.

or, if you like, mimetically:

> The characters proclaim their loves and loathings dimpled with breadcrumbs, adorned with swellings, fiddling with troublesome socks.

One danger is that the reviewer's novel may stand in the way of the author's. Sometimes the two are incompatible: when the Canadian writer Marian Engel describes the adulterous hero of *Injury Time* as having been 'instructed to clean up his act', another, mid-Atlantic Beryl Bainbridge is brought to mind. A further danger is that mimicry may become parody (one of the standard ways of dismissing a bad novel is of course to ape its mannerisms), and a reviewer adopting the manner of the novelist may do the novel an injustice where no injustice was intended.

When a reviewer mimics a novel simply as a way of describing it (without, that is, any pejorative intentions) he is in some sense taking it over, as if he too could predict how the characters might behave. Those contemporary novels that disclaim verisimilitude make it difficult for the reader to enter their world; indeed, by making an issue of their own fictiveness they deliberately set up barriers against it. In their more extreme Sarrautian forms they may invite him to participate in the invention, but that in itself is a way of pointing up what would in these cases be seen as the fallacy that fiction imitates life. More realistic novels by contrast offer the reader a whole new world with new friends (or enemies) and new places to go to. 'We follow the life of her heroine,' a grateful reviewer reports, 'through a circuitous route where we meet a plethora of well-drawn characters and visit a number of interesting places.' But reviewers in discussing this world are inclined to be over-eager:

> Perfectly observed details—a steaming mug of tea in a transport
> café, a misfired blind date in a lurid pub—make you feel you're living
> Desmond's life.

It may be that the best fiction has a reality that reality itself hasn't got (however well we know the details of other people's lives we don't often feel we're living them), but the examples here don't support the claim that is made for them, and the reviewer, mistaking familiarity for something better, has been hasty in casting aside her own life in favour of Desmond's. It's the same with characters' emotions which too readily become the emotions of the reviewer: 'I relaxed as much as the hero and his wife do when she burns her ovulation charts.' It's hard to believe in that degree of empathy.

A critic who professes to share all the characters' ups and downs tells us too much about his own responses. David Lodge reviewed Mary Gordon's *Final Payments*. He thought it a good novel and one of its qualities, he said, was that it engaged the reader's sympathies on the heroine's behalf: 'It says much for the power of Ms Gordon's writing that the reader feels a genuine sense of dismay at the spectacle of the heroine's mental and physical breakdown.' The point he is making is very like the one being made by the reviewer who said she relaxed when the hero's wife burned her ovulation charts, but he is putting the emphasis on Gordon's writing rather than his own sensibilities.

Generally speaking, the more highbrow the publication the more self-effacing—or apparently self-effacing—the reviewer. A critic in a popular paper may, rightly, claim that but for him a whole section of the literate public might never hear of certain writers and that this enjoins on him the necessity to be forthright and uncomplicated. Auberon Waugh, who reviews novels in the *Evening Standard*, is such a writer. One of his habits is to complain of personal suffering—excruciating boredom, a pain in the ass—on reading novels he doesn't like; another to award prizes—'my gold medal . . . a peerage or some luncheon vouchers to go with it'—to those he does. Waugh sees himself as deploying the common sense of the common man: a reviewer in a more serious journal or newspaper has to suggest expertise, give evidence of special qualifications (though even here there are some who choose to make their comments personal as an excuse for slipping out of responsibility— to say 'I enjoyed it' is sometimes a way of saying 'little me I enjoyed it').

Whatever the publication, it is probably fair to say that most readers of reviews do not go on to read the novels themselves: in that sense
reviews act as substitutes for the novels, incorporating as a further
dimension the experience of the reviewer in reading them. Hence perhaps the documentary interest reviewers show in the lives that are led
in novels (the more sociologically particular the world that is described,
the more confident the praise: 'exactly conveys the tone and feel of a
theatre'; 'quite faultless in its delineation of every aspect of the cinema'). Experiment, symbols, allegory: reviewers don't often like them
('there may be an allegorical meaning here that I've missed; if there is,
Mr Keating isn't pushing it, and I'm all for that'), and novels that have
a grand plan or an easily detected message are rarely well received.
Time and again a book is praised for understating its intentions:

> *Getting Through* leaves so much unsaid that what is left—the story
> itself, pared down—becomes the reflection of great things.

> The purpose of their encounter is never formulated by authorial
> commentary or by the intrusive use of imagery.

> The book never loses its distant innocence of expression—as if the
> full surface of the world can only be conveyed by a prose that neither
> moralises nor obtrudes.

Authorial unobtrusiveness ('clear spare sentences', 'direct factual
observation', 'clear but unemphatic patterns'); modesty of effect and
affect—these are the qualities reviewers speak well of. What is wanted
is not 'hectic' plotting but 'a meticulous circumstantiality', 'not clash-
ing symbols but uninsisted juxtapositions'.
    On the other hand, it is the reviewer's business to make explicit

what the author has been commended for rendering inexplicit; to spell out ('in their interaction they retrace the patterns of social intercourse familiar to us all') and to extrapolate ('Violence, Bainbridge seems to be saying, is as casual, as impersonal as the shadows we know'). Novelists may not be allowed to moralise but reviewers do it all the time:

> To him, the conquest of pride is ultimately more important than the conquest of Prague. It takes a lot of courage to suggest this, but the only real antidote to the think-alike, talk-alike herd instinct of Marxism is the liberation of your own soul from second-hand thinking and borrowed feelings.

> I don't accept any form of racism and I applaud Mr Brink's honest novel.

And if writers don't moralise, or are told that they ought not to, they are nonetheless praised in moral currency: 'Where [the characters]—and Miss Sagan—truly shine is in the sections that describe their acknowledgment of a colleague's cancer.'

Praising is the reviewer's most difficult task. Allocated, in most newspapers, 1,000 words in which to give his views of three or four novels of average merit, he hasn't the space to build up the case for each one and must therefore resort to an encomiastic shorthand. In what is usually the first part of a review, where we are told what sort of novel it is and what happens to whom, the novel itself does much of the work; and if a reviewer gives a coherent account of it and makes the characters seem interesting, he has already done a great deal to commend the book to the reader's attention. A skilful reviewer will also interweave judgment and description. 'Bernice Rubens's new novel is convincing about the need for people to see plots in their lives': that 'convincing' carries conviction because of what follows it; if it had been placed at the end of the review—in the phrase 'a convincing novel', for instance—one would scarcely have heard it.

Since the vocabulary of praise is limited, the same words occur again and again, while some acquire emblematic loadings. *Truth*, for example. When a reviewer says a novel has 'an overall ring of truth', he may just be talking about 'plausibility' and making it sound like something more important. But it is the final adjectival blast that offends. *Marvellous*, *delightful*, *brilliant*: it is hard for a reviewer eager to say good things about a novel to avoid such words, yet they have been used so often in connection with novels which, when compared, say, with *Our Mutual Friend*, are merely mediocre that readers may find some difficulty in giving them credence. It's true they are important to publishers, who use them in their advertisements, and a reviewer anxious to promote a novel will be sure to include a few for the publisher to quote, just as many literary editors, alert to the danger of one novel review sounding very like any other novel review, will want to cut them out.

Reviewers are varyingly responsive to these embarrassments, but the stratagems they may resort to for avoiding the clichés used by their less self-conscious colleagues quickly become clichés themselves. One doesn't often come across the simple phrase 'a marvellous novel' nowadays: the fashion is for triads of adjectives ('exact, piquant and comical', 'rich, mysterious and energetic') or for adjectives coupled with adverbs—'hauntingly pervasive', 'lethally pithy', 'deftly economic'—in relationships whose significance would not be materially altered if the two partners swapped roles—pervasively haunting, pithily lethal etc. The praise is made to sound less bland by the use of negatives ('a completely unponderous story') or of oppositions indicating that a novel hasn't made too much of its virtues ('stylish but troubling', 'unforced yet painful'); and by various minor syntactic devices: one novel 'is saved by energy from pretension', another is rescued from overfamil-iarity 'by the author's evocation of certain oblique and mysterious states of consciousness'; one 'gives us a feel for our own loony culture that is so recognisable we blink with shame and embarrassment', another produces 'shocks so true to life that they hardly seem paradoxical'.

Some reviewers, it's obvious, are better writers than others, but even among good writers there are recurrent mannerisms. Wordplay is one: 'Amid stern actualities, Kundera gamely concocts (like Sterne, and hence unsternly) stories about people playing games.' Verbs are preferred to adjectives: a 'story spurts and fizzes', a 'sense of humour crackles'; and so sometimes are nouns, usually in their plural form—*intricacies*, *acutenesses* and so on. The abstract and the concrete may be unexpectedly juxtaposed: 'details slither rat-like into their lairs'; and rather than speak directly of a novelist's talents, reviewers have lately been much inclined to anthropomorphise the novel: 'grinding on like that is, Hanley's fiction knows, the hardest of all feats.' The desire to avoid clichés is strong and commendable, but leads to some perplexing formulations: 'Through all such knots and breaks of time, a rare aptitude for patience is the unassuming form of Trevor's irre-placeable imagination.'

Novel reviews don't of course end like novels: novelists seldom finish off their work by praising or scolding their characters, though they may (or may not) award them happy lives. But what is wanted of a reviewer is much the same as what is wanted by the reviewer: a modest, unemphatic originality, a meticulously circumstantial account of the novel's merits, and a plausible (or should I say truthful?) response to them.

1. 'Ninety Years of Novel-Reviewing', August 1929.
2. 2 November 1978.
3. *New Fiction*, No. 18 (1978).
4. 7 April 1978.

Narcissism and Its Discontents

Staying in Castries for the wedding was a young man called Mr Kennaway. When he watches me I can see that he doesn't think I am pretty. Oh God, let me be pretty when I grow up.

Jean Rhys was 12 at the time of the wedding in Castries, on the island of St. Lucia. At the age of six a photograph had been taken of her: she looked very pretty then in a new white dress. Three years later, she realised 'with dismay that I wasn't like it any longer': 'It was the first time I was aware of time, change and the longing for the past. I was nine years of age.'

The memory of the dress—'over and over I would remember that magic dress'—worn for the first time with a frangipani wreath, was compounded with the memory of the place where she had been given it, Bona Vista, an estate in the Dominican hills, bought by her father in a moment of financial optimism, 'very beautiful, wild, lonely, remote'. It had to be sold soon afterwards, 'and we never went back': 'Bona Vista too had vanished.'

Jean Rhys didn't really change much after the age of nine. A sense of loss, which was primarily aesthetic, and a consequent sense of being at a loss, seem to have dominated her life—or the record she wished to give of her life—as they dominate her writing. Their circumstances and their resourcefulness may vary a little, but almost all Jean Rhys's heroines, both in her novels and in her short stories, suffer from a similar incapacity to wake up from a dream. They know this about themselves, but the world seems to them too harsh and they lack the 'nous' to deal with it: 'Take my advice and grow another skin or two . . . before it's too late,' a young man remarks to the nous-less heroine of 'Till September Petronella'. Jean Rhys's mother, who didn't like her very much, worried about her ability to look after herself: 'I can't imagine what will happen if you don't learn to behave more like other people.'

One reason she found this difficult, even as a child, was that she didn't know which other people to behave like. On the one hand were the island's black inhabitants, about whom she had complicated feelings. When she was very young she had wished she was black, would pray for a transformation each night and in the morning 'run to the looking-glass . . . to see if the miracle had happened'. Later on, she envied them their lives—'they had a better time than we did'; and wondered whether, being Catholics, they also had 'a better chance in eternity'. Above all, she envied them because they were 'more a part of the place than we were', and being a part of the place mattered to her a great deal: 'It's strange growing up in a very beautiful place and seeing that it is beautiful . . . I wanted to identify with it, to lose myself in it. (But it turned its head away, indifferent, and that broke my heart.)'

The place wouldn't have her, and for all her wanting to be one of them, the black population wouldn't either; *Wide Sargasso Sea* wonderfully describes her feeling that there was a conspiracy between the two to unsettle the settlers, to drive them out by driving them mad. One of her early memories is of a black nurse called Meta, full of magic and malevolence, who played harsh jokes on her, told her, for instance, that at night cockroaches would fly into her room 'and bite my mouth and that the bite would never heal'. When eventually Meta left, Rhys says, with a characteristic sense of un-undoable damage, it was already too late: 'Meta had shown me a world of fear and distrust, and I am still in that world.'

Her family didn't know what Meta was like; they didn't even know, or so she felt, that the blacks didn't like them:

They hate us. We are hated.
Not possible.
Yes it is possible and it is so.

Wherever she went later in her life, she always had a strong sense of being hated, which confirmed her in her view that she saw the world more clearly than other people.

Jean Rhys's father was a Welsh doctor, interested in the newspapers that came from England more than anything else, but 'kind and gentle to me' unlike her mother, a shrewd and capable woman, descendant of an old slave-owning family, and apparently quite uncomprehending of her daughter: '"You are a very peculiar child," said my mother.' She seems to have said it rather often. If they had a companionable (or even characterisable) family life, Rhys gives little sense of it (she had several brothers and sisters but scarcely mentions any of them): instead, in a sequence of short chapters very like her short stories, particularly the later ones, she evokes her own isolation in a place full of pleasing sights and frightening people. The white world was no more welcoming to her than the black ('I'm very much afraid of the whole bloody human race,' one of her heroines remarked) and she in turn was either ingratiating or aloof, finding the ways of thought of her family and their friends acutely puzzling—and, it's implied, rightly so. She may have been unfit for the world, but it isn't clear that she considered the world fit for her. And she didn't altogether dislike not being a part of it: 'I preferred being an outcast by myself,' she observes, after describing a snub from one of the few girls she tried to be friends with.

There remained the terrible problem of looks (the girl she had wanted to be friends with had been chosen on the grounds that she too was plain) and of her incapacity to please despite the efforts she made. Thomas Staley, in his study of Rhys's fiction, discusses the sad fate of her heroines at the hands of 'a male-dominated bourgeois society' and refers to them as victims of 'negative narcissism', a condition 'where the female, treated exclusively as an object, reaches an emotional state in which the exclusive object of her psychic energy is the self'. There is something (more obvious than the words suggest) in that. In the world in which Jean Rhys grew up women were expected first to be pretty, then to flirt, and finally to marry. But Mr. Kennaway didn't think she was pretty, and Mr. Gregg didn't like her ('I knew that for the rest of his life, whenever he thought of me, Mr Gregg would send out a small shoot of dislike'). 'I dreaded growing up. I dreaded the time when I would have to worry about how many proposals I had, what if I didn't have a proposal?' One could say that a world in which girls grew up in dread of not being proposed to was a bad bourgeois world: but in the case of Jean Rhys it isn't the only thing to say.

Even worse in her eyes than not getting a proposal was being seen not to get one. 'When you sink you sink to the accompaniment of loud laughter,' Sasha Jansen remarks in *Good Morning, Midnight*, speaking for all the women Jean Rhys has written about. In the family dining room in Dominica there was a picture of Mary Queen of Scots going to her execution—'her right foot eternally advanced, walking daintily to extinction'. The crowd behind her, Rhys comments, 'was male . . . I have often since seen their narrow eyes, their self-satisfied expressions.'

When she was 17 Rhys left Dominica for England, convinced that it would be the most wonderful place on earth. But in all Rhys's stories, including her own, hope is set up only to be dashed. England, as anybody knows who has read her novels, represented a kind of extinction. It was cold, grey, and full of smug hostility: 'Later on I learnt to know that most English people kept knives under their tongues to stab me.'

When Jean Rhys died in 1979, only the first part of her autobiography, the account of her West Indian childhood, was ready for publication; the second part, which covers the years from 1907 to 1920 or 1921, had been taken down from dictation by the novelist David Plante and was still substantially unrevised. A third section consists of fragments from a diary of the 1940s. The second part is dull by comparison with the first, though the events are interesting enough: a brief period at the Perse School in Cambridge; her time as an acting student and then as a chorus girl; her first love affair and the unhappiness that followed; her work in a soldiers' canteen; and after the war her move to Paris and her marriage to the mysterious Jean Lenglet, about whom she seems to have known unaccountably little. She had now started to live the kind of futile, penurious life so well described in her first four novels: sleeping a lot, drinking a bit, clinging to sadness ('I would have missed it if it had gone'). Reluctant to make any move unassisted by fate, she simply waited for men to arrive and then to depart. In her first published story she speaks, rather crudely for her, of the 'curse of Eve': 'the perpetual hunger to be beautiful and the thirst to be loved'—as always, she was talking about herself.

It was a curse she never allowed her heroines to overcome. Fate was kinder to her. 'I must write,' she noted in her diary. 'If I stop writing my life will have been an abject failure.' Between the end of her first affair and the beginning of the war, she moved for a short time to a bedsitter in World's End. Here, appropriately, fate—as she describes it—took her in hand. With no apparent purpose in mind, she bought some new pens and several shiny exercise books and then, in some kind of daze, wrote down everything that had recently happened to her. She didn't look at the books again for many years, but took them with her wherever she went—'this is one of the reasons I believe in Fate.' Fate subsequently introduced her to Ford Madox Ford and the notebooks 'were the foundation for *Voyage in the Dark*': with that uncharacteristically proud announcement the autobiography ends.

'Have all beautiful things sad destinies?' asks the sarcastic Mr. Rochester in *Wide Sargasso Sea*. His first wife said no, but she was pretty and came to a sad end. All Jean Rhys's women thought obsessively about looks although having them never did them much good. A feminist argument would not be inappropriate here, nor would Professor Staley's 'negative narcissism', but it might still be the case that good looks are a currency which can be put to good use or to bad. Take Liane de Pougy, 'celebrated *cascadeuse* of the Belle Epoque', as Anita Brookner has described her. She was, for most of her life, one of the most beautiful and elegant women in France, had a triumphant career as a courtesan ('the nation's Liane'), married in her late thirties a Romanian prince—which didn't stop her having a good time—and ended up in the arms of God, or at any rate the Church. Maimie Pinzer provides another, more complicated example. She was a good-looking Jewish girl, born in Philadelphia in 1885. When she was 13 she had to leave school to work in a department store. There she started going with men and although her subsequent career was full of pain, she was in no doubt that she had escaped from an intolerable background.

Prostitution, as one of the editors of *The Maimie Papers* points out, is a form of upward mobility. An unwholesome form perhaps—at least in the eyes of those who have dedicated themselves to reclaiming fallen women, or women *tout court*—but prostitutes have not invariably found it so. A pretty but impecunious girl might not see any good reason for giving up the notion that her face could be her fortune in a world where, thanks to their faces, respectable girls regularly made respectable fortunes. 'She has been told twenty times a day by her mother, since she was five years old, that she's a beauty of beauties . . . that she was born for great things, that if she plays her cards she may marry God knows whom': Christina Light, the future Princess Casamassima, was uncommonly beautiful but there was nothing very unusual about her mother's ideas for her. Gladys Deacon, another American and, according to Chips Channon, 'once the world's most beautiful woman', made it her life's business to marry the Duke of Marlborough (though she hated him almost as soon as she married him). Then, too, one has to consider the available alternatives. Jean Rhys, down and out in London, preferred to take money rather than take work of any kind. Maimie Pinzer, a contemporary of Gladys Deacon's, was 'rescued' by a very Christian gentleman who, though he had no trouble in persuading her that going with men was a low activity and unworthy of her, could not convince her that the other occupations open to her were preferable. 'I don't propose,' she said, 'to get up at 6.30 to be at work at 8 and work in a close, stuffy room with people I despise, until dark, for $6 or $7 a week! When I could, just by phoning, spend an afternoon with some congenial person and in the end have more than a week's work could pay me.' In recent years, for God knows what awful reasons, prostitution has been moving away from the old idea of good times to a new idea of good works—or lay therapy.

There are, however, other connections between fortune-hunting and good looks of which economic necessity or the wish to be rich and well married may only be a part. It's a matter of expectations and how they can be met. 'I was not born. I happened,' Gladys Deacon, who was famous for her 'brain power' as well as her looks, once said; and although she was by then very old and selectively senile, it had always been her view that the facts of life—both biological and social—didn't apply to her. In her confidence that she could improve on what nature had already so generously done for her she had paraffin wax injected into the bridge of her nose—nature had its revenge when the wax started to shift to other parts of her face. An exalted idea of her own destiny, of having been 'born for great things', was confirmed but not assuaged by a great deal of looking in the mirror (Mabel Dodge Luhan said that Gladys 'was content to lie for hours alone on her bed, happy in loving her own beauty, contemplating it') and a legion of famous admirers—Proust, Montesquiou, Berenson, Hofmannsthal, the Kaiser's son, and a hundred others. Her extraordinary sense of herself was matched by an extraordinary contempt for other people. When the *Titanic* sank she was appalled that a friend of hers should have died when so many 'nasty *femmes de chambre*' were saved: 'I can imagine the way they howled, cannot you?' she wrote to her mother.

Later in her life, she came to admire Hitler, who had, as she put it, 'a telling personality': 'When you think how hard it is to create a rising in a small village, well, he had the whole world up in arms.' She too had disturbed some part of the world: unfortunately, the search for acknowledgment of her powers—her marriage to the Duke of Marlborough—proved wholly unsatisfactory, and after that there was only age and an increasingly wild eccentricity.

Liane de Pougy preferred Mussolini: 'How envious I am of Italy with her Mussolini! Our leaders are old, white-haired, flabby.' Moderation, respectability, convention: good-looking women seem to have some special difficulty in bearing with them, as if life must be made to live up to the reflection in the mirror. 'I would rather have the highest or the lowest in everything. I find that instinctively I avoid being where I have to mix and mingle with the half-bred, the half-souled and the half-educated,' Maimie Pinzer wrote in one of the letters to the Bostonian Fanny Quincy Howe that make up *The Maimie Papers*. Later on, when she had set up a shelter for young prostitutes in Montreal, she described her favourite among them as being 'the opposite of "bourgeois"'. Neither Gladys Deacon nor Liane de Pougy had much knowledge of the 'lowest', except in their own behaviour, where looks were knowingly taken to be licence. 'For me,' the latter said, 'there was nothing between being pure and being dissolute.' When Gladys Deacon was an hour and a half late for an appointment with the playwright Giraudoux, he felt, apparently, that this was 'the minimum' time to wait for someone of her beauty. Jean Rhys was more unhappy and more nihilistic: 'I am a stranger and I always will be, and after all I didn't really care'; and because her heroines didn't really care either, they were capable of the same capriciousness as those two far more confident and extravagant women.

In all these lives men feature prominently and not at all. Jean Rhys for long stretches of her life was wholly dependent on them, emotionally and financially: but there is nothing to suggest that she enjoyed their company. As suitors and victims, payers of compliments and buyers of presents, they provided necessary recognition. Liane de Pougy was famous for having been given the most expensive string of pearls in France but the sensuous scenes she records are scenes between her and other women: 'At about three o'clock my Flossie [the much-written-about Nathalie Barney] arrived. We lay down to rest in the overwhelming scent of flowers. She took me in her arms and . . . we were both equally stupefied by tenderness.' Though there is little evidence to support her claim that she was 'nervous . . . in the presence of men', it's clear that she could find them gracelessly 'other'. In her later years, she even had some difficulty in coming to terms with Jesus: 'Your incarnation,' she said, addressing him one night, 'makes me see too much of the man in You, and that puts me off.' Maimie Pinzer, though not put off by the man in men, was most strongly attached, for much of the period covered by these letters, to Mrs. Howe, the upper-class woman she would have liked to have been. Staley even suggests that the heartless Jean Rhys found her best moments in the companionship of women.

Mon semblable, ma soeur . . . The world now is full of sisters, who have persuasively argued the case against looks, seeing them largely as a matter of men's vanity and women's collusion: but it may be that they do women an injustice in overlooking the question of women's vanity and men's collusion. Nor would everyone necessarily be happier if the sense of good looks were eradicated, as some radical feminists would have them be, in the cause of sexual equality. Even narcissism has its rewards, as well as its discontents. Most of Liane de Pougy's and Gladys Deacon's friends were artists ('she implored Epstein to come and talk about art'), with whom they shared their contempt for the bourgeois world and their unusual commitment to appearances. It's possible there is some connection between a sense of looks and an idea of art. Jean Rhys is not rightly praised, as Staley praises her, for a 'comprehensive' understanding 'of what it is to have been a woman in this century': her understanding is maddeningly limited to what it is to have been Jean Rhys. She was a narcissist who described herself beautifully.

Books reviewed:
Smile Please: An Unfinished Autobiography by Jean Rhys
Jean Rhys: A Critical Study by Thomas Staley
My Blue Notebooks by Liane de Pougy, translated by Diana Athill
The Maimie Papers edited by Ruth Rosen and Sue Davidson
Gladys, Duchess of Marlborough by Hugo Vickers

Death and the Maiden

Alice James died in London at the age of 43, regretting only that she would not have the pleasure of knowing and reporting herself dead. The reporting was done instead by her favourite brother: 'I went to the window to let in a little more of the afternoon light, and when I went back to the bed she had drawn the breath that was not succeeded by another,' Henry James wrote to their eldest brother, William, in America, as if, in the now fashionable way, defining death to a Martian. Eager to do what justice she could to the occasion, Alice had sent William a farewell telegram the day before, which Henry later confirmed. William, nonetheless, feared that her death might simply be an illusion: 'her neurotic temperament & chronically reduced vitality are just the field for trance-tricks to play themselves upon.' It was very like William—or her idea of William—to try to rob her of her greatest, her only achievement.

She died in March 1892. Looking back on the previous year, she made a note in her diary of the books her brothers had written or published and added: 'not a bad show for one family. Especially if I get myself dead.' The James family was exhilarated by the thought, and the proximity, of death. 'When that which is *you* passes out of the body, I am sure that there will be an explosion of liberated force and life, till then eclipsed and kept down,' William wrote to Alice when he learned that she was dying. It was the lesson their father had taught. 'We have all been educated by Father to feel that death was the only reality and that life was simply an experimental thing,' Robertson James, the youngest son, said after their mother's death. 'We feel that we are more near to her now than ever before, simply because she is already at the goal for which we all cheerfully bend our steps . . . The last two weeks . . . have been the happiest I have known.' So exalted was the James idea of death that it sometimes seems as if they thought 'the distinguished thing' was too distinguished for anyone who wasn't a member of their family.

Being a James was a complicated business, and the five children all too obviously divide into the two who succeeded, William and Henry, the two who did not, Wilkie and Robertson (who once said he thought he was a foundling), and Alice, the youngest and the only girl, who both did and didn't. It was complicated principally because their father made it so. Henry James *père* had spent his own childhood and youth haunted by his father's stern Irish Calvinism, which he both flouted and feared; and the kind of father he eventually became was a direct repudiation of the father he had had. Where his father had exacted discipline he exacted freedom, where his father had been remote and authoritarian he was loving and indulgent. It's been said that the only right the James children didn't have was the right to be unhappy, but they weren't allowed to think badly of themselves either: to have done so would have been to admit what their father's philosophy proscribed—the presence of evil in the James household. Jean Strouse, in her excellent biography of Alice, points out the difficulty that all this positive thinking caused James's children: 'To be innocent and good meant *not to know* the darker sides of one's own nature. To love and be loved . . . required the renunciation of certain kinds of knowledge and feeling.' It was a renunciation that Alice couldn't in the end manage without renouncing practically everything else.

James Sr.'s idiosyncratic philosophy derived by an eccentric route from Swedenborg: in 1844, on a visit to England, he had what he came to see as a Swedenborgian 'vastation', an experience of 'perfectly insane and abject terror', from which he emerged with a new faith in God's benevolence and man's spiritual capacities. From then on his faith was his occupation. Henry, troubled by the fact that his father had no recognisable job, asked him how he could describe what he did to the children at school. 'Say I'm a philosopher,' his father replied, 'say I'm a seeker for truth, say I'm a lover of my kind.' Henry continued to look with envy on the friend who told him 'crushingly . . . that the author of *his* being was in the business of a stevedore'. Their father's philosophy didn't make much impression on the world at large (William Dean Howells said of his book *The Secret of Swedenborg* that James had 'kept it'), but it dominated his children's lives as his own father's Calvinism had dominated his. None of them ever altogether rejected it.

He was ambitious in his expectations of his children, but what he required of them was intangible: neither achievement nor success but 'just' that they should '*be* something'—something unspecifiably general, which could loosely be translated as 'interesting'. Their education was eclectic—'sensuous' was the word their father used—designed to develop their sensibilities rather than train their minds; and both Alice and William later wondered whether they had any. Alice, typically, consoled herself with the thought that to have had one would, as she put it, 'have deprived me . . . of those exquisite moments of mental flatulence which every now and then inflate the cerebral vacuum with a delicious sense of latent possibilities'.

'A delicious sense of latent possibilities' was precisely what their father wished for in his children, and as they grew up he went out of his way to discourage them from settling down to any one activity. The fact that the family had money, and that their father had never had to do anything, made choice more difficult. In 'Notes of a Son and Brother', Henry summed up their father's expectations, and in doing so incidentally revealed how closely the cast of his sentences mirrored the cast of his father's mind—the claim that James's fiction elaborately borrowed from his father's Swedenborgianism is something else again. What James Sr. wanted, Henry said, was 'something unconnected with specific doing, something free and uncommitted, something finer in short than being *that*, whatever it was, might consist of'. *That*, on the other hand, might have been a good deal less strenuous.

What place Alice had in her father's grand design was unclear. She was much closer to him than she was to her mother, celebrated by Alice as the 'essence of wife-and-motherhood', but seeming to lack any more colourful qualities. Henry was Mary James's 'angel', and there is no evidence to suggest she had a special interest in her daughter. Alice, unlike her mother, was imaginative and quick, and her father found the company of this 'heir to the paternal wit', as he called her, enchanting. 'Her presence is a perfect sunbeam to Father,' her mother remarked. Yet while her father took the family first to Europe, then from country to country, in search of the right atmosphere and the right school for her brothers, Alice merely sat at home, learning a bit of this and that, partaking of the atmosphere. Her father took pleasure in her intelligence but did little to encourage it, and for most of her life she had a fierce sense of her capacities and an equally fierce sense of their not being wanted.

James Sr.'s ideas about what women should do with their lives differed from conventional ideas only in that he thought they were too good to do anything. 'The very virtue of woman,' he wrote, 'disqualifies her for all didactic dignity. Learning and wisdom do not become her.' Alice, his clever daughter, was—unlike her brothers—to make nothing of her cleverness. Was she then to be like her mother and her mother's sister who lived with them? 'Large florid stupid seeming ladies' was how the pert Lilla Cabot described them: 'the very incarnation of *banality*'. 'Oh, Alice, how hard you are,' her father once said to her and many years later she was still worrying about the remark: it was a fault in her—a lack of womanliness—not to have a gentler nature. She was, her family said, highly moral, the implication being that she was too highly moral, a Calvinist at heart. The sad fact is, as Ruth Yeazell says in the subtle and sophisticated biographical essay with which she introduces her selection of Alice James's letters, that Alice, who wasn't what her father said 'woman' ought to be, a 'form of personal affection', a lover and blesser of men, who never did anything, indeed who spent most of her life wanting it to end, came closest to fulfilling her father's wish that his children should just *be* something.

Alice started to think about dying before she reached adolescence. 'I had to peg away pretty hard between 12 and 24, "killing myself", as someone calls it—absorbing into the bone that the better part is to clothe oneself in neutral tints, walk by still waters, and possess one's soul in silence.' She wrote this in the diary she began when she was 40, so it may be that her memory was coloured by the experiences of adult life. But when she was 17, William, on an expedition in Brazil, sent his love to Henry and Alice and asked: 'Does the latter continue to wish she was dead?' It may simply be that she saw no way forward for herself. Her father—who had taken on himself the task of defining reality for the rest of the family—had not offered her one; and her mother's example was inappropriate: she wasn't like her mother. Leon Edel, in his *Life of Henry James*, sees Alice as a casualty not so much of the family as of the age: 'In our time,' he says, 'she might have learned to play tennis, to swim, to row, to ski, to drive a car.' It's hard to think of Henry in any age skiing his way out of his difficulties: but certainly, as Edel goes on to suggest, if Alice had been able to conceive of a life away from her family and an occupation other than wife-and-motherhood, she might not have spent so many years 'chained', as she said, 'to a sofa'. 'When I am gone,' she wrote to William as she was dying, 'pray don't think of me simply as a creature who might have been something else, had neurotic science been born.' The remark is characteristically proud as well as far-sighted: there is no sense in dwelling on what her life could have been in an age of psychoanalysis or Valium.

The family returned from Europe in 1860 and settled down to a New England life, first in Newport, then in Boston, finally in Cambridge. Alice went to school, made friends, took up riding, swimming, and sailing—the very activities Edel prescribes. Yet it was 'under the low grey Newport sky' that she took the decision to clothe herself in neutral tints. A 'palpitating' Alice, subject to mysterious pains and prostrations, now began to appear in family letters, and within a few years almost every reference to her was a reference to her health. Invited to spend a few days with the Emerson girls, she had to refuse because the excitement was too much: like other famous 19th-century invalids, and no doubt many who weren't famous, she had started to limit her choices by being ill; and when Henry said of her in 1889, 'she only gets on so long as nothing happens,' he might have been speaking of the whole of her life.

'Nerves' were current in the family in the 1860s, as her brothers faced up to the necessity of leaving home and deciding what to do. The two younger boys went off to the Civil War and to their lives of un-Jamesian obscurity and failure, though they too sent back reports of illness and despair. Neither William nor Henry was fit to go: William indeed was in a state of hypochondriacal depression that was to last for something like 17 years—in effect, until his marriage. Their father loved his children even more when they were ill or in difficulty ('there is nothing . . . so full of hope and joy to me as to see my children giving way to humiliation'), so as the claims of Alice's ill-health grew more pressing her share of parental attention steadily increased. 'To be menaced with death or danger [has] been from time immemorial . . . the very shortest of all cuts to the interesting state,' James wrote in the preface to *The Wings of the Dove*. Alice's body, however much she was to revile it, had done for her what her mind had been unable to do: it made her 'interesting'.

In 1866, when she was 18, she spent six months in New York receiving a form of treatment for her nerves that was described as 'motorpathic'—it consisted largely of physical exercises to stimulate the muscles and bracing homilies to depress (in the old sense) the mind. A year and a half later she had her first breakdown. It lasted several months and her family praised her for enduring it so virtuously. While each of her unhappy brothers was blamed in turn by their mother for being 'morbidly hopeless', Alice was praised for her valour: 'The fortitude with which our daughter carries the load which has been given her to bear is truly beautiful,' Mary James wrote to the unlucky Robertson. Alice's highly moral nature had at last found an area in which it was allowed to operate.

Twenty years later, after reading an account that William, by now a professor of philosophy at Harvard, had written of the work the French physician Janet had done with hysterics, Alice gave a memorable description in her diary of the 'violent turns of hysteria', as she rightly called them, which she had suffered in her late teens:

> As I used to sit immovable reading in the library with waves of violent inclination suddenly . . . taking some one of their myriad forms, such as throwing myself out of the window, or knocking off the head of the benignant pater as he sat with his silver locks, writing at his table, it used to seem to me that the only difference between me and the insane was that I had not only all the horrors

and suffering of insanity but the duties of doctor, nurse and
straitjacket imposed upon me too.

While the pit of her stomach, the palms of her hands, the soles of her
feet suffered their discrete insanities, her mind remained 'luminous
and active', unaffected by what was happening to her but quite inca-
pable of stopping it. 'Her mind does not seem at all involved in it,' her
mother observed. Jean Strouse alludes to what Charcot called the *belle
indifférence* of the hysteric, but it could equally have been the healthy
indifference of the stoic. It's tempting, given her later history, to settle
for stoicism.

'Alice is busy trying to idle,' Mary James wrote to Henry as Alice
recovered. For the next ten years her life alternated between getting
better and getting worse: these were her two chief occupations. When
she was better, she cycled and gossiped and picnicked with other sisters and daughters of Cambridge intellectuals, wrote them letters that
were often heated and sentimental when they were away in Europe,
which they frequently were, took part in sewing bees and amateur the-
atricals. Occasionally she was fit enough for short holidays away from
home and her parents; and in 1872 she spent a triumphant summer in
Europe with Henry and her aunt Kate. Although she was sometimes
ill, and although Edel suggests that anxiety on her behalf undermined
Henry's pleasure, it was the only period in her life of which one can say
that she enjoyed herself. Five years afterwards, she wrote to a friend: 'I
am frightened sometimes when I suddenly become conscious of how
constantly I dwell on that summer I spent abroad.' Part of the enjoyment derived from the realisation that her sensibilities weren't after all
inferior to her brothers': 'Imagine the bliss of finding that I too was a
"sensitive".' When she returned to Cambridge, her family, impressed by
her enthusiasm and vigour (William said she was in all respects more
'elastic'), concluded that the 'journey was a great thing for her in every

way'. Yet there was no question of repeating the experience. 'Her greatest delight would be to go again and stay longer,' Mary James wrote
to Henry, adding that this would not, of course, 'be possible during
Father's lifetime'. He 'would not', Jean Strouse comments, 'sacrifice his
pleasure in her company to her pleasure at independence.'

Strouse's dim view of Henry James Sr. and his accomplice wife
is catching; and after a while it becomes difficult to resist the thought
that James's oppressively (Strouse would say selfishly) loving personality and eccentric (equally selfish) ideas were in many ways to blame
for Alice's fate. One might call this the Laingian version, and it's rein-
forced here by the fact that her history up to the death of her parents is
largely presented through her parents' eyes: not what she was but what
they said she was—i.e., what they made her into. To some extent, this is
a consequence of the material that is available, but it also accords with
some—very persuasive—comments that Strouse herself makes about
the effect on Alice of having such a father. (Looking at what Edel has
to say about Alice, one may feel that the two writers are describing
different sets of parents.) The Laingian view isn't, of course, the only
possible view of Alice's troubles—nor the only one Strouse takes. She
writes very well about her relation to her times, and particularly about
her health and its relation to the times. It is, however, the case that the
Alice who is the subject of her book is a victim whereas the Alice in
Yeazell's essay is her own worst enemy.

There was nothing very unusual in Alice's condition (so far); and
many reasons for this kind of nervous weakness can be found both
in the social history of well-to-do young women, whose uselessness
reached its lowest point in the second half of the 19th century, and
in the history of medicine, which was just beginning to address itself,
through the new science of neurology, to diseases that were not entirely
to do with the body and not entirely to do with the mind. Hysteria was
thought to be a female affliction, but beyond that most neurologists

didn't know what to make of it: 'It were as well called mysteria,' said the excellent Weir Mitchell. Different doctors optimistically devised different treatments, the majority of which were tried on Alice, but most shared the view of Charles Taylor, Alice's first doctor in New York, that the body should be stimulated and the mind soothed. From this it was only a short step to saying, as several neurologists did, that too much education was a bad thing for a woman. 'For patience, for reliability, for real judgment in carrying out directions, for self-control,' Taylor was to write, 'give me the little woman who has not been "educated" too much, and whose ambition is to be a good wife and mother . . . Such women are capable of being the mothers of men.' Jean Strouse picks up the fact that Alice's diary description of her hysterical attacks had pictured her either in her father's library or in the schoolroom, as if the attacks only occurred when she was trying to use her brain. On the other hand, it may be that these were the occasions when she most resented their occurrence. Whatever the reason, Alice had concluded that 'conscious and continuous cerebration' was 'an impossible exercise'—thereby incidentally, or not so incidentally, proving both her father and her doctor right: thinking was an unsuitable occupation for a woman. What is missing from Strouse's common-sense, as well as sisterly, account of Alice's maladies is the interpretation that Freud would have put on them. Yeazell, quite properly, points out the similarities between Alice's symptoms and those of some of Freud's most famous patients. It's impossible to believe that there wasn't a strong sexual element in Alice's sufferings.

As her twenties progressed, and more and more of the women she knew got engaged, her letters to her few remaining unmarried friends began to fill up with catty remarks:

What do you suppose I heard the other day? Nothing less than that those dreadful Loverings had had no end of offers . . .

Between ourselves, can you conceive what the youth wants her for? You may say money, but after all she hasn't got enough in her own right to make it worth while and her mother may live half a century . . .

Sargy [the man who was to marry Lilla Cabot] always had the capacities of a cormorant, so he is able to swallow her whole, not having to think about her as she is going down must make it much easier . . .

One or two young men briefly took her fancy, but they had no interest in her and she remained proposal-less. Strouse observes that her family never encouraged her to think of marriage (Too delicate? Father wouldn't have liked the idea? Too obviously a spinster?), while she confined herself to jokes about 'unattractive youths' who couldn't see her qualities. The only man to flirt with her was her brother William. The romance with William—or the appearance of romance, it's not easy to tell how much of it was irony—had begun when she was a child, and in the 1870s he was still, for example, addressing her as 'sweetlington' and 'beloved beautlet' in letters charged with amorous suggestion. In 1878, when Alice was 30, he announced his engagement to another Alice, a 'peerless specimen of "New England womanhood",' according to Henry. The first Alice was unable to go to the wedding—she had again collapsed.

This time, too, she had physical symptoms: her stomach was a 'nest of snakes coiling and uncoiling themselves', her legs gave way, and a year later she could still barely walk. She was, however, much more unhappy than she had been during her first breakdown, and talked to her father about killing herself. Characteristically, he gave her permission to do so—or, as he put it, granted her the 'freedom to do in the premises what she pleased'—attributing her unhappiness to 'our trouble as a race' (the human race, that is) and 'the burden of the mortal life'. He was confident that once he had given his permission she wouldn't do it, and he was right. However, if her diary is to be trusted, she found a way round him. 'The fact is,' she wrote shortly before her death, 'I have been dead so long and it has been simply such a grim shoving of the hours behind me . . . since that hideous summer of '78 when I went to the deep sea, its dark waters closed over me and I knew neither hope nor peace, that now it's only the shrivelling of an empty pea pod that has to be completed.'

There were another 14 years to go. In 1881, her mother died of an attack of bronchial asthma, and Alice didn't collapse as everyone expected her to do. The usual bulletins were issued: she was seen by Robertson to 'thrive under the ordeal of nursing' her sick mother, and after Mary James had died Aunt Kate reported that 'her mother's death seems to have brought new life to Alice.' She was happy, or 'almost happy'—content to think of her mother as a 'beautiful illumined memory'—and enjoying her new responsibilities. At the end of 1878, talking about her recent breakdown, she had said in a letter: 'For a young woman who not only likes to manage herself but the rest of the world too, such a moral prostration taxed my common sense a good deal.' Now she had a chance to manage and for the most part did it well. What she dreaded was that her father, too, would die, and soon enough he did. Whether or not he had an illness isn't clear: for the most part he wanted to die, 'yearned unspeakably' to do so and thus rejoin his wife, who grew ever more perfect in his eyes. He stopped eating, complained that 'this dying' was 'weary work', and according to Alice's new friend Katharine Loring, got over 'the delay in dying by asserting that he [had] already died'. His last words were for his sons—'*such* good boys'. Henry returned from England two days after his father's death and, true to the family metaphysic, read aloud over his grave a farewell letter from William that had arrived too late to be read at his bedside. Henry told William he was sure their father heard it 'somewhere out of the depths of the still, bright winter air'.

This time Alice did, briefly, collapse: but now she had Katharine Loring to look after her (at least when Miss Loring was able to get away from the sick members of her own family). They had become friends some years earlier when Alice was recruited to teach history—it was the only thing she ever 'did'—by a group of Boston women who had started a charitable correspondence course for women: Katharine was head of the history department. It may sound like the beginning of a True Romance: in effect, it was the start of what was then known as a 'Boston marriage'—of which there were quite a few among the James family's acquaintance. 'I wish you could know Katharine Loring,' Alice wrote to Sara Sedgwick, 'she is a most wonderful being. She has all the mere brute superiority which distinguishes man from woman combined with all the distinctively feminine virtues. There is nothing she cannot do from hewing wood & drawing water to driving runaway horses & educating all the women in North America.' Katharine was indeed an admirably practical woman—and an all too inspiring nurse. None of the other Jameses seems to have been at all fond of her (William's wife suspected that she was Alice's lover, which seems unlikely, and if any part of their relationship is described in *The Bostonians*, it's clear that Henry didn't like it), but they agreed that she was an unusual 'blessing' to Alice.

In 1884, Katharine Loring brought Alice to England, where she would spend the rest of her life, most of it in bed. She was now a full-time invalid, one pain succeeding another without interruption; and everything that happened to her, whether she was living in a room in Bournemouth or in a room in Leamington, happened within that room. There are many descriptions in her letters of what it was like to be so confined and so uncomfortable, all of them written with a robustness that seems to contradict their subject matter. There is also a great deal that isn't about illness: but about the friends she liked and, more often, those she half-liked, about Henry and his work, about England, the contemptible English and their contemptible politics. 'I never expect to be deader than I am now,' she wrote to William and then attacked him for his 'bourgeois' attitude to *The Princess Casamassima*. The poverty of the English poor, unemployment, strikes, the inequities of the Empire, and especially the Irish Question, were treated in her letters and her journal with a radical passion that is the only evidence we have that she may—possibly—have regretted not leading a more active life. As it was, she consoled herself with the thought that it was 'a wonderful time to be living in when things are going at such a pace'.

It was in any case Alice's view, so she said in her diary, that 'the paralytic on the couch can have if he wants them wider experiences than Stanley slaughtering savages.' Yes and no: but the notion mattered to her. At the end of her life Alice had found a philosophy which enabled her both to accept what was happening to her and—more important—to think well of herself. It wasn't a grandiose vision such as her father's discovery of Swedenborg had offered, but it made a virtue of her non-life. 'We do not take our successes with us only the manner in which we have met our failures, that never crumbles in the dust,' she wrote to the unfortunate Robertson's wife. She read the three volumes of George Eliot's *Journal and Letters* and despised her for her 'futile whining'. It's reasonable to suppose, as everyone who has written about her does, that some part of Alice's English decline can be attributed to a desire to have Katharine Loring's full attention—and quite a bit of Henry's. As before, her body said one thing and her mind another. She didn't complain and made no explicit requests for sympathy. William, who always got it wrong, irritated her with pitying remarks about her sufferings and frustrations. To a letter in which he had her 'stifling slowly in a quagmire of disgust and pain and impotence' she replied that she had roared with laughter, 'for I consider myself one of the most *potent* creations of my time, & though I may not have a group of Harvard students sitting at my feet drinking in psychic truth, I shall not tremble, I assure you, at the last trump.' By then she had made not trembling at the last trump the thing that mattered most.

In 1891, her doctor at last diagnosed a plausible (and fatal) organic illness: she had cancer of the breast and it was incurable. 'To anyone who has not been there,' she wrote in her diary, 'it will be hard to understand the enormous relief of Sir A C's uncompromising verdict, lifting us out of the formless vague and setting us within the very heart of the sustaining concrete.' Impending death brought to her life the definition she required. It also brought her Katharine Loring's absolute devotion. 'As the ugliest things go to the making of the fairest,' her diary reported, 'it is not wonderful that this unholy granite substance in my breast should be the soil propitious for the perfect flowering of Katharine's unexampled genius for friendship and devotion.' She died, not trembling, but, Katharine Loring said, 'very happy' in the knowledge that the last trump was at hand. 'Her disastrous, her tragic health,' Henry wrote after her death, 'was in a manner the only solution for her of the practical problem of life—as it suppressed the element of equality, reciprocity etc.' It isn't clear whether he meant that life was too much for her or that she was too much for life: both are distinct possibilities. 'I have always had significance for myself,' she had said in one of her retorts to William; after she died her brothers, reading her diary for the first time, found she had significance for the family too: the diary, they both agreed, constituted 'a new claim for the family renown'. Unfortunately, Henry, fearing some 'catastrophe of publicity', didn't want it given 'to the world', and it wasn't until 1964 that the full text, edited by Leon Edel, was finally published. Katharine Loring never had any doubt that it was written for posterity to read.

Books reviewed:

Alice James by Jean Strouse

The Death and Letters of Alice James edited by Ruth Bernard Yeazell

Divorce Me

Twelve years ago Jonathan Gathorne-Hardy got divorced after ten years of marriage. In the unhappiness that followed he thought about himself and about society: would it break down too? In 1969, the year Gathorne-Hardy got his decree nisi, there were 60,000 divorces in Britain: in 1980 there were 150,000. 'During the last century of the Roman Empire, as a great civilisation collapsed, a raging epidemic of divorces roared unchecked.' A terrifying parallel? Seemingly not. 'Even quite general knowledge about the past can have a calming effect,' Gathorne-Hardy says, and he should know because his knowledge is very general. 'Roman culture' was 'too superficial to withstand the temptations that beset it', and 'the result was a moral collapse which we do not only not approach but can barely envisage.' (The source for Gathorne-Hardy's remarks about the Roman Empire is Jerome Carcopino's *Daily Life in Ancient Rome*, published in translation by Routledge in 1941, when Carcopino was minister of national education in the Vichy government.) What's happening to us is much grander:

a 'vast reorganisation of the modern psyche', a 'profound change in human consciousness'.

'I see you have written a book about yourself and called it *The World Crisis*,' Arthur Balfour once said to Churchill. Gathorne-Hardy is the author of two well-known books, *The Rise and Fall of the British Nanny* and *The Public School Phenomenon*: records not of his life but of his kind—tribal history. *Love, Sex, Marriage and Divorce* translates into world history the three-year analysis he underwent in the wake of his divorce. Now he is the doctor and we (his readers) the patient. 'We must begin,' he says, 'like any sensible analyst does . . . by looking into the past.' And what we see when we look into it is that it was never all that stable or all that virtuous. ('Until the late Middle Ages frequent changes of partner were quite usual.') It follows that there is nothing peculiarly bad or difficult about the present: 'This is an age, uniquely, of anxiety and stress. You find this obvious—a cliché even? A cliché it certainly is. I don't for one moment think it is true.' Analysts are always inclined to make light of their patients' troubles. Least said (by the analyst), soonest mended.

Psychoanalysis, as its critics have never been slow to point out, is a form of treatment resorted to by those who, in a sociological sense, have nothing to worry about. The troubles that preoccupy Gathorne-Hardy can similarly be construed as the product of unusual good fortune. His title is deceptive. Love, sex, and marriage are contingent: what interests him is the divorce they lead to. The first cause of divorce is sex—not its failure but its staggering availability. This is the work—in Gathorne-Hardy's telling, the single-handed achievement—of Kinsey, who 'turned sexual freedom, from being a trend among the elite and literate, into a mass movement, possibly for the first time in history'. That Kinsey—Alfred C. Kinsey, Professor of Zoology, as he liked to be known—was a thoughtful man is indicated by the first paper he wrote:

'What do birds do when it rains?' He was by nature a collector, and in his early years was devoted to the wasp: so devoted that he was eventually in a position to give the Natural History Museum a collection of four million different wasps. Although he disclaimed any interest in altering behaviour (Gathorne-Hardy: 'This is rubbish'), he was always eager to point out that it was the most respectable people who had the busiest sex lives—'time and again a lawyer who has masturbated forty times a week,' Gathorne-Hardy notes, 'will be "distinguished in his profession"'—and, conversely, that adolescents who came to sex early were, in Kinsey's words, more 'alert, energetic, vivacious, spontaneous, socially extrovert and/or aggressive individuals in the population' than those who got to it late.

After the annals of sexual prowess, the annals of sexual infirmity. After Kinsey, Masters and Johnson—'it was around the clitoris that they made major discoveries.' Sex is a problem because it is no longer supposed to be a problem. 'Throughout history men have boasted of their conquests, and in liberated ages, women too,' Gathorne-Hardy writes: 'this is the first time conquerors and conquests have worried about how and how often they both come.' (In this context it seems we must praise Kingsley Amis, who has given us, in *Jake's Thing*, our only song of impotence and experience.) Gathorne-Hardy isn't sure whether sex is a symptom or a cause of domestic unrest: 'sex is central but also extremely elusive.' At the end of his book, however, under the heading 'Some Solutions to the Problems of Marriage, Sex and Divorce', he painstakingly describes the complicated procedures devised by Masters and Johnson for the treatment of sexual 'dysfunction' ('the sensate focus sessions inch towards the genitals') and gives them credit for considerable feats of marital retrieval: 'if their technique were applied generally', premature ejaculation, 'like some sexual smallpox', could be 'completely eliminated in ten years'.

The second cause of divorce is women. 'There is a Japanese TV programme which specialises in getting back missing people. Twenty years ago, it was 70 per cent men running away; now it has reversed—70 per cent women clearing off.' In Gathorne-Hardy's view, so many women clearing off isn't necessarily a bad thing. Not only because it's reasonable that women should want to get away from the dusting and the cooking ('the main, indeed only, point about housework is that for large numbers of people it is awful'), but because it gives men the chance to replace them—not with the duster (this isn't mentioned) but with the children. 'As the ideology of the 1950s was dismantled and a new one erected to allow women to work, someone had to take the mother's place in the family. Father.' The ideology of the 1950s was the ideology of Winnicott and Bowlby: 'Winnicott, a brilliant child psychologist, raised the mother's role, especially the role of her breast, to lyrical heights . . . It seems possible that Winnicott wanted to *be* a nursing mother.' It seems even more possible that Gathorne-Hardy wants to *be* a mother *tout court*. Certainly the passion that animates his book is that of a father whom divorce has separated from his children. In Denmark, he says, there are fathers who kidnap their children 'just to force Bowlby-stuck judges to realise that fathers *can* look after their children'.

Self-obsession, what Christopher Lasch calls 'pathological narcissism', is the third cause of our advanced divorce rate. Gathorne-Hardy doesn't mention Lasch, but in a chapter entitled 'The Privilege Bulge' he writes about the same 'rage to grow'—through yoga or through remarriage—which Lasch in his book finds so enraging. It all began, according to Gathorne-Hardy, who has a notable dislike of multiple causes, with the 'Privilege Bulge Generation', born in the 1930s and 1940s (his generation), and brought up under the influence of psychoanalytic ideas to expect the happiness that a childhood without repression was bound to bring. Forty years later they're still expecting it; and as evidence Gathorne-Hardy cites the fact that 'a major proportion' of contemporary love stories have middle-aged heroes and heroines, which 'as far as love goes is historically new'. Therapies designed to soothe and to enlarge proliferate; and 'if marriage doesn't lead to "growth",' which after ten or fifteen years it may well not, the solution is simple: 'dump it.'

Love is the last reason—'the entrancing delight of romantic love'. 'Even the practical users of a marriage bureau aim to and "generally do fall in love",' Gathorne-Hardy says before asking the deep question: 'What is this love they fall into?' An English disease, Cobbett said: 'it produces self-destruction in England more frequently than in all other countries put together.' A romantic death wish, said Denis de Rougemont, whose book *Passion and Society* (1956) is the model for Gathorne-Hardy's discourse on love from the Crusaders ('a gang of vicious and often drunken thugs, murderers and fornicators') to the novels of John Updike. In the old days—stretching from the 12th century to the Second World War—there was marriage and there was adultery (or thoughts of adultery): on the one hand, stability, a house and a dowry; on the other, longing, desire, and despair. This distinction held society together, according to de Rougemont, who feared what would happen when it disappeared. What has happened is that a large number of people get married more than once. 'I don't want you as a mistress; our lives just aren't built for it,' the hero of Updike's *Marry Me* says to the woman who isn't his wife. 'Here there's no institution except marriage. Marriage and the Friday night basketball game.'

Monogamy, not marriage, is under threat: 'no matter how you phrase the statistics, one thing is clear—the institution of marriage itself still rests on a bedrock of statistical stability.' Between the end of the 16th century and the start of the 19th, the average length of a marriage was 20 years (the figures are Peter Laslett's). Today, couples who don't divorce can expect to be together for 40 or 50 years—'for a good number of people it is a great deal too long.' In this context Gathorne-Hardy's seemingly daft proposition, 'divorce—the modern death', can be seen to make sense. 'Divorce him quick,' I heard an American child say to his mother when he thought his father was about to drown. Marghanita Laski, discussing Colin Murray Parkes's *Bereavement* in the *LRB*, commented on 'his perverse avoidance of marital desertion as the obvious analogue to bereavement by death', and added that in the first case the pain is 'made worse by the knowledge that all the misery has been caused, not by chance, but by human choice'. On the other hand, pain caused by 'human choice' is easier to resist; there is even pleasure in doing so.

Gathorne-Hardy has no inclination to play down the many kinds of unhappiness that divorce can bring: here, at least, he is on home ground. He may not be sorry that 'the grim, granite monogamy until death' is on its way out—but the way looks pretty bumpy. He speaks of the 'terrible fires of divorce', of 'the terrible cries of pain which rip through our late 20th-century prose', of the 'acute, almost physical pain the ripping apart can cause', and quotes some of the 'victims', among them a crane-driver. 'I'd be sitting up there in the crane,' he says, 'and suddenly I would burst into tears.' It's the only eloquent sentence in the whole book.

All the difficulties divorce entails are attended to, however cursorily, from the shame and embarrassment (especially for women, who, when they lose their husbands, are assumed to be longing for any creep's attentions) to the unhappiness of children, many of whom—'rich and poor alike'—never give up the idea that their parents will get together again: 'The *Times* obituary of Alexander Onassis said that he and his sister had "always entertained hopes for a reunion between their parents".' Some of what Gathorne-Hardy says is idiosyncratic. He claims, for instance, that the misery is equal for the leaver (who is usually, though he doesn't say so, the husband) and the left (i.e., the wife)—which seems unlikely and possibly self-aggrandising. Of the financial difficulties he remarks, 'the most general, most concrete and one of the most painful results of divorce is an immediate crash in the standard of living,' and then goes on to say that the middle classes suffer most in this respect. The 'lowest-paid simply exchange one form of poverty for another'. As always, he is full of optimism. He discusses the loneliness, but also the useful things people can do to find new partners and new ways of life. Clubs for the divorced 'sound fairly grim', and also 'petit-bourgeois', but 'on the whole they work'; communes have their silly side but can 'help one-parent families through the most difficult years with their children'; even marriage bureaux aren't to be scoffed at. Heather Jenner's agency 'has arranged 15,000 marriages'—and several of her former clients have said they would 'send' their children to find partners in the same way. Taken together, these 'developments' are a good thing, some of them, he says, more often seen on television than subscribed to in real life, but nonetheless 'a sign that we are at the start of something'. One more thing: the bad years can be creative. 'Bertrand Russell produced during the harrowing period after his first marriage broke up the work for which he will always be remembered: the *Principia Mathematica*.'

One difficulty means more to Gathorne-Hardy than any of the others. In the old days before divorce really got going, couples whose marriages were slipping sometimes decided to have a child in order to acquire a common interest. It's not like that any more. The majority of divorces occur within three years of marriage, or, to put it differently, no sooner is the child born than its parents decide to part. 'Children tend to detract from rather than contribute to marital happiness,' the sociologists say. Children interfere with their parents' 'growth', Gathorne-Hardy says. So one child in three now lives with only one of his parents, usually his mother—and mothers can be mean. 'The central injustice in divorce today is that of depriving fathers and their children of each other.' It's all right for the mothers: they have the child and 'centuries of gossip-and-support traditions to call on'—fathers 'are often *completely alone*'. Some might say fathers in the main have jobs— but no matter. They also have their 'growth' to think about. Still, it's true that in the vast majority of cases mothers are given custody of the children and that some exercise their bitterness by making it difficult for their former husband to see them: 'The playwright Terence Frisby went to the high court to ask that his access—one *afternoon* a fortnight—should be extended to one a week. The judge turned the application down flat on the grounds, some mad fragment of jargon floating into his head, that he was "in grave danger of becoming too possessive".' The law, Gathorne-Hardy says, should be changed, and 'the principle underlying the change should be that a child has an inalienable right to two parents, and that each parent has an equal right to see and have its child.' It sounds all right but how could it be done? Partition? In the meantime, even without changing the law, 'the situation would be immediately and immeasurably transformed for the better if a few mothers were sent to prison for denying children and fathers access to each other.' A feminist, I suppose, would have to agree.

After the 'terrible fires of divorce', the 'high blue sky of the future'— i.e., remarriage. The psychoanalytic view is that second marriages are even less likely to succeed than the marriage(s) that preceded them. According to Dr. Edmund Bergler, for instance, 'the chances of finding conscious happiness in the next marriage are exactly zero.' (What about unconscious happiness—could one settle for that?) Statistics bear him out. Never mind, Gathorne-Hardy says: 'Being a couple is naturally nicer.' And if there has to be another divorce, there's always the chance of yet another marriage. Besides, the pain is easier to bear the second time round. What's nice about Gathorne-Hardy is that he seldom says a discouraging word. Whatever's happening it's for the best. 'A profound and exhilarating sense of power, of lifting vision, of release' is within reach. 'Seventy-three per cent of strongly religious women are now orgasmic all the time.'

Book reviewed:

Love, Sex, Marriage and Divorce by Jonathan Gathorne-Hardy

Patty and Cin

'I grew up,' Patricia Hearst says, describing what life had once been like for the granddaughter of Citizen Kane, 'in an atmosphere of clear blue skies, bright sunshine, rambling open spaces, long green lawns, large comfortable houses, country clubs with swimming-pools and tennis courts and riding horses.' It must have been a nice life, and would look pretty in the cinema, but heroines endear themselves by their difficulties and until the SLA kidnapped her Patricia Hearst's only difficulty was that she was a bit short. Five foot two—not a dwarf, but her girlfriends were taller. 'Most things came easily to me,' she says a little later, 'sports, social relationships, schoolwork, life. I had only to apply myself to them and I found I could do them well, to my own satisfaction.' Is she trying to tell us that it was especially brutal of the SLA to intervene in a life that ran so smoothly, or is it that she wants us to know that she wasn't some kind of neurotic who could be expected to crack up in difficult circumstances?

She may have been rich but she wasn't laid back. Her mother was strict, a 'Southern lady of the old school', and the girls (five of them) didn't smoke, drink, take drugs or 'go out anywhere' in jeans. Her father taught her how to use a gun. She trusted her parents and they trusted her. When some teachers found fault with her she refused to apologise—she knew they were wrong and her father agreed. It was, she insists, a normal and happy childhood, the implication being that if she seemed later to turn against her family, it was very much against her will. It's true these 'gracious', almost perfect parents had a tendency to moralise, but she soon learned to 'tune out while seeming to participate'—a trick of some importance in her later life. Today her book is wholesomely dedicated to 'Mom and Dad'—a touch that puts one in mind of Sylvia Plath's *Letters Home*.

When she was 17, she fell in love with one of her teachers ('I suppose I threw myself at him but I hoped not in any obvious way'), a young man of 23, called Steven Weed—not a name that would necessarily wish fame upon itself. He won a teaching fellowship at Berkeley, and she went with him, enrolling as an undergraduate, eventually to do art history—'I had been surrounded by art all of my life.' It was then 1972; the student rebellions of the previous decade, 'abhorred' by her mother 'for trying to destroy the traditional values that make America great', had 'withered away': 'when a young socialist forced a leaflet into my hand in Sproul Plaza, I took special delight in dropping the message into one of the dozens of nearby trash cans.' She and Mr. Weed rented a flat together, 'a bright sunny duplex in a nice neighbourhood'; and it was there, at nine o'clock on the night of 4 February 1974, that the SLA found her, dressed only in her knickers, bathrobe, and alpaca slippers.

She was tied up, gagged, blindfolded, and taken away. Her destination was a cupboard, six and a half feet long, where she was to remain, blindfolded, for 57 days. After she'd been there a couple of hours, the cupboard door opened and the leader of the gang introduced himself: 'I am general field marshal of the Symbionese Liberation Army. My name is Cin.' ('Sin,' she thought—'these people must be evil incarnate.') His speech, part General Westmoreland, part urban guerrilla, was a sort of post-Vietnam gobbledegook. The SLA, he said, had declared war against the United States: a war of the poor and oppressed against fascism. She should consider herself 'in protective custody' and would be treated according to the Geneva Convention. The first thing the SLA had to see to were her manners. 'If you gotta go pee,' one of them told her, 'say "I gotta go pee"; if you gotta go shit, say "I gotta go shit." That's the way poor people talk.' Other combat units had taken other prisoners that night, they said: the SLA was a huge army with important international connections. It wasn't long before she came to believe that this might well be true. She was told of secret agents eavesdropping in restaurants 'to hear first-hand the troubles and the problems voiced by the people'; of SLA medical units practising 'battlefield surgery by going out in the woods and shooting dogs in order to learn how to administer to gunshot wounds'; of summer camps where children were taught to handle machine guns. When she was released from the cupboard, she asked about the other units:

> The question surprised them and they all seemed to look to Cin for an answer. After a moment's hesitation, his face cracked and he burst out laughing.
>
> 'What other units? This is all there is, baby. We're the army. You're looking at it.'
>
> They all laughed at the big deception.

It was an army of eight soldiers, three men and five women. Some of them, unlike Patricia Hearst, had a sense of humour, of a kind.

The SLA had made itself known in California by murdering a black school superintendent—a choice of victim that made them look like idiots to other left-wing groups with which they were in competition. It's unlikely that they had a precise idea of what they might achieve by 'arresting' Patty Hearst, as they put it, but no one could say that she wasn't a suitable candidate for a kidnapping. In the event, what she did for them probably exceeded even their wild expectations. Like all such groups, they longed for publicity. Once they had persuaded her to speak on their behalf, they could rely on every news bulletin in California giving its version of what the SLA had done that day. She was well aware of her contribution—'with me in their clutches, the SLA was a household word'—and, as time went by, was glad to have a contribution to make. Financially, she proved less useful. Their first idea of what to do with her had been to have her ask her father to provide 70 dollars' worth of food for every poor person in the state. It would have cost him 400 million dollars and even he couldn't manage that. Cin, who, as always, was in charge, found this hard to believe. 'This man with little or no education was clearly over his head in dealing with million-dollar projects' is Patty Hearst's rueful comment on the episode. When eventually terms were agreed and the food was distributed, the SLA still wasn't pleased. No one gave them credit for their generous thought; the food, they said, was being thrown at the people—'one woman had been hit by a turkey leg and seriously injured.' They reached the conclusion that her father was trying to force them to kill her.

Sitting in her cupboard, Patty Hearst found it hard to know what to make of the SLA. Their reactions were unpredictable and mostly violent; Cin claimed to be instructed by God and they were obsessed with the idea of their own death. However, they kept threatening to kill her first, and the one thing she was certain of was that she didn't want to die: 'I wanted to get out alive and see them all sent to jail . . . for what they were doing to me.' It didn't take her long to realise that getting out alive meant co-operating with them and she didn't hesitate to do so. Harangued all day long about the evils of capitalism, she 'accommodated' her thoughts 'to coincide with theirs'. Only once does she say that she regrets not having been more strong-minded:

I wish I could say now that I stood up well under Cin's interrogation, that I refused to reveal vital information, that I lied and fooled him . . . Terrorised, threatened constantly with being hung from the ceiling for being an unco-operative prisoner . . . I only wanted to co-operate and not to make them angry at me. I was afraid and weepy, hardly the heroine.

Her tone of voice, for the most part, is defensive, and sometimes priggish, as if answering those critics who said of her when she was released that she'd been all too eager to do whatever the SLA asked of her. She writes both about herself and about the SLA with an alienating gracelessness and her story has been 'querulously' received (Joan Didion's word) by American reviewers who felt that she hadn't told the whole truth. It could simply be, however, that what happened to her, and her response to it, was more complicated than she is able now (or was old enough then) to deal with. Writing about her early life, she says, 'I thought I knew what was right and what was wrong for me,' which suggests that she was less interested in what was right and wrong in general; and talking about the SLA's attempts to re-educate her, she says: 'Actually, I did not really care one way or another about any of the things they told me. I had always been apolitical and still was.' Had she cared more, she might have kept a better grip on herself. On the other hand, she might not have survived.

The failure of the food programme—by which was meant its shabby treatment in the media—may have been taken by the SLA as evidence that 'the fascist corporate state' wasn't interested in negotiating her release. But now it turned out that they didn't feel like killing her either: 'You're kinda like the pet chicken people have on a farm—when it comes time to kill it for Sunday dinner, no one really wants to do it.' A possible alternative was found: if the rest of the SLA agreed, she might be allowed to join them. She was given a torch and a supply of books—Eldridge Cleaver, George Jackson, Marx, Engels, the SLA Codes of War—and was tested on her reading of them. They became more friendly, changed her code name from 'Marie-Antoinette' to the more affectionate 'Tiny', gave her cigarettes, told her she could 'fuck any of the men in the cell'. Sex, they said, wasn't ever compulsory, but 'if one comrade asked another, it was "comradely" to say yes.' That day, the young 'Cujo' followed her into the cupboard; they took off their clothes, 'he did his thing' and left; she thought about the others listening in the room outside. She had long since given up any hope of being released or rescued alive—'I had lived in fear of the SLA for so long that fear of the FBI came naturally to me'—and as each member of the cell in turn questioned her about her sincerity in wishing to join them, she became increasingly ingenious in telling them what they wanted to hear. Asked to record a message that had been written for her, denouncing her parents and praising the SLA, she did so 'with vim and vigour'. For the SLA it was a triumph. For her the whole business of proving herself a convert to their cause was another instance, though she doesn't quite say so, of being able to do what was required of her, easily and to her own satisfaction.

Her formal induction into the SLA was handled with some solemnity. The others were sitting in a circle on the floor when she was led out of the cupboard, still wearing her blindfold. 'In the silence I heard Cin say: "The sisters and brothers have all voted for you to join this combat team." A wave of relief spread through my body.' Invited, after a short swearing-in ceremony, to take off her blindfold, she was dismayed by what she saw: 'Oh God,' she thought, 'what a bunch of ordinary-looking, unattractive little people.' When she was put on trial a year and a half later for her part in the first SLA bank robbery, the outcome hinged on whether or not she could realistically be said to have been brainwashed. The jury did not believe she had been, but it would be difficult to find another explanation for the fact that, having once been so contemptuous of Berkeley lefties, she should now be disappointed that her new comrades were so . . . weedy: 'Their physical appearance just didn't match my image of them as revolutionaries. I had expected them to look bigger, stronger, more commanding.'

She still had her bad, bourgeois moments: she didn't like using the communal toothbrush and was appalled to discover that while she'd been in her cupboard, the other women had been wearing her bathrobe. (Later on, she was to see her sister on television wearing one of her old jackets—that was another bad moment.) Some of her comrades complained that she continued to 'talk like a rich bourgeois bitch' and it was evident from the 'combat position' she had been allocated in the event of an FBI raid that she was still an expendable member of the team—but by and large she felt that she had now 'crossed over'. They kept busy, training, drafting communiqués, thinking up future 'actions' and berating themselves for not thinking up future 'actions'; two people stood guard every night, guns at the ready.

At the beginning of April, they decided to rob a bank. Their preparations were meticulous: 'I knew more about the Hibernia Bank branch at Noriega Street and 22nd Avenue,' Patricia Hearst reports, 'than I know about my parents' home in Hillsborough.' When they went to bed the night before, Cin announced that 'he would be carrying a list of doctors, one or more of whom would be kidnapped at gunpoint to remove bullets, if need be'; and the next morning no one was allowed to have breakfast lest they were 'gut-shot' by the police. When it was over, Patty Hearst, who was the only one not to wear any kind of disguise, had become 'a wanted criminal' and, she was able to gather from what was said on the news, deeply hated by the American public. She was, she says, 'sick to my stomach' at seeing herself on the television screen 'so publicly identified with the SLA'. But it doesn't stop her noting (with a hint of pleasure?) that there was 'a hint of awe' in the media accounts of the robbery.

'A team,' it was said in the SLA, 'operated together, succeeded or failed together, lived or died together.' Within a few weeks of the bank robbery, the flower of the SLA was dead. Patty Hearst's first outing after the bank was to a sports shop, where she was sent, disguised in an Afro wig, to buy some heavy socks and underwear. She went with two of her fellow soldiers, a married couple known as 'Yolanda' and 'Teko' (their real name was Harris). The revolution, the SLA were convinced, would begin that summer and they were busy preparing for it: preparing for combat (hence the need for heavy socks) and preparing for death, about which they now talked all the time. Patty Hearst may have been happy enough to practise killing other people but she found her comrades' way of thinking about their own deaths increasingly alien: 'Being ever practical, I could not understand why they were fighting for something which they did not believe they would live to see accomplished.' There was an incident at the sports shop (after paying for the socks Teko tried to steal a bandolier): the three of them escaped, shielded by a hail of bullets from Patty Hearst's gun, but they were careless and the other six members of the SLA were tracked down by the FBI in their Los Angeles safe house. Miss Hearst and her two companions took refuge in a motel next to Disneyland and watched on television the battle that was taking place between their comrades and the Los Angeles police force: 9,000 bullets were fired, the safe house went up in flames and its occupants were burned to death. None of them had even tried to escape; the coroner, a shrewd man, was to say that 'they died compulsively.'

The three Disneyland survivors were now, Miss Hearst boasts, 'the most wanted trio in the United States'. The Harrises briefly considered joining their comrades in death, but fortunately decided against it ('Cin would have wanted us to live and to fight on'). When the last news bulletin was over, Teko, who had taken over as general field marshal, announced that it was time for bed. 'Yolanda turned to me and solicitously asked "Do you want to make love with us tonight?" "No thanks," I said and climbed into the other bed, alone.' What had upset her most about the shoot-out was that she could so easily have been there and no one would have cared: 'The police had not asked me, Patty Hearst, to step outside when they opened fire.' It confirmed her in her view that 'there was no turning back': 'I was a soldier in the people's army. It was a role I had accepted in exchange for my life.' What is extraordinary is that she hung on to that role during the 18 mostly miserable months she was to spend with the Harrises before being captured, even though there were many occasions when she could have escaped. It isn't even clear that they would have minded being shot of her: they treated me, she says angrily, like 'a moronic army recruit'.

The three of them still considered themselves at war, but the revolution that was to take place that summer was postponed while they lay low in rented houses in various country resorts on the East Coast which had been found for them by a radical sportswriter connected with *Ramparts* called Jack Scott, whom Spiro Agnew had once described as 'an enemy of sport'. Scott's idea was that they should raise money for the revolution by writing a book about the SLA: it was bound to be successful and a corporation could be set up in Lichtenstein so that they wouldn't have to pay tax on the money they earned. A writer was sent to help them, whose claim to fame, according to Patty Hearst, was that he'd once been arrested in England for, as he put it, 'shitting on a picture of the queen'. It was, like everything else that summer, a dismal business. They quarrelled with the writer, with each other, with Scott and his wife, whom Teko decided to murder, though he never got round to it.

In the fall, they went back to California and with a group of new recruits—the SLA's status had been much enhanced by the deaths of their former comrades—resumed the normal life of revolutionaries.

They robbed some banks and a woman was shot—'this is the murder round,' Teko said brightly; and tried their hand at making bombs, though Teko stuffed them with so much lavatory paper they failed to go off. Patty Hearst's own position was at last improving: she got on well with the new recruits, was invited to write a 'position paper on the SLA version of radical feminism' and ran her own gun classes. Presumably it was the self-confidence that followed from this that enabled her to start thinking about a return to civilian life. When she told the others that she felt like jacking it in, they were shocked. 'You can't do that,' they said, or she says they said: 'You're a symbol of the revolution. You give the people hope.'

The issue was decided for her by the FBI, who arrested her one balmy day in the early autumn of 1975. She wasn't at all pleased. 'As the flash-bulbs went off in my face, I remembered the press pictures of Susan Saxe, a revolutionary who had recently been arrested, and, like her, I smiled broadly and raised a clenched fist in salute.' It was the last thing she did to give the people hope. At first, remembering Cin's lurid fantasies about the FBI, she refused to co-operate. When her family visited, they seemed 'unfamiliar', 'as if from another world', while they in turn hardly recognised her, 'curled up like a foetus', barely able to speak. As it became clear that not only was she to be prosecuted for taking part in the Hibernia Bank robbery, but that her trial was to take precedence over that of her two former comrades, withdrawal turned to sullenness and then to outrage. She was outraged by the Federal marshals, who 'seemed to equate fame with danger' and dragged her about in chains; outraged by the lawyer found for her by her father—he had made his name defending My Lai's Captain Medina and the Boston Strangler—who bungled her case, while insisting, as part of his fee, on the exclusive right to write a book about her; outraged by the judge, who gave an interview before her trial in which he boasted that he knew 'Randy Hearst' (which he didn't) and wasn't impressed by his money; outraged by the jury, who believed that her family had arranged for the press to be sitting opposite them in court in order to intimidate them; outraged by the press, 'who behaved like sharks in a feeding frenzy': but outraged above all at being treated like a criminal rather than as the victim of a kidnapping.

No doubt she is right to say that it all happened this way because the public was more interested in 'an heiress' and 'a celebrity' than in 'two unknown radicals called Harris'. 'The government had to prosecute me,' she says, now very much the sadder and the wiser woman, 'in order to prove that there was equal justice for all in America.' On the other hand, it is likely that had she, at any point during her trial, condescended to say that she was sorry for what she had done, she might well not have been found guilty or, if found guilty, not been given the maximum penalty of seven years in prison. The trouble was that she didn't feel sorry. 'I would do it again,' she told her interrogators. 'It saved my life.' It has never been in her character to apologise. In the end, celebrity brought its reward. After 'one of the largest campaigns for clemency in the history of this country', her sentence was commuted by the kindly Jimmy Carter.

Every Secret Thing is not an attractive book; it's flat and it's repetitive: but it tells a good story and has the ingredients for a better movie. It is, after all, very possible that what Patty Hearst would have said if she were more honest is that she enjoyed some of her time with the SLA, that she was captivated by Cin (or sin), that she liked being part of a gang of outlaws, that, as the prosecution alleged at her trial, there was more to her relationship with Cujo than she later wished to admit—certainly there is little about him here—but that doesn't mean that in her heart of hearts, wherever that might be, she was determined, as the phrase once was, to overthrow the government of the United States. She is as she describes herself, 'ever pragmatic'. Many American reviewers and some English ones came to the conclusion, after reading Patty Hearst's book, that it could only have been written in order to make money: 'dreamy notions', Joan Didion says, 'of what a Hearst might do to turn a dollar'. It may well be, however, that she just wanted to show that everything she did was right—for her.

Book reviewed:

Every Secret Thing by Patricia Hearst and Alvin Moscow

Hagiography

One evening in December 1975 David Plante called on his friend, the novelist Jean Rhys, who was staying in a hotel in South Kensington: 'a big dreary hotel', she said, 'filled with old people whom they won't allow to drink sweet vermouth'. She was sitting in what the receptionist called 'the pink lounge', wearing a pink hat. She was then in her eighties. He kissed her and told her she was looking marvellous. 'Don't lie to me,' she said. 'I'm dying.' After supper and a great deal of drink, they went up to her room: 'sometimes her cane got caught between her legs and I had to straighten it.' They drank some more and talked about her life. Five hours later, David Plante got up, took a pee, and told her he had to leave. '"Before you go," she said, "help me to the toilet."' He took her there and left her, in her pink hat, holding on to the washbasin. Sometime later she called to him:

> I opened the door a little, imagining, perhaps, that if I opened it only a little, only a little would have happened. I saw Jean, her head with the battered hat leaning to the side, her feet with the knickers about

her ankles, just off the floor, stuck in the toilet. I had, I immediately realised, forgotten to lower the seat . . . I stepped into the puddle of pee all around the toilet, put my arms around her, and lifted her.

'I'll try to walk,' she said when he offered to carry her to her bed. So he propped her up against a wall and 'took off her sopping knickers'. When he got her onto the bed, he rang Sonia Orwell, who arrived to take charge of the situation: 'For God's sake, David,' Mrs. Orwell said, 'don't you know when someone's drunk?'

A few days later, he again visited Jean Rhys, who in the meantime had been moved by Mrs. Orwell to another hotel, one which no doubt allowed its guests to drink sweet vermouth. She was feeling better. 'Now, David,' she said, 'if that ever happens to you with a lady again, don't get into a panic. You put the lady on her bed, cover her, put a glass of water and a sleeping pill on the bedside table, turn the lights down very low, adjust your tie before you leave so you'll look smart, say at reception that the lady is resting, and when you tell the story afterwards, you make it funny.'

David Plante has little trouble making his stories funny: he could probably have made them even funnier had he wanted to, but telling funny stories about your friends is a tricky business if you intend to go on having friends; and on the evidence of this book, Plante, an American novelist who lives in England, has quite a busy social life. Sonia Orwell once said to him that the life he led was 'very chic': too chic, she thought, for a writer. But he has got his own back on her now. *Difficult Women* is a memoir of three women whom it was once very chic to be friends with, and the one whom it was most chic to be friends with was Mrs. Orwell, though she told Plante that in Paris she knew some 'very very ordinary' people. It's an unflattering book, especially in its account of her, but whether Plante has any sense that he might have betrayed their friendship is hard to determine since, while making her sound entirely unlovable, he keeps telling us how much he loved her.

Jean Rhys died in 1979; Sonia Orwell, George Orwell's widow, a year later. Plante's third subject is Germaine Greer, who, as well as being a friend with a house near his in Italy, was his colleague for a term at the University of Tulsa ('from Tulsa I wrote letters to Sonia, one long one about Germaine Greer'). Of these women, Germaine Greer seems to have been the one he liked best, but now she thinks him 'a creep' for having written this book. Former friends of the other two will have worse things to say of him: indeed, some pretty hard things have already been said by people who didn't know either of them, and it seems possible that a lot of dinner parties of the kind he describes will now be taking place without him. As a foreigner, Plante claims in self-defence, he is unable to grasp the distinctions the English make between public and private life—which sounds convenient but could, I suppose, be true. No one who records everything he sees his friends do and hears them say does so without malice, yet something besides malice must have prompted Plante to write up his diary for publication, especially as he can't make his friends look silly without looking pretty silly himself.

Mrs. Orwell, being a sociable woman, gave a great many dinner parties ('Sonia is knowledgable about and gives a lot of attention to her cooking, which is mostly French'). He didn't enjoy these parties. 'I would get home from an evening of being victimised, angry and depressed, and swear I'd never see Sonia again. The next morning, however, I'd ring her to say what a lovely dinner party . . . and how I longed to see her again.' Plante, of course, is a snob for whom there was pleasure in the thought of being an intimate of the well-connected Orwell, or a personal friend of Jean Rhys or a close companion of the electrifying Greer; and pleasure, too, in being the kind of nice young man who can get on with everyone, however rich and famous. He is also a homosexual, though he doesn't precisely say so; and he has a weakness for unaccommodating women—the kind actors call 'outrageous'. He often refers to this weakness in explaining his affection for these 'difficult' women but says little to elucidate it. 'You could jump to a Freudian conclusion that this had to do with my mother,' he said in an interview. And then added: 'But I absolutely reject that.'

It may be that 'difficult women' are a luxury that straight men can't afford in their lives. But if there is some truth in this (men who have to live with women, if they have any sense, must prefer them to be easy-going), there is none in its converse: lesbians don't sing any songs in praise of difficult men. It would be against their code of honour to do so, and quite unnecessary since heterosexual women do it all the time. Given that the history of the world can in a sense be seen as a history of the difficult men who have run it, it seems appropriate to register a protest against Plante's title. No one has yet written a book about three moderately famous men who happened to have known each other and called it 'Difficult Men'. (Or even 'Nice Men: A Memoir of Three'.) Still, there's no sense in being curmudgeonly, or in pretending that there's no such thing as a difficult woman—the chances are that if you aren't 'difficult' no one will write a book about you. Plante is very good at describing some of the ways in which women can make life hard, while insinuating that no merit attaches to being friends with someone it's easy to be friends with. 'Difficult women', it turns out, can make you like yourself better for liking them.

Take Jean Rhys. Of the three relationships Plante describes this was the one that troubled him most, largely because he knew that he wanted something from it that wasn't just friendship, and he didn't like this in himself. 'I wondered if my deepest interest in her was as a writer I could take advantage of,' he reflected at an early stage in their relationship. 'I did not like this feeling.' The feeling recurred when she accepted his offer to help her write the autobiography she wanted to write but could no longer manage. ('I can't do it myself and no one can help me,' she said, as she always said.) Their collaboration was long and painful. The same material was gone over again and again: sometimes she liked it, often she hated it; she would drink, become confused, shout at him, say it was worthless, that there was no point going on. He would put a thousand disparate fragments into chronological order and she would drop them on the floor. Then, looking at what she had done, she would again say, 'I don't know if this will ever be finished, it's in such a mess.' After Jean Rhys died, Sonia Orwell explained what Plante had no doubt understood all along: that Rhys was overcome with terror at the thought of another writer taking over her book. Her fears are easy to sympathise with. Unfortunately, they tie in all too well with the paranoia of a woman who, while always asking for help, never ceased to find fault with those who helped her; who would say 'I don't want to see anyone,' and ten minutes later: 'No one ever comes to see me.' It's clear from David Plante's account of her, as it is from everything she wrote both when she was young and when she was an old lady, that she depended on, and was inspired by, a sense of being treated badly.

Plante describes a tearful afternoon when he tried to dictate a passage about the loneliness of old age:

> She said no one helped her, she was utterly alone. She said she had had to come up to London on her own, when in fact Sonia and her editor had gone to stay in the village for three days to get her ready, and drove her up to London to the flat they had found for her. She asked me to read the whole thing out. She said, afterwards: 'Well, there are one or two good sentences in it.' I wondered how much of the 'incredible loneliness' of her life was literature, in which she hoped for one or two good sentences—all,

she often said, that would remain of her writing, those one or two good sentences.

She was always incredibly lonely because in her own mind no one else existed. Sonia Orwell told David Plante that she wished he had known how charming Jean Rhys had been when she was younger, but the charm is there for everyone to see in the heroines of her novels, all of whom are versions of herself and all of whom are charming and very pretty. 'I don't think I know what character is,' she admitted to Plante. 'I just write about what happened.' By which she meant what happened to her. And it wasn't only as a novelist that she found the notion of character elusive: everyone she knew in life was a mystery to her. 'I don't know much about my husbands,' she told Plante, confessing that she had no idea why her first and third husbands had spent time in prison. Max Hamer, her third husband, was married before, she said, 'but whether he had any children or not I don't know.' She herself had two by her first husband, Jean Lenglet. After they divorced, the daughter (prudently) stayed with her father: the son had died in early infancy. 'What did it die of?' Plante asked. 'Je n'sais pas' was her reply: 'I was never a good mother.'

It was characteristic of her that while she talked a great deal about her writing and writing in general, both of which seemed to matter a lot to her, she was prepared to turn her back on everything she had done for the sake of a couple of sad sentences: 'I'll die without having lived . . . I never wanted to be a writer. All I wanted was to be happy.' What is hard to understand is the part Jean Rhys's obsession with herself played in other people's affection for her. 'For some mad reason, I love you,' David Plante said to her one day and then wondered, not why he had said it, but why he loved her. 'The most enormous influence on me in the four and a half years since I met her,' Scott Fitzgerald once remarked of his wife, 'has been the complete, fine and full-hearted selfishness of Zelda.' Perhaps there is something unfailingly attractive about pretty women whose self-absorption makes them unable to cope with anything. 'It took me three visits to teach her how to open a compact she had been given as a gift,' Plante writes in passing about Jean Rhys: maybe it was the gallantry her selfishness inspired that made him think he loved her.

David Plante had first met Jean Rhys at a 'luncheon party' at Sonia Orwell's house; and when he was working on her autobiography he liked to discuss her with Mrs. Orwell. Heaven knows why, since Sonia could not bear to let him think that he knew anything about Jean that she didn't already know: 'Everything you've said about Jean that she's told you I've known, in greater detail, from her and there is a great deal she has told me which she hasn't mentioned to you.' That's the way Sonia Orwell, who thought, perhaps rightly, that 'most people' didn't like her, talked to her friends, as if telling them anything that didn't make them feel awful would encourage in them a terrible sense of well-being. 'When I was with her,' Plante writes, 'her effect was to make me see my life as meaningless, as I knew she saw her own life.' It's a funny reason for wanting to be someone's friend. 'I was in love with that unhappiness in her,' he continues. Mrs. Orwell, who had more common sense than David Plante, thought it was self-indulgent to say that kind of thing about oneself—and she had a point.

Plante acknowledges her qualities, her generosity with her time and her money, and what he calls her 'disinterested devotion' to her friends: but it is the many unpleasantnesses, or 'difficulties', of her behaviour that are assiduously reported. He took her to Italy to stay in his house, though her friends warned him against it ('When I said I was going to Italy with Sonia Orwell, he said: "You're out of your fucking mind"'): she didn't like it there and the bits he was particularly proud of she particularly hated. She was often drunk; she didn't like anyone she didn't know (and a large number of people she did know): 'The writer mentioned friends of hers. Sonia said: "They're swine."' One or two people, her protégés, she respected, but mostly she was contemptuous of other people's endeavours and even more contemptuous of their reputations: '*Freddy Ayer. He doesn't think . . .* My God. I know Freddy Ayer. I know he doesn't think.' Having wanted to write and, in her own eyes, failed, she was particularly hard on writers, especially those who hoped for success: a writer was congratulated in her presence on a book he had recently published: 'Sonia said: "I won't read it. I'm sure it's awful."' It seems likely, however, that she found her own behaviour more repellent than Plante did. 'Sonia was difficult, but she was difficult for a reason. She wanted, demanded so much from herself and from others, and it made her rage that she and others couldn't ever match what was done to what was aspired to.' It's an admiring remark but the rage wasn't always admirable. When she was ill, a friend came to stay with her: 'In the late morning, she'd bring a tray up to her, and would either find Sonia in a darkened room, her head lifted a little from the pillow, saying angrily, "You fucking well woke me up just when I'd fallen asleep," or, in a bright room, sitting up in bed, saying, as she stubbed out her cigarette in an ashtray: "*Enfin.* I thought breakfast would never come."'

Sonia Orwell disapproved of Jean Rhys for making a meal of her miseries, but she didn't invariably do better herself. On the other hand, she at least had some idea of what she was up to:

'Yesterday a young woman stopped me in the street to ask me the time. I shouted at her: "Do you think I can give the time to everyone who stops me in the street?" Afterwards, I wondered why I had been so rude to her. Why? Why am I so filled with anger?'

I said nothing.

She said: 'I've fucked up my life. I'm angry because I've fucked up my life.'

David Plante doesn't tell us a lot about Jean Rhys that Jean Rhys hasn't. His portrait of Mrs. Orwell is persuasive: but there is little reason for people who never knew her—who have never even heard of her—to know now how much and with what cause she loathed herself. Novelists have more tactful ways of saying what they think about their friends.

The year Sonia Orwell stayed with David Plante in Italy he decided to spend a few days with Germaine Greer before returning to England. The first thing he saw when he arrived at the house with Greer was a baby sitting at a table under a fig tree playing with finger paints. 'That's not the way to use fucking finger paints,' Greer shouted at the child, who 'looked up at her with a look of shocked awe that there was a wrong and a right way to use finger paints'. Plante went into the house while 'Germaine taught the baby the use of finger paints.' Inside the child's mother was reading a magazine. 'Where the fuck are you while your baby is making a fucking mess out of the fucking finger paints I paid fucking good money for?' Greer shouted from the garden. Germaine Greer knows a lot more than the right way to use fucking finger paints: as Plante describes her, there isn't a single fucking thing she doesn't know how to do. The next morning he finds her doing drawings for a dovecot she wants to build:

I said: 'It looks as if you're designing a whole palazzo.'
'I'm simply doing it the way it should be done,' she said.

They visit a local coppersmith: Greer and the coppersmith speak to each other in the local dialect:

Outside I asked: 'But how do you know the dialect?'
'Don't you?' she asked. 'You live here. Shouldn't you know the dialect?'

They go to a garage where the mechanics stare at her: 'they have never known a woman who could swing her hips from side to side and clasp her hands to her breasts and pucker her mouth and know as much as they did about shock absorbers.' Wherever Greer and Plante go together, in Tulsa or in Tuscany, it's the same story: she is in complete fucking command; he is flummoxed. The only expertise they seem to share is an ability to take care of their own sexual requirements:

> At dinner with six others, Germaine said to me across the dinner table: 'I haven't had sex in weeks, not since I got here.' 'Neither have I,' I said. She said: 'Well, I've been happy enough in my little white room taking care of it all by myself.' 'I'm pretty content in that way, too,' I said.

Clearly Plante is dazzled by her: dazzled by the sight of her breasts shining in the candlelight as she sits in a bath with burning candles all along the edge, dazzled by the sight of her pubic hair peeping out through the gaping buttons of her skirt, by her 'bodily presence', by her looks (until he noticed her 'stubby' feet, he had thought she 'was beautiful beyond any fault'); dazzled by her sex life, her stories of fucks in the sea with used-car salesmen and the descriptions of her 'long, violently fluttering orgasms'; dazzled by her 'knowledge of the whole world and what was happening or not happening in it'; dazzled by her understanding of 'what it is to be a woman' (what is it?): 'Her intelligence was to me the intelligence of a woman, because she had, as a woman, thought out her role in the world; the complexity of the role required intelligence to see it, and she had seen it, I thought, thoroughly'; dazzled, above all, by the splendour of her public persona. The chapter ends with a description of the wondrous Greer giving a lecture at the Unitarian Church in Tulsa:

Powerful lights illuminated the stage so TV cameras could film the lecture; in the intense light, Germaine appeared to have a burning silver sheen about her. As she talked, she moved her arms in loose soft gestures, and I found myself being drawn in, not to a public argument in support of abortion as she defined it, but a private revelation about love . . . I thought: She's talking about herself. And yet she wasn't talking about herself. She was talking about the outside world, and in her large awareness of it, she knew it as I did not; it was as if she had a secret knowledge of it, and to learn that secret from her would make me a different person. I wanted to be a different person. I had never heard Germaine give a public lecture; I had never seen her so personal. I thought: I love her.

What is surprising is not that Germaine Greer finds him a creep but that after everything he says about her he finds her difficult. If that adjective can encompass both the helpless Jean Rhys and the very able Germaine Greer, what hope is there for the rest of us?

Book reviewed:
Difficult Women: A Memoir of Three by David Plante

Vita Longa

'Contemplating a worn piece of green velvet on her dressing table, I felt my whole being dissolve in love. I have never ceased to love her from that moment.' The person who said that was known as Christopher St. John, though her real name was Christabel Marshall. We know how she felt about the object of her passion, Vita Sackville-West, because she kept a 'love-journal' in Vita's honour. Sackville-West, who had recently (and most unusually) been abandoned by another woman, allowed St. John to hold her hand. She even allowed her, Victoria Glendinning reports, to accompany her in her car 'all the way' to Tonbridge: in Tonbridge Christopher was put on a train back to London. But on the way out of London—on the Westminster Bridge Road, to be precise—Vita had 'stretched out her left hand' and told Christopher that she loved her, and when they got to the station in Tonbridge Vita parked the car in a side street and gave Christopher 'a lover's kiss'. ('I never knew unalloyed bliss with V. except on that November day.') The lover's kiss was followed by 'one night of love'. Then it was all over.

Glendinning's book is mostly about love: Vita falling into it, dying for it, falling out of it; being adored, being swept off her feet, glimpsing paradise, getting bored. At the time of her affair with Christopher St. John Vita was 40: Christopher, Glendinning writes, was 'very ugly and in her late fifties'. (Virginia Woolf, called on to intercede with Vita on Christopher's behalf, described her as 'that mule-faced harridan of yours'.) Vita didn't drop Christopher: she liked people to go on loving her, provided they didn't expect much in return, and Christopher eventually settled for a phone call every Friday night. She didn't stop being in love with Vita, however, and 20 years later, at the age of nearly 80, was still in love with her: 'my dearly loved Vita—my soul's joy'.

All the women who loved Vita Sackville-West loved her with that kind of intensity. 'I have loved you all my life,' Violet Trefusis wrote: 'loved you as my ideal, my inspiration, my perfection.' And in most cases Vita's feelings, for a while at least, ran equally high. There can't be many people who were so much involved in bliss. Vita's son Nigel Nic-olson, attempting to give some account of what went on between his mother and Violet Trefusis, speaks of the two women being 'carried on the breezes towards the sun, exalted and ecstatic, breathing the thin air of the empyrean'. One might, more meanly, say that an important part of their extreme love for each other was the sense it gave them of their great superiority to everyone else. In a life in which what mattered most was to be grand and free and take risks and have adventures and generally be carried on the breezes towards the sun, there is something to be said for a minor character like Christopher St. John who made a note of what exactly happened to her, however meagre, and what the street was called and where the car was parked.

The young Vita Sackville-West, living at Knole, prepared for her adventurous life in a variety of literary forms—'all romantic and all long', as Virginia Woolf said of the works of the young Orlando. Tremendously dissatisfied with herself—'I must have been quite dreadful'—Vita filled her exercise books with elaborate and high-minded reconstructions of the past. Her heroes were aristocratic and overdressed: Richelieu and the Medicis and her own Sackville ancestors. 'My Vita,' Harold Nicolson was to say of his wife, 'is a heroine to everyone including her own darling self.' But it took her a while to figure out what sort of heroine she was going to be. When she had finished a 65,000-word novel celebrating Edward Sackville, a modest hero of the Civil War, she added a coy 'author's note'—she was then 14—in which she wondered whether he could see her and if he knew 'how I wish to be like him'. (This coyness is infectious: Glendinning in *her* author's note says that she thinks Vita 'would like' the form her biography has taken.) She was more bold in her next novel, at any rate about her wish not to be a girl, and told her mother that its young hero, Cranfield Sackville—'he held his tongue and committed his thoughts to paper only'—was intended to be a portrait of herself.

Even better than dressing up as a boy in a novel was dressing up as a boy in real life. When she was 17 she wrote a verse drama on the life and death of Thomas Chatterton: dressed in a white shirt and a pair of black breeches (run up for her in secret by Emily, her maid), she would act it out alone in the attic at Knole and every time be 'moved to tears' by her own performance. Twenty years later, in a flamboyant account of her own adolescence attributed to the heroine of *All Passion Spent*, Vita described her thoughts as having been 'of an extravagance to do credit even to a wild young man. They were thoughts of nothing less than escape and disguise: a changed name, a travestied sex and freedom in some foreign city.' But by then she wore breeches every day, though she wore them with pearls, and had disguised herself as a man to go dancing with Violet Trefusis. She had even, at the height of her passion for Violet, changed her name, faked her sex, and, briefly, found freedom in a foreign city. It wasn't only Vita herself, or the giddy Violet, who found her trousers a turn-on. Virginia Woolf told

Vita that it had been the sight of her gaiters that inspired *Orlando*, Virginia's homage to Vita's androgyny.

Vita, unlike most women who would rather be men (let alone men who would rather be women), had good reason to be discontented: had she not been a girl she would have inherited Knole. The house, given to Thomas Sackville by his cousin Elizabeth I, was, in its way, quite magnificent, with 52 staircases and one bedroom for each day of the year; seen from across the park, as Vita put it, it seemed 'less a house than a medieval village' (wandering into the Great Hall one day, she came face to face with a stag sheltering from the cold). Virginia Woolf didn't think much of it ('too little conscious beauty for my taste'), but for Vita it was the most fierce, and most lasting, of her many attachments. 'I cannot bear to think of Knole wounded and me not there to be wounded with it,' she told Harold Nicolson when she heard that the house had been hit by a bomb. It wasn't simply that she thought she and Knole were the same thing, though she often did. The house also provided her with visions of herself extending back over hundreds of years. Glendinning makes the point that 'she never wrote a fictional version' of its loss: 'Vita's heroes are always in possession of their ancestral homes'—but one could also make the point that her heroes always have ancestral homes to be in possession of.

Vita didn't altogether dislike being a woman and wasn't wholly a lesbian. 'I don't object to homosexuality,' she said to Harold Nicolson several years after the end of her affair with Violet and at the beginning of her relationship with Virginia Woolf. She was talking about her cousin Eddy but it may leave one wondering what subtle category she had in mind for her own and her husband's behaviour. As a young girl she had two relationships of the kind Glendinning calls 'exciting', one with Rosamund Grosvenor ('what a funny thing it is to love a person as I love Roddie'), the other with Violet Keppel. By the time of her engagement to Harold Nicolson, in 1913, when she was 21, there were four or five women telling her that they loved her—'*de tout mon coeur*—and more every day, if that is possible'. It's true that there were also young men, some described here as 'unsuitable' and some as 'brilliant', who seemed to want to marry her and whom she teased but kept at arm's length. 'Men did not attract me in what is called "that way",' she wrote in her 'Autobiography of 1920', first published in 1973 as part of Nigel Nicolson's *Portrait of a Marriage*. 'Women did. Rosamund did.' 'She and Rosamund,' Glendinning explains, 'shared a diffuse and sentimental sensuality, but never, then or later, did they technically "make love".' Apparently, 'they did not think of it,' but that kind of thing is hard to ascertain.

'What fun,' was Vita's comment on meeting Harold Nicolson. In the three years between their meeting and their marriage she spent a lot of time worrying whether she wouldn't have more fun with someone else, with Rosamund or Lord Lascelles, or 'in a tower with my books'. Glendinning, always mindful of the possibility that readers may find Vita 'unlikeable'—she has some difficulty later on with her snobbery and her anti-Semitism—at this point nods wisely and remarks, 'There is nothing peculiar to the modern mind about a vivid, clever, attractive, complex girl of twenty being unwilling to tie herself down for life,' the implication being that if it isn't peculiar now it must have been peculiar then. One could wish that Glendinning had said more about the context in which Vita led her wayward life. 'Physical fidelity,' she tells us apropos of Vita's parents, 'wasn't greatly valued in the marriages of the British upper classes,' but that doesn't quite cover all of Vita's behaviour. In 1960, when they had been married 47 years, Vita told Harold in a letter that everything that happened when they were young had been 'partly your fault':

I was very young and very innocent. I knew nothing about homosexuality. I didn't even know that such a thing existed—either between men or between women. You should have told me. You should have warned me. You should have told me about yourself, and have warned me that the same sort of thing was likely to happen to myself. It would have saved us a lot of trouble and misunderstanding.

She added for good measure that he wouldn't even now like her letter: 'you never like to face facts.' But in her 1920 autobiography she knew enough to say that at the time she hadn't thought it wrong that 'I should be more or less engaged to Harold, and so much in love with Rosamund'. And what about the many affairs she had in middle age—with Hilda Matheson and Evelyn Irons and Olive Rinder and any number of other women ('she falls in love with every pretty woman, just like a man,' Virginia Woolf told Ottoline Morrell)? As for Harold's homosexual friendships with young men, it seems he simply took them for granted. To Harold, as his son observed in *Portrait of a Marriage*, 'sex was as incidental, and about as pleasurable, as a quick visit to a picture-gallery between trains.' Another thing the British upper classes didn't greatly value was the old idea of taking their secrets with them to the grave.

'In her awakening womanhood she desired nothing but that she might yield to him the most abased subjection.' Coming from Vita the remark, made in an unpublished novel written at the time of her marriage, may seem a little overstated, but no more so than many things she said of herself, especially in her fiction. She conceded that with Harold she 'never knew the physical passion I had felt for Rosamund', and was later to complain to her mother of his lack of sexual enthusiasm. (Her mother reported—poor man—that 'H. is always sleepy and has her in a desperate hurry.') On the other hand, he was, she said, 'like a sunny harbour to me'. In the 1920 autobiography she wrote that 'for sheer joy of companionship' the first years of her marriage were 'unparalleled or at least unsurpassed', and in 1915 noted in her diary that 'we are more in love than ever. I thank God I have known absolute happiness.' A friend was proudly cited who had told her that 'the doors of our house are like glimpses of paradise.' Until late middle age Vita was either extremely happy or extremely miserable, or both at the same time.

The period of absolute happiness with Harold came to an end in the autumn of 1917 when he caught a venereal infection from one of his young men. Vita was not so much wounded as unleashed, and the long-drawn-out affair with Violet was the consequence. 'I suppose I am too cultured and *fin de siècle* to impose my virility,' Harold sighed, while she told him that she longed for 'new places' and had had enough of ordering lunch. On 10 February 1920 the two women eloped.

> We will lead you such a dance
> If in Belgium or in France,
> But we aren't going to trifle very long,

Vita wrote on the train from Boulogne to Amiens. On 14 February Harold and Denys Trefusis flew to Amiens in a two-seater aeroplane and reclaimed their respective wives. ('Quite like a sensational novel,' Lady Sackville noted in her diary.) The relationship didn't really end until some time in 1922. Wild oats are all very well, Vita wrote to Harold, but not 'when they grow as high as a jungle'.

Nigel Nicolson was three the year his mother eloped. Vita didn't take much interest in her children until they were grown up and then took too much. 'They rush after me whenever they see me, simply because they have nothing else to do,' she complained to Harold when the boys were home from prep school or Eton. And when he reminded her that responsibilities were not something 'to regard with shame', she asked him how he would like to have entire charge of two children for four months of the year:

Supposing that someone—say Eddy—told you that he had to look after two boys and that it was too much of a good thing, you would instantly agree. It would never cross your mind to say he was being unreasonable. Why then is it different for me? Sex, I suppose. Well, I don't see that it makes any difference, so there.

So there. Looking after her children came under the general heading of 'Acid X'—something she didn't want to do but Harold (or the world) said she ought to. What concerned her mostly when she thought about them at all was whether she preferred Ben to Nigel or Nigel to Ben and which of the two was more like her.

One might have expected Nigel Nicolson to hold all this against his mother. One might have expected it were it not for the habit that leads the upper classes to celebrate their own and each other's bad behaviour. If Vita was cruel, he says of the episode with Violet, 'it was cruelty on a heroic scale.' Had the fault been more modest would it have been less admirable? Glendinning, untroubled by these distinctions, speaks of Vita's 'potential for criminal carelessness'. That, too, seems dramatic but certainly Vita came and went at her own terrible pleasure. Some years later she had an affair with the art historian Geoffrey Scott. Of this incident Nigel Nicolson writes: 'Vita had not been kind to Geoffrey—she had smashed his life and finally wrecked his marriage—but what part does kindness play in love?' No doubt the question doesn't expect an answer but even Vita could on occasion express unease about what she saw as the 'savage' side of her character, though she was more afraid for herself than worried about the damage done to others.

The affair with Violet was followed by the much more sober affair with Virginia Woolf. 'Florid, moustached, parakeet coloured, with all the supple ease of the aristocracy, but not the wit of the artist', Virginia Woolf noted in her diary for 15 December 1922. She had met Vita for the first time the previous evening. The Nicolsons were introduced into Bloomsbury by Clive Bell and generally considered a bad thing: 'I mean,' Woolf wrote, 'we judged them both incurably stupid. He is bluff, but oh so obvious; she, Duncan thought, took the cue from him and had nothing free to say.' Virginia never changed her mind about Vita's intellectual capacities. Even when she and Leonard were making considerable sums of money out of her books—*The Edwardians* sold 800 copies a day—she would praise them to Vita's face and describe them behind her back as 'those sleepwalking servantgirl novels'. 'Her real claim to consideration,' she told Jacques Raverat, 'is, if I may be so coarse, her legs.' Harold warned his wife to be careful—'it's like smoking over a petrol tank'—and this time, more admiring, less engaged, she was: 'I *have* gone to bed with her (twice) but that's all.' 'Do you really like going to bed with women?' Vanessa Bell asked her sister in a loud voice as they were buying some pills in a chemist's shop. 'And how d'you do it?' That is one thing Glendinning alas doesn't tell us. The two ladies went to the zoo together, they ate muffins in teashops, Vita taught Virginia how to drive and when passion faded they remained friends. Vita took up with Hilda Matheson and Virginia was consoled by Ethel Smyth.

After Hilda came Evelyn and Olive and Mary Campbell and all sorts of others; some were established lesbians with jealous partners, others, like Mary Campbell, had jealous husbands; several had never slept with a woman before. And so it went on, despite age and arthritis, till her death in 1962.

During all this time she and Harold never stopped being friends, never stopped saying (or Vita never stopped saying) that they loved each other more than any two people in the world: her love for him, she told him in 1929, was 'immortal'. 'All the gentleness and femininity in me,' she wrote in her autobiography, 'was called out by Harold alone.' But she was not so wifely (or even, to be broad-minded, husbandly) as to show an interest in what he was doing. When the Foreign Office posted him to the embassy in Berlin she paid him a brief visit and came home. When he was invited to join the British delegation at the League of Nations she didn't know what the League of Nations was. He would ask her to accompany him to Buckingham Palace: she wouldn't go—'I shall just have to lie low, and you will have to lie high if anyone asks where I am.' If she spent any time thinking about what he did it was only in her unrelenting effort to persuade him to give it up. 'People like you who can write marvellously should not waste themselves in a lot of humbug and fubsiness.' By 'humbug and fubsiness' she apparently meant the preliminaries to the Second World War. When eventually he left the Foreign Office he was miserable. (So miserable that he joined Mosley's New Party. Vita, who disapproved, consoled herself by securing a job for one of her girlfriends' girlfriends on Mosley's newspaper.) 'It would be an overstatement to say that Vita wrecked Harold's career,' Nigel Nicolson remarks. But in the overstatement there's a statement of some kind. 'I know that there is no such thing as equality between the sexes,' Harold noted in his diary in 1934, 'and that women are not fulfilling their proper functions unless subservient to some man.' In that overstatement, too, there is a statement of some kind.

Book reviewed:

Vita: The Life of Vita Sackville-West by Victoria Glendinning

Sisters' Keepers

Keeping women, like keeping horses, is one of the many things the rich can do that other people can't. They may do it for reasons of financial prudence, but if so it's the sort of prudence that only the rich can afford. One of the girls Edna Salamon talked to met her man in a lift: 'I told him that I was really hard up and if he wanted to go out with me he'd have to pay me . . . He asked if £500 was enough.' She said £50 would do and hasn't been hard up from that day to this. There must be men who don't find it easy to keep a mistress as well as a wife, but the ones Salamon met in the course of her researches generally claimed that 'it made more economic sense' than going through a divorce. 'He didn't want me to have any less luxury than his wife,' a middle-aged Texan said of her lover: 'I always had a new car to drive—lovely clothes—memberships at the best private clubs.' The prudence may be as much emotional as financial: an abandoned wife whose former husband didn't want her to have any less luxury than his girlfriend would have less reason to feel grateful. Or it may not be a matter of prudence at all. Even the nicest husbands must have more fun buying zippy cars for their doxies than sedans for their wives.

Salamon is careful about the distinctions to be made between one man's wealth and another's—'to describe all the men as rich obscures the extreme variations possible'—but she can only guess at the wealth of the men she came across: the rich are always eager to spare their interlocutors the embarrassment of knowing exactly how rich they are. There are extreme variations, too, in the currency in which these men expect to be repaid. One woman has met her lover every day in the middle of the day for the past 26 years. Another spends four weekends a year with her man, and for that he has so far paid out a quarter of a million pounds. It may be that for him, and for many of the men involved in these relationships, the greatest pleasure is simply the pleasure of spending their money.

That isn't what they say, of course. Most of Salamon's book is taken up with describing the different kinds of women who are, or who seek to be, kept but in her last chapter she compares what she has learned from them with what their lovers have told her. 'Men,' she says, 'are much more likely to claim that their appeal to their partners is personal virility while women tend to play down the sexual side of the relationship.' These men aren't young: the man who spends four weekends a year with his mistress is in his sixties. However much they may boast about what they do in bed, their women see it differently and talk behind their backs about 'middle-aged problems' and the 'male menopause'. Neither the men nor the women were happy to talk about financial arrangements. But it seems likely that for both keeper and kept money is a larger factor than what it can't buy.

'A cat wearing a jewelled choker does no more than reflect glory on the owner,' Salamon (cattily) observes, and she has a point. The question is: what kind of glory? A man who goes out with a girl whom he has dressed in diamonds may think he is saying something about his virility, but the only hard evidence the diamonds provide is the evidence of hard cash. And the cash exercises its own kind of tyranny. The Texan woman whose boyfriend wanted her to live in the same luxury as his wife told Salamon that the only difficulty between them was that she wanted to have a career and 'he wanted me to be free to do the things I wanted to do.' The striking thing here isn't his claim to know what's best for her but his insistence that she should only want what money can supply. Salamon sometimes talks about these women sinking into a life of 'conspicuous consumption'. One might also think in terms of the conspicuous presumption of the men they are involved with.

Salamon came to London from Canada in 1980 to write a thesis at the LSE about the reasons women stay with dreadful husbands, but finding it difficult to collect representative samples of every kind of marital disaster, she took her hairdresser's advice and settled for the subject of kept women, of whom her hairdresser knew a great many. Her book is a shortened version of that thesis, dedicated to her supervisor but got up by her publisher to look like a box of chocolates. On the back there is a large photograph in which she looks very glamorous, her face half-hidden by all sorts of layers of curls. One can see that she might have occasion to visit her hairdresser quite often and one can also see why some of the men she interviewed found the experience confusing. (One of them offered to take her to Acapulco for Christmas and added, presumably when he saw the look of horror on her face: 'You don't have to fuck me unless you want to.') Unlike the majority of women who write about women, she doesn't appear to do so out of a sense of personal discontent and though concerned to show that kept women are not necessarily less nice than other women, she isn't her sisters' keeper.

Heaven forbid. Salamon is a scientist and shares no one's illusions. 'I would argue,' she says in the course of some remarks on the

conservatism of kept women and their lovers, 'that the sexual liberation of women is as authentic as the Loch Ness monster.' Having got
her PhD, she has gone back to Canada, where she teaches criminology
at Simon Fraser University. Her subject, however, is unlikely to be
crime, which, in university departments, has largely yielded to something called 'deviance'. Kept women, for example, are 'sexual deviants'
and so too, very nearly, are those who take an interest in them: 'In
writing on sexual deviance you are thought at least marginally devi-
ant yourself,' Salamon writes in her preface. 'Adie! How could you!'
shrieked one of her friends. In this case the term is misleading, however, since what it signifies are not unusual acts (there is nothing out
of the way about the things these women do in bed, no mirrors or
funny underwear or 'unnatural' practices) but only an unusual social
arrangement—which turns out not to be very unusual at all. Salamon
asked one of her interviewees whether there was a part of London
where mistresses tended to live. 'If there was you'd never get in for the
traffic,' he replied. The trouble with 'deviance' is that those who study
it may have an overdeveloped sense of what is being deviated from.

The same, perhaps not surprisingly, might be said of kept women
themselves. Most of the ones Salamon writes about were quite happy
to talk about sex, although, like the men they have it with, it doesn't
always feature much in their lives: 'With the sheik I probably have sex
a couple of times a year—that's not much is it?' Nor do they make a
pretence of loving the man who keeps them—some do love him and
some don't. One woman who makes a habit of being kept, as many
of them do, refers to all her keepers as 'Willie': Willie I, Willie II,
Willie III, Willie IV—like the kings (or keepers) of England. Similarly, they aren't on the whole disturbed by the thought that their
lovers are married to someone else. In fact, it sometimes seems that
one of the pleasures of being kept is that it enables you to be more
wife than a girlfriend and less wife than a wife. 'I think it's a fine

game and no small work of art,' one of them boasted: not only did she 'travel extensively and enjoy the company of world-renowned classical musicians' but her fellow, while making all this possible, also 'mows the grass and takes out the garbage'. One might be forgiven for thinking—though it isn't the impression Salamon wishes to give—that these women live in a perfect world. The chief evidence that they don't is their extreme reluctance to talk about their means of support. The reason no doubt, as Salamon surmises, is their fear that they might be mistaken for common or garden prostitutes: a fear made all the more intense by the fact that what largely drives them into taking money in the first place is their greed for social success: 'I have arrived—so to speak!' said the woman who enjoyed the company of classical musicians.

The social success that they want is of course the kind that only money (or, in some cases, power) can bring, and one of the most striking things about them is the distinction they make between the money that supports them and can't be spoken of and the money that is casually spent on them and is spoken about all the time. Some kinds of kept women—Salamon calls them 'professional opportunists'—spend their lives cooking up situations in which their lovers will find themselves in a shop handing out cash in preposterous quantities. She cites the case of a woman who 'manipulated her lover into a top boutique in Switzerland, selected several outfits and feigned astonishment when the bill came to slightly over £11,000'. Another on her first date always suggests a rendezvous at Harrods. 'If he fails to buy her something from the vast assortment featured there he is definitely not attracted enough to be worth her while.' The point of these expensive acquisitions goes beyond their mere expense. The more a man spends on you, and the more 'tasteful' the things he buys, the greater the status he confers. 'She contrasted her own situation with that of her friend who was kept by an Arab man. She commented that while her friend had dozens of pairs of shoes, none of them was handmade and while her friend's lover had bought her a house in a fashionable London mews, it was not really a very nice mews house.' Many of Salamon's opportunists are upper-middle-class women with degrees, confident that what they are getting in return for their favours is simply what they deserve to have.

Not all kept women are equally cynical. Even in Salamon's book there are women who fall in love with men who just happen to be rich. Nor are they all equally interested in money. 'If he hadn't been so good at his job I wouldn't have looked at him twice,' Salamon was told by a 'senior executive' in a cosmetics firm who was being kept by the managing director: 'I'm very ambitious myself and I need that mental stimulation in a relationship.' Women who are kept by their bosses—'career women' in Salamon's categorisation—may be glad of the opportunity to talk about work to their lovers in the way husbands talk about work to their wives. What must be even nicer, however, is the encouragement they get—'my lover is my true friend because he wants me to make the most of myself'—and, nicer still, the chance to make it to the top smoothly and ahead of everyone else. Colleagues may not like it but that's their bad luck and easily attributed to jealousy or incompetence. 'Although they have achieved high positions through dubious means, the members of the Career Woman category appear aggressively sure of their own abilities,' Salamon reports with admiration and dismay. The anxieties of deviance might have seemed more impressive if we had heard from women who'd been kept and dumped.

The impression one gets from reading Salamon's book is that the unusual element in these women's lives is merely the unusual degree to which they allow ambition (or self-interest) a free rein. Women, as feminists often tell us, are the victims of their own wish to please. No one would say that of the women Salamon writes about, though one might, if one were tender-hearted, say it of the men who keep them. 'What is past is past,' she was told by an American who'd been kept by four different men. 'During the relationship I usually enjoy myself and grow as a person. And from there one just goes on.' Maybe, as the women themselves argue, they're not that different from everyone else—'I think I am quite normal in saying that I love to be spoiled with attention and gifts'—but know what they want and worry less than students of deviance think they should about how they get it.

Book reviewed:

Kept Women: Mistresses in the Eighties by Edna Salamon

Fortress Freud

Psychoanalysts have a difficult relationship with the rest of the world—or, as they sometimes call it, 'the goyim'. Janet Malcolm's two very striking books of reportage, *Psychoanalysis: The Impossible Profession* and *In the Freud Archives*, make this clear. Freud's wife, according to her grandson, 'divided the world into those who knew of grandfather and those who did not'. The latter, he said, 'did not play any role in her life'. In that sense every analyst is Freud's wife and lives in a world entirely taken up with psychoanalytic concerns. Sometimes it seems that they hardly know what may happen in real life and fear it accordingly. On the night of the New York blackout in 1965 someone I know was with his analyst. As the lights went out the analyst—not the patient—jumped out of his chair and shouted: 'They're coming to get me.' Psychoanalysts have had good reasons for considering themselves beleaguered, but for the past 20 years at least, the world, being less interested in them, has been less interested than they imagine in finding them out. 'No decent analyst would let his picture appear in the *Times*,' one New York analyst snapped at another, as if he had caught him sneaking his image into the temple of Baal. Malcolm speaks of the 'chilly castle of psychoanalysis' and admires its austerities. One might less admiringly think of it as Fortress Freud and question whether it too needs to be so insistently defended.

The idea that psychoanalysis is something to be guarded from the world was of course Freud's: 'we have been obliged to recognise and express as our conviction,' he said in 1933, 'that no one has a right to join in a discussion of psychoanalysis who has not had particular experiences which can only be obtained by being analysed oneself'; and Malcolm, who is unusual in being nice as well as astute, wants us to know that he regretted this—'you can believe me,' she quotes him as saying, 'when I tell you that we do not enjoy giving an impression of being members of a secret society.' Though she concedes that he went too far in speaking of a 'right' to talk about psychoanalysis, she also believes that he had no alternative: 'From the resistance that even card-carrying Freudians put up against the Freudian unconscious, the resistance of the non or anti-Freudians may be deduced.' But the idea of 'resistance' is an old Freudian wheeze for dismissing other people's opinions; and one doesn't have to cite the shortcomings of the rest of the world in order to account for Freud's attempt to declare psychoanalysis a total exclusion zone.

Despite what is said by loyal members of the taskforce, Freud was never entirely on his own, though it's true that in the years of 'splendid isolation', as he called them, the years of his friendship with Fliess, no one shared the confidence he had in himself. By 1902, however, a psychoanalytic society met every Wednesday around a table in his waiting room; and if to start with it had only four members, its discussions were still considered sufficiently interesting to be reported each week in the Sunday edition of the *Neues Wiener Tagblatt*. At the end of his life, when he made those remarks about giving an impression of belonging to a secret society and not enjoying it, his ideas were 'detonating' (Malcolm's word) throughout the intellectual world. He was passionately determined to make his mark as a scientist, and it could be that the most effective way of persuading the world that he'd seen further than any of his rivals, especially those among them, like Adler and Jung, who had been obliged to pack their bags and leave the Freudian house, was by surrounding his secrets with secrecy. 'I am nothing by temperament but a conquistador,' he said in a letter to Fliess, and he fought hard to make his sovereignty over the unconscious secure. In the world at large Freud's revelations were assimilated in all sorts of ways. Psychoanalysis, however, was a family matter.

The situation has scarcely changed even now. Take, for example, Freud's own reputation. Present-day analysts, so Malcolm asserts, are unruffled by what is now routinely, though not always persuasively, said about Freud: that he persecuted his colleagues, that he took unfair advantage of them, that he faked his evidence, that he fucked his sister-in-law. 'Most Freudian analysts,' she writes, 'can take or leave Freud himself,' and reading that sentence, one may briefly wonder what can have happened to make them all so reckless, but her real meaning, to judge by the analysts whom she herself cites, is that they can take or leave what is said about Freud by anyone who isn't an analyst. Within the profession security is almost as tight today as it was when Freud was in charge, and it is still the case, Malcolm reports, that 'outsiders wishing to join in the discussion of psychoanalysis are in effect told to go away and maybe come back after they've been analysed.' No analyst would say in public that he had doubts about Freud.

The first of Malcolm's two books is an account of the contemporary psychoanalytic profession largely based on the experience of one middle-aged New York analyst whom she calls 'Aaron Green'. He is an edgy, discontented man, committed to Freud's legacy in its most classical form and at the same time acutely aware of the profession's shortcomings. He discusses, for example, the period when he was in training at the New York Institute of Psychoanalysis:

'I had several friends who were asked to resign.'
'After a long time in training?'
'Yes, sometimes after many years.'
'What does it mean when someone is dropped?'
'I don't know. These things are shrouded in mystery.'

Far from having been abandoned, the ways of the secret society have been institutionalised. Authority relies on silence and mystification to get its effects and no one knows on what grounds candidates for membership have been blackballed: they simply vanish into the daylight. Malcolm, whose own feelings about psychoanalysis aren't at all easy to gauge, talks about 'the narrow, inward-turning path of psychoanalytic therapy' and represents the training institutes and analytic societies as 'decrepit mansions with drawn shades' planted along 'hidden, almost secret byways . . . marked with inscrutable road signs'. What she seems to have in mind is something drawn by Charles Addams, homes for ghouls rather than the headquarters of what is commonly assumed to be a form of therapy.

Once an analyst has completed his training he begins to hope that he will, in time, become a training analyst himself; or, as Green puts it, be admitted into the inner sanctum of psychoanalysis, his own analyst's bedroom. 'Not everyone,' he says, 'feels like that—some people drop out of the institute world and go their own way—but the majority, like me, for whatever infantilely motivated reason, hope that they will get into that bedroom: that they will become training analysts.' Once they are in the bedroom that's where they want to stay. Analysts, it seems, spend most of their time in each other's company—at meetings, over supper, in matrimony; they worry to an unusual degree about each other's good opinion and, as they say themselves, find little to talk about with people 'on the outside'; the members of a given institute speak the same way, even dress the same way. 'Aaron's attitude towards the NYU Institute is . . . affectionate': for the Columbia analysts 'he has nothing but bitterness and scorn':

> 'But the schism was years ago,' I said. 'What's the matter with them now?'
>
> Aaron frowned, and said in a low, dark voice: 'They're sharp dressers.'

In the early 1960s I used to see a middle-aged analyst who found it impossible to accept that the reason some of her patients wore miniskirts was that most of their friends wore them too: it must, she insisted, have some deeper significance.

There are many analysts—Green is one—who would agree that analysts spend more time closeted with each other than is good for them; and the question of what psychoanalysis can and cannot sensibly account for is more unstable, or ambiguous, than most patients realise when they are lying on the couch wondering why their analyst hasn't spoken for the past three-quarters of an hour. For example, Malcolm says of Freud that 'it has become a kind of cliché that he was "no *Menschenkenner*"' (i.e., no judge of people). To those who are not au fait with the subtle, self-protecting, teasing ways in which psychoanalysis both tries and refuses to connect with the external world this may seem surprising. 'Throughout his life', Malcolm continues, Freud 'was beset by the affliction of overestimation', but since the overestimations she cites—which are the ones that are usually cited in this context—are his overestimations of Breuer, Fliess, and Jung ('the most prominent of those who came within the orbit of Freud's propensity for idealisation followed by disillusionment'), one might suspect that the cliché, however well founded, is also a convenient way of making it seem that there was nothing in Freud's behaviour that could decently be thought reprehensible.

Psychoanalytic theory offers no grounds for expecting analysts to be wiser than anyone else: its view of human nature and its capacity for change, let alone improvement, is far too gloomy for that. According to Green, 'such small edge as analysts have they exercise in only one situation in life—namely, the analytic situation.' Malcolm is more eloquent. 'The greatest analyst in the world,' she says with seeming admiration, 'can live his own life only like an ordinary blind and driven human being,' but the unjustified sinner, the really ordinary human being, may think there is something tricky about a science that claims so much and so little for itself and its adherents. Her remark, intended perhaps to release psychoanalysts from the uncomfortable burden of other people's expectations, at the same time makes it plain that analysis should not be seen in the way it is conventionally seen—as a means of assisting people to get their lives in order. What it provides is, appropriately, both more modest and more magisterial: an initiation into its own way of thinking.

On the other hand, if it's the case that the greatest analyst in the world can't get any more grip than the rest of us, why have Freudians laboured so hard to keep up the image of Great Father Freud? And why have so many people, most of them loosely or formerly connected with psychoanalysis, felt it necessary to work away at the destruction of that image? It has often been said, and not only by its detractors, that there is too much of the family romance in psychoanalysis (consider the number of analysts who, as Green points out, boast that their analyst was analysed by X who was analysed by Freud or Abraham or Ferenczi—though I've not yet come across any who've boasted about being analysed by my relative Max Eitingon): maybe a history in which filial passions have played such a critical part can itself be taken as evidence in favour of Freudian theory.

The current black sheep and family snitch is Jeffrey Masson, the principal subject of Malcolm's second book. Masson made his first appearance in the international psychoanalytic community in the early 1970s and the community was dazzled. 'He wasn't,' writes Malcolm, who has an eye for these things, 'like the other analytical candidates one sees at congresses—quiet and serious and somewhat cowed-looking young psychiatrists who stand about together like shy, plain girls at dances . . . Masson was dancing with some of the most attractive and desirable partners at the ball.' He was a student of Sanskrit at Harvard when he first had recourse to psychoanalysis ('my main symptom was total promiscuity'). From Harvard he went to Canada to teach Sanskrit at the University of Toronto and on the day the term began realised he would have to give it up. ('I couldn't sit there with four students, all eccentric, and read this little script. I just couldn't.') So he decided to embark on a training analysis at the local institute in preparation for a second career. As with everything else in his life, he was first enraptured, then bored—though to begin with, he was bored only with psychoanalysis in Toronto: 'when I get to the real heart of things,' he told himself, 'it will all be different.' In 1974, at a meeting of the American Psychoanalytic Association in Denver, he gave a paper on Schreber and Freud: 'Canada,' a New York analyst said, 'has sent us a national treasure.'

It was at the Denver congress that Masson met his man. Kurt Eissler is one of the grandees of contemporary psychoanalysis, the guardian of Freud's good name (he once wrote a review of Freud's *Collected Letters* to which he gave the title 'Mankind at Its Best') and, more to the point, the exceedingly jealous guardian of the Freud Archives in Washington. Like Freud when he first met Jung, Eissler was enchanted by Masson. 'He embodied all that Eissler most cherished in people: intellect, erudition, energy, zest, colour, sparkle, even a certain wildness—qualities that the early analysts evidently had in abundance but that today's sober practitioners entirely lack.' In his turn, Eissler, who, at the time of their first meeting, was exactly twice Masson's age, represented everything that in a perfect life a son might want of his father; and not only did he, as Malcolm reports, love Masson 'quite beyond all expectation', he also promised him the freedom of the archives—which, given that Masson's interest in analysis was almost entirely historical and that large sections of the archives are closed to everyone else, was like giving him the keys to the kingdom.

In October 1980 Masson was appointed the archives' projects director, to the dismay of many members of the analytic community, which was by then losing confidence in him. ('This man,' they said, 'is a mistake.') Even worse, when Eissler retired Masson would be taking his place. But Eissler didn't read the papers Masson was sending him and, it appears, didn't listen to the things he said. In October 1981, after two articles appeared in the *New York Times* announcing to the world and to his unsuspecting patron that Masson had developed new and heretical ideas about Freud, his appointment was rescinded. 'I'm going to recommend to the board that you be terminated,' Eissler is supposed to have said: the implication being that, in ceasing to be acceptable to the family, Masson would also cease to exist—another casualty of the ancestral propensity for idealisation followed by thoughts of assassination.

In the Freud Archives was initially published in the *New Yorker* after Masson had been expelled from the analytic community but before the appearance of his own book, *Freud: The Assault on Truth*, which, he believed, would blow away the foundations of psychoanalysis. It will be like the Ford Pinto, he told Malcolm: they will have to recall every patient since 1901. But when the book came out last year, though it had many reviews, no patients were recalled and the only effect it's likely to have is to ensure that no one else makes it into the archives for many years to come. Not even the anti-Freudians welcomed it. Frank Cioffi, for example, whose opinion of Freud could scarcely be lower, took the view that Masson had 'achieved the remarkable feat of concocting an account . . . no less tendentious and unreliable than Freud's own'. Yet for all Masson's excesses and his wrong-headed scholarship, there is something sympathetic in what he says about psychoanalysis.

The subject of his book is the seduction theory, which Freud held between 1895 and 1897 and then dropped—in Masson's view, suppressed. In April 1896, in a paper on 'The Aetiology of Hysteria', Freud argued that sexual abuse in infancy or early childhood was the invariable cause of the hysterical symptoms which so many 19th-century women (and some men) developed in adult life, that these experiences 'could be reproduced through the work of psychoanalysis', and the symptoms thus relieved. This, in brief, is the seduction theory. Its importance for Masson is that it was based on the idea that people are made ill by something that really happened to them. The paper was delivered to the members of the Vienna Society for Psychiatry and Neurology and, Freud reported to Fliess, 'met with an icy reception from the asses'; Krafft-Ebing, who was in the chair, said that it sounded 'like a scientific fairy tale'. At the time Freud was enraged (his colleagues, he told Fliess, could go to hell), but it wasn't long before he, too, began to think he'd been wrong. His patients weren't getting better, for one thing—and in those days patients were expected to get better pretty quickly.

The seduction theory eventually yielded to the theory of infantile sexuality and the Oedipus complex; 'psychical reality' took over from 'material reality'; when patients talked about childhood seductions they were no longer thought to be talking about something that had really happened to them but about something they wished had happened. This has generally been taken to be one of the great moments in the history of psychoanalysis: a victory for common sense (it was, after all, unlikely that so many children were either assaulted by their fathers or seduced by the maid—Jocasta, as so often, barely features in the story), and one of Freud's decisive contributions to the way we think of ourselves. Masson, however, sees it differently: 'by shifting the emphasis from an actual world of sadness, misery and cruelty to an internal stage on which actors performed invented dramas for an invisible audience of their own creation, Freud began a trend away from the real world that, it seems to me, is at the root of the present-day sterility of psychoanalysis and psychiatry throughout the world.'

There are many sober, dark-suited analysts, Freudians as well as post-Freudians, who might agree with much of what is said in that sentence (provided they didn't know it was written by Masson) without wishing to see the seduction theory brought back to life or sharing Masson's hectic suspicion of the reasons that led Freud to ditch it. Reviewers of Masson's book have had no difficulty in persuading their readers of the sloppiness of his research or the simple-mindedness of the conclusions he draws from it: indeed one doesn't have to have read the whole of Freud to see that Masson got much of it wrong and that his book is chiefly interesting insofar as it constitutes another inglorious episode in the long-drawn-out family romance. It is still, however, the case that the relationship between orthodox psychoanalysis and the reality of patients' lives is ambiguous and often unhelpful; and that when analysts say to their patients, as most of them do, 'I'm not interested in what happened to you but in what you have made of it,' the patients may reasonably feel that hermeneutics are not enough. As Leonard Shengold, one of the most sympathetic of the analysts

Malcolm talked to, said in a paper on child abuse, 'the patient must know what he has suffered, at whose hands, and how it has affected him.' It's an important point, and not exactly arcane, yet the issue is far too often evaded.

The behaviour of the analyst I used to see varied with the time of day when I saw her. On Tuesdays and Thursdays I saw her early in the morning and these 'sessions' were, I imagine, like everyone else's, low-key and fairly formal. On Mondays and Fridays my appointment was at six and she was usually more friendly and forthcoming. On Wednesdays, however, I went at 6:30 or 7 and often she used to make odd, disconnected remarks and sometimes her speech was slurred. I couldn't figure out what was going on, but from time to time I would nerve myself the following morning to ask her whether there'd been anything wrong the night before, to which she always responded by asking me what it was about me that caused me to find reasons for alarm in other people's behaviour. The last time I saw her, around five o'clock in the afternoon, she was quite bananas and kept repeating questions I'd already answered. Afterwards, wanting to make my peace with psychoanalysis, I talked to other analysts, whose response was always much the same as hers. Fifteen years later someone told me what should have been clear to me at the time: that the woman was an alcoholic. If it wasn't so easy for analysts to deny the reality of their patients' lives (to use a phrase of Masson's) and if this analyst's colleagues had been less concerned to protect her and more willing to grant that patients have an important stake in their own perceptions, I might not, despite six dutiful years of analysis, have ended up with such fiercely ambivalent feelings about it. Similarly, if the keepers of the fortress were less concerned to protect Freud's good name, to preserve the mysteriousness of his mysteries and to foreclose discussion, if, for example, their archives, like most archives, were open to scholars,

Masson and others like him might not become so inflamed every time they succeed in prising away a bit of evidence that shows (or may show) that Freud was (or may have been) less than totally perfect.

Book reviewed:

In the Freud Archives by Janet Malcolm

Lady Rothermere's Fan

'We missed you at Chantilly,' Ann Fleming wrote to Evelyn Waugh in 1956, after she'd been to visit Diana Cooper in France. 'Mr Gaitskell came to lunch and fell in love with Diana . . . He had never seen cocktails with mint in them or a magnum of pink champagne. He was very happy. I lied and told him that all the upper class were beautiful and intelligent and he must not allow his vermin to destroy them.' Mrs. Fleming wrote a great many letters to Evelyn Waugh, telling him where she'd had lunch and where she'd had supper and who'd been there and made a fool of himself. It can't be said that there's anything in them that the rest of the world badly needs to know; and some people might find her tone of voice offensive. On the other hand, the letters were written for Waugh and he liked them. The question that's hard to answer is: why are we reading them now?

The *Observer*, who serialised the letters, described their publication as 'the literary event of the season', which shows a doubtful sense of what's what. Ann Fleming was married for 12 not very happy years to Ian Fleming, with whom she'd been infatuated for most of her life.

Her previous husbands, Lord Rothermere, the owner of the *Daily Mail*, and Lord O'Neill, never counted for much, though she had had a glamorous life with Rothermere and had been in love with him for a few years when still married to O'Neill. Being in love, unlike being married, is part of having a good time—and good times are what she chiefly writes about. After a supper at Petworth where Harold Macmillan had been present, she told Waugh that 'except for a weakness for anecdotes about the peerage, everything he said was interesting,' but added: 'I doubt if he would enjoy a jolly jokes evening.' That, to the extent that it's fair to judge from these letters, is what she liked best: jolly jokes evenings with her friends. She was witty ('that's the cosiest *Fan tutte* I've ever heard,' she said after she and her friends had been listening to it round an open fire with cushions and blankets); gave good, and when she was married to Rothermere spectacular, parties and is generally remembered as the sort of woman who could create a conversational fizz.

Her friends, as one would expect, were all grand, even those who weren't straightforwardly upper-class. On the one hand, Boofy Arran; on the other, Lord Goodman. Mark Amory inadvertently sets the scene when he says in his foreword that he'd had to tidy up her spelling because 'she never spotted the first "a" in Isaiah.' 'People born in all sorts of strata of society enjoyed the fruits of success,' Cecil Beaton wrote apropos of the party she gave to mark Cyril Connolly's 50th birthday. 'And no one wasted their time in banalities.' Not everyone—especially not her husbands—could handle so much brilliance, but there was always a chance that the outsider's bemusement would further enhance the occasion. Invited to Chatsworth for 'a high society pheasant shoot', she reported to Waugh that the other guests, 'Sandyses and Radziwills', had 'fled to their bedchambers alarmed by Mitford and Cecil wit'. But then three of them were foreigners and the fourth 'a humourless politician'.

Except in her letters to Fleming she doesn't say much about herself beyond noting her often 'sorry' state of mind and prevailing Waugh-like animosities. The point of the letters is to broadcast the news: how everyone's feeling ('Cyril so down he was forced to spend ten days at the Ritz') and behaving ('by the time coffee appeared Randolph and Claud were unconscious beneath the table and June was uncontrollably weeping'); the effect the guests had on each other and the quality of the conversation at the various occasions she'd attended ('Noël was making eminent playwright conversation to the leading lady . . . He should be used as a cabaret and not as a guest . . . the deserts of pomposity between the oases of wit are too vast'); the look of delight on George Wigg's face when Debo Devonshire asked him if he would tap her telephone and the 'terrible tension' on Evangeline Bruce's when her husband took up 45 minutes of dinner-party time to answer a simple political question. She enjoyed embarrassment and records with pleasure the gaffes that she and other people made ('You know Jamaica well, is the native problem worse than in Nassau?' the Duke of Windsor asked Lord Rothermere, when it was her lover, Fleming, who had a house there). She played on the uneasy relationship between Waugh and Cyril Connolly by reporting to one the disparaging remarks made by the other; and if times were dull invented exchanges for the sake of the discomfort they would cause, or coaxed people into saying things she would later give them reason to regret.

Waugh with mock-envy thought of her as 'living at the centre of the political web', but though she enjoyed the company of politicians, provided they weren't humourless, and liked to know what was going on, she says little about events at the political centre—which would in any case have been outside her stylistic range. The rights and wrongs of Suez are not raised, nor do we know what she thought about Eden's abrupt resignation. The Edens' subsequent touchiness, however, is a constant cause of complaint—it was so hard to know with whom they could safely be asked to supper—and a recurrent source of amusement, as in: 'I went to the Second Empire exhibition in Paris and by force prevented James Pope-Hennessey sending Clarissa a postcard of "La Parure du Canal de Suez".' (The *parure* in question appears to have been a collection of necklaces and brooches presented to the Empress Eugénie.) One of her best moments comes when she is telling Waugh about 'a noisy evening with Avons and Devonshires': 'there was a great uproar and lots of four-letter words; Debo said to Roy Jenkins: "Can't you stop them by saying something Labour?"'—'but this,' she says to Waugh, 'is something Roy has never been able to do.' There's an interest, of course, in all this tribal chit-chat, but however stylishly done, it doesn't exactly constitute a literary event.

Mark Amory, the editor of the letters, who was a friend of Ann Fleming's and her literary executor, has a strong tribal sense, as his many snobbish footnotes make clear. Apart from the footnotes, which aren't always accurate, he has written an introduction that tells the story of her life up to 1946 when the letters begin. She was born in 1913; 'during the last of the long hot summers before the First World War', he notes, reviving yet again the idea that the country and the weather lost their charm at the same time. (I thought the summer of 1911 was the really hot one.) Her parents were both the children of Souls, her mother a Tennant, her father a Charteris. She was brought up by her grandmothers, spent a term at Cheltenham Ladies' College (it wasn't a success) and a few months at the Villa Marie Antoinette in Versailles—a finishing school. In retrospect she didn't think she'd been happy. 'None of us,' she said afterwards, 'had any affection in our tempestuous childhood,' but Amory doesn't altogether believe this, citing the letters she wrote to her father about her pet rabbits. In 1931 she came out, went to dances, had beaux, and settled into the rest of her life.

Several young men proposed to her and for no reason that anyone can now remember she said yes to Shane O'Neill, a tall young man with a job in the City, whose family, Amory reports, is 'the most ancient in Europe that it has been possible to tabulate'. (There may be other contenders—but who's tabulating?) At her memorial service Noel Annan told the story—it's repeated here—of how 'at a dance she heard O'Neill ask his partner to sit out on the stairs. "I don't want to do that," objected the girl, "I'll ruin my dress." "I don't mind ruining my dress," said Ann, and plonked herself down beside him.' They were married in 1932 and it wasn't long before she was ready to ruin her dress again.

Yet the years dragged by without any harm being done to her dresses, and by 1936, she said later, she'd 'given up all hope of falling in love'. In August 1935 she met Fleming by a swimming-pool in Le Touquet—no dice. The following August, in Austria, her luck turned. Esmond Harmsworth, the future Lord Rothermere, was 38 and, according to Amory, 'devastatingly good-looking, athletic and a sophisticated lover'. He also had a wife and three teenage children, but they don't feature much here. That he was a rich and powerful press tycoon was another thing that, in later accounts, Ann always played down: 'I regarded newspapers as I did the arrival of groceries and milk and paid but little attention,' she wrote in 1955 to her brother Hugo Charteris. For six years, so she said, she lived only for physical contact with Rothermere while, in some sense at least, being both in love with the more difficult Fleming and married to tall O'Neill. In October 1944 O'Neill was killed in Italy; and eight months later she married Rothermere. On the night before the wedding she had supper with Fleming and went for a long walk with him in the park: 'if he had suggested marriage,' she wrote afterwards, 'I would have accepted.'

Had he done so, metropolitan social life might never have recovered from the war, or so Amory would have us believe. 'With her emergence as Lady Rothermere, Ann's life entered its most spectacular phase.

She was 32. She had the money, the style, and the energy to brighten the drabness that had descended on London, and set about doing so.' These were the great party-giving years and Warwick House, where the Rothermeres lived, was 'filled with the sound of the rich, powerful and amusing at play'. (It's sometimes hard to resist the impulse to make disagreeable remarks about the extent to which Amory seems to wish that he too had been there.) To begin with, her guests—apart from the aristocracy who were already her friends when they weren't her relatives—were mainly politicians and journalists, but gradually the balance shifted towards painters and writers (in the first instance, Lucian Freud, Francis Bacon, and Peter Quennell, who was known— someone had to be—as 'Lady Rothermere's fan'): Amory cites this as evidence of her capacity to 'develop', and however off-putting a notion, it may be true. Rothermere with his devastating good looks is now seen as a kind but colourless figure who was nice to her two O'Neill children but couldn't cope with her new friends: 'Esmond was hardly allowed to speak as they roared rude remarks past him,' an anonymous well-wisher is quoted as saying.

Her chief interest apart from her parties and Fleming was her husband's newspaper, which she thought him scarcely fit to run. Discussing a possible new editor with her brother Hugo, who, like Fleming, worked on the paper for a time, she says: 'he is as good a mould as one could get to pour our liquid chairman into and hope that he will set.' It's a memorable phrase. Fleming admired her editorial interventions: 'you play with the little finger of your left hand a greater part in Esmond's business than any other woman I know in any other husband's business,' he wrote to her in 1950. The remark might seem double-edged but probably wasn't: fearfulness for the paper appears to have been a factor (among many) that caused the two of them to hesitate before going off together.

Two months after her marriage to Rothermere, Fleming sent Ann a letter telling her—presumably for the first time—that he loved her. A month later he seems to be saying little else. Partly because of the life he led and partly because of his novels Fleming has always had a bad press: 'selfish', 'spoilt', 'unreliable'—and full of the kind of moody self-pity that women are inclined to find attractive in men. 'Someone cut the cards wrong at the beginning,' he says in the first of the letters printed here, 'and it's been like that all along.' It isn't clear whether he's talking about his current travel arrangements or the whole of his life, but it doesn't seem to matter either. Amory ascribes his unfortunate character to the fact that he 'had grown up in the shadow of just about the most promising young man in the country'—his brother, Peter—'and had little alternative to becoming a black sheep', which sounds a bit too much like the kind of observation Buchan's characters used to make. Fleming, less Buchan than buccaneer, had broken any number of hearts and had any number of rich and wonderful mistresses in the time Ann had known him; and she was always conscious that an attempt to pin him down would cause him to run. On the other hand, it can't be said that she was in every way different from him: most of the damaging epithets that were applied to Fleming could just as fairly or unfairly be applied to his wife, though she had qualities he didn't have and wrote more entertaining letters. It is at least possible, for instance, that she found it even more difficult than he did to give all her attention to one other person. By 1956, Amory says, each of them had a lover but nothing more is said about hers: on grounds of libel, presumably, though everything in the letters suggests that it was her friends who were Fleming's chief rivals. He, meanwhile, continued to take mistresses and to think of himself as alone.

By the time Fleming died in 1964 their relationship had long since soured: 'If you were well and we were both younger our marriage would be over,' she said to him in 1962, while also telling him that she loved him and in letters to her friends giving animated accounts of how they weren't getting on. 'Thunderbird's only happiness,' she wrote to Waugh, 'is pink gin, golf clubs and men . . . I don't like an empty house at sunset—d'you suppose Bowra or Sparrow would live with me?' Fleming warned her before they got married that they 'would be happy together beside the blue lagoon but not in Kensington Gore'. It's a banal remark—not at all the kind of thing *she* would have said—but accurate enough. They'd been very happy chasing lobsters in the Caribbean: now he couldn't stand her friends and she was embarrassed both by his novels and their success. Given these facts and their characters, it seems amazing that they managed to live together for so long.

The social round continued after Fleming's death; she made new friends and was often thought to be about to marry Lord Goodman. When Waugh died in 1966 she asked Nicholas Henderson to replace him as her chief correspondent but her letters to him don't have the same éclat—she'd had to work harder to keep Waugh entertained. With the deaths not long afterwards of her father, then her brother, and the suicide, in 1975, of her son Caspar Fleming, the letters—at any rate those printed here—become more infrequent and much shorter. Adversity was another thing that fell outside her stylistic range, and she said as little about her own as in previous years she'd said about other people's. (In 1951, when her nephew Richard Charteris was drowned, she'd begun a letter to the boy's mother: 'My Darling Virginia, I should have written sooner but there was a rush of plans for holidays, a promotion party for Noël Coward, a television party . . .') In this she was at least even-handed, asking for no more sympathy than she gave. She spent a week in a nursing home because she'd been drinking too much; and told Patrick Leigh Fermor that Diana Cooper had rung her there 'and said, "Hear you're in a home for inebriates": she then came along, seduced all and sundry and left after booking a bed to die in; my prestige *much* improved by the visitation.' When in 1981 she wrote to tell her friends she had cancer her tone was scarcely less bright. Amory, no doubt quite properly, pays tribute to her courage, but it was the sort of courage that's more eloquent in life than in letters.

Book reviewed:

The Letters of Ann Fleming edited by Mark Amory

Quarrelling

'You must explain to me why Cyril wants Barbara,' Evelyn Waugh wrote to Ann Fleming in September 1955, a year after Barbara Skelton's marriage to Cyril Connolly had formally ended. 'It's not as though she were rich or a good housekeeper or the mother of his children.' The following year Edmund Wilson asked Connolly, now two years into his divorce, why he didn't get someone else. 'I'm still on the flypaper,' Connolly replied. 'I've got most of my legs loose, but I haven't yet quite got off.' A few months later Skelton married her next husband, George Weidenfeld. Connolly took to his bed, where his ex-wife, according to Wilson, sometimes brought him a bowl of soup.

It was very like Connolly to make a fuss of his wife once he had lost her and very like his ex-wife to keep a bloke in hand when the one she wanted was still in the bush. Everyone had expected their marriage to be a disaster. It was and it wasn't. 'Saturday,' Skelton tells us, 'was the gayest day of the week.' In the morning they shopped, then they had lunch, then they quarrelled. After that, they did some more shopping, went to the cinema, had supper, and quarrelled again. Even more than quarrelling, they enjoyed making plain their dislike of each other. 'Seeing some red wine all over his face, I say: "What have you got all over your face?" "Hate," says Cyril.' On another occasion he is lying half-naked on the bed. 'Is there anything you want?' she asks him. 'That you will drop down dead. That's all I wish, that you will drop down dead.' At Christmas she goes to Fortnum's to buy her husband a present and chooses something she knows he won't like.

Instead of a child, they acquire Kupy, a small animal that bites. It also sits in its hut in the garden eating its tail while, upstairs in his room, a despondent Connolly sucks the sheets on the bed. Other people didn't often come to the house: for one thing, the Connollys couldn't afford to feed them. The household had a reputation, however, and sometimes Connolly's friends wanted to see it for themselves. Ann Fleming, in her malice, arranged for a party of toffs to call in there for tea: 'A few days later reports of the visit drift back. They were all disappointed a. they had expected our surroundings to be far more squalid, b. because Kupy had not come out of her hut and bitten some-one's penis and c. because I had not been thoroughly rude to everyone.' With another year of the four-year marriage to go, people were telling each other that they had already separated. Her former lover Peter Quennell, eager for bad news, invited her to lunch at the Etoile and asked about her sex life. But that day she didn't feel like doing Connolly down, so Quennell soon got bored and asked for the bill. While Cyril dined out on their quarrels, his wife, recording the insults day by day in her diary, listed the titles of the books he threw at her in his rage.

They were both equally capable of monstrous behaviour (Connolly famously marked his place in a book he had borrowed with a rasher of bacon), but it's clear from all the memoirs and letters their contem-poraries have published over the past 20 years that allowances were made for the boorish Connolly which few people—lovers apart—were prepared to make for his wife. Unlike Connolly, however, who cared desperately about other people's good opinion, Barbara—vain in quite a different way—appears not to have given a damn whether anyone liked her or not. 'What a terrible waste of time people are,' she writes in her diary after seeing the Flemings—and the Flemings are the one couple she likes. With Connolly's friends she finds fault at every turn: their houses are filthy, their butlers incompetent, their cooks a disgrace. Her own friends, too, are a miserable lot: 'I telephone Jocelyn Baines and meet him for a quick drink . . . I think him a silly arse, of course.' Worst of all, on a bad day, is her 'slothful whale of a husband' with his fat, bad-tempered face—'Hubby has put on an inch of jowl since Christmas'—and his 'Chinese-coolie legs'. He lies in bed all morning shouting 'Pooey' so loudly that he can be heard through two closed doors, spends hours soaking in the bath, and keeps her awake all night by muttering 'Poor Cyril!' in a stage whisper over and over again ('while lying sprawled on his back with one eye open to see if I have heard').

'Barbara,' Edmund Wilson decided, 'is really a bad lot': so bad that when David Pryce-Jones came to write his memoir of Connolly he thought it best to say nothing about her at all. On the other hand, it is part both of her disobliging character and its attraction that in compiling her own memoirs she does nothing to minimise her outrageous capacity to give other people a hard time. Her evil reputation evidently pleases her and she records her own bad behaviour with the same meticulous delight as she records the slights and disparagements directed at her. No doubt a vast number of ill-natured remarks about her friends, her lovers, and her husband have been excised from the diary extracts which make up most of her book: but the many which remain make it plain that she couldn't care less about showing herself in what would vulgarly be thought of as a favourable light.

Her life before Connolly was a rackety business: a matter largely of frocks and lovers and food. It was the sort of life you could lead only if you had looks: and 'Mrs Connolly,' Maurice Bowra wrote to Ann Fleming, 'is plainly a cup of tea at a high level.' It isn't easy to tell from photographs why she was thought to be such a catch, but she wouldn't have pulled such faces in them if she hadn't thought she had something; and that something was good enough for an awful lot of men, beginning with her Uncle Ivan (known in the family as 'that dreadful dago'). Driving along the High Street, he told her she'd find some sweets in his pocket: but all she found 'was a hole and something warm and slithery'. Connolly's friends, who spoke reprovingly of 'the power over men of her prettiness', blamed her face for everything: for his fateful decision to marry her and for his subsequently finding it so hard to get his legs—his Chinese-coolie legs—off the flypaper.

Skelton's mother was a former Gaiety Girl—'Mummy was a beauty'—who married a regular army officer with weak health and 'no outstanding ability'. Mummy didn't much like her and Daddy 'was a great disappointment'—to which fact 'a clever Freudian' (mummy might have called him 'a clever Jew') attributed some of her later proclivities. Neither parent was a match for the infant Jezebel and when she was four she was sent off to boarding school in the belief that the discipline might do her some good—might stop her, for instance, attacking people with a carving knife when she couldn't have a second helping of lunch. She doesn't say much about school, except, characteristically, that there was one from which she was expelled after a bundle of love letters was found in her desk. It turned out that the 'Fred' who had signed them was merely a name she had given herself. (In later life she must have had innumerable love letters from one Fred or another: it would be interesting to know what, if anything, she said in response.) At 15, she set out for London, Daddy having agreed to pay for her keep. Thanks to his rich friend Sidney, Daddy didn't have to go on paying for long.

Sidney found her a job selling dresses in a smart shop in

Knightsbridge; then he took her to Brighton for the weekend. She doesn't say whether she liked him, but she must have done her best to be nice because he gave her an allowance and moved her into a large *poule-deluxe* flat in Crawford Street with an Axminster carpet and green velvet curtains. A grand tour of Europe soon followed:

> A suite at the George V. Champagne luncheons at Fouquet's . . . Holland. Belgium. Italy. Gelati. Ghiberti. The Ethiopian crisis. In Bologna, tomatoes were thrown at the chauffeur seated at the wheel of the Alvis. In Rimini, the hotel was full of Italian beauties dining with German officers à la Stroheim. In Basle we lodged at the Hôtel des Trois Rois.

The litany is nicely turned and gives a good idea of the extent of her interest in the rest of the world: at best, it runs to a verb. On her return, she finds she is pregnant and terminates first the child, then the relationship—'for no rhyme or reason, just out of boredom'. Anyone else would have given a passing thought to the abortion—not Skelton, however, who doesn't really like to be seen thinking at all. It's more chic (or more upper-class) just to drift from one thing (or one bloke) to another, and to represent one's life as a sequence of anecdotes. Someone suggested she get a life settlement out of Sidney: 'Feckless like my parents, I was not cut out for that sort of thing. The future would take care of itself!'

A spell in India, where she stayed with her uncle, a general in the Indian army, confirmed her dismaying power to cause trouble and think nothing of it. She fell in love with a young poet who was also a captain in the Royal Engineers; when she left India he stowed away on the ship that was taking her home; was discovered, court-martialled, and banished to the North-West Frontier. She was staying with her parents in the country when she heard his death announced on the *Six*

O'Clock News. Back in London, she finds a last letter from him, which she quotes—and that's the end of him, he isn't mentioned again.

It is now the late 1930s. Until her marriage, 11 or 12 years later, to Connolly, Skelton, wishing to keep her age a secret, doesn't give any dates. She is employed as a model at Schiaparelli, while playing fast and louche in a demi-monde of rich men and excitable women. Gradually the merely rich drop away and the names of the men become more familiar: 'Another habitué of the Café Royal then was Goronwy Rees. He joined the writer Peter Quennell and me for dinner and, while Peter was engrossed in paying, managed to slip an invitation to lunch between the pages of my book.' At the beginning of the war Madame Schiaparelli shut shop and Skelton moved in for a while with a Free Frenchman ('Monsieur Boris was desperate for a woman and I seemed to fit the bill'): 'Every morning, he prepared the coffee, then dressed in army uniform and a képi and, carrying a briefcase, walked briskly out heading for the French headquarters, where he relayed broadcasts to the French people. Standing at the window, I would watch him stride away, then utterly exhausted return to bed and go on dozing.' No point in getting up when the news was so awful and the Curzon Street Sherry Bar didn't open till 12.

Earning a living wasn't a problem: her lovers did it for her. But she dreaded being put into the WAAFs or the Wrens and so got a job as a secretary with the Yugoslav government in exile. (The main thing there was the lavatory: her Yugoslav colleagues were 'none of them great plug-pullers'.) It must have been during the war that she started keeping a diary and what has so far been a charming but perfunctory narrative is now filled out with a succession of scenes from her life which could also be scenes from a novel about a woman who lived in London during the war and never gave the war a moment's thought. Lovers are the burning topic and how to divide her life between them: 'Peter telephoned to say he would come at 11. Feliks rang to suggest he did the same thing.' In a cast of four or five regulars they are the principal players: Quennell 'for a feeling of security' and Topolski for his company. The clever Freudian might have had something to say about the messiness of these arrangements, but what he said wouldn't have interested her. It wasn't exactly a good time she was after (though she did like good food), still less true love and domestic peace. Difficulties were the thing she enjoyed, the ones she made for herself and, even better, those she made for other people—which is one reason her marriage to Connolly made more sense than it might seem to.

Sacked by the Yugoslavs 'for arriving late at the office every morning for two months', she followed Donald Maclean's good advice and offered her services to the Foreign Office as a cipher clerk. In due course she was sent to Egypt, where she had an affair with big King Farouk ('I was never bored'), then on to Italy and Greece. Her tour of duty cut short by the Greek civil war, she came back to London and more of the same, except that now rich John Sutro was her principal beau, with Connolly in hot pursuit. Predictably what clinched it for Connolly was a holiday she spent in Geneva with Sutro.

The wedding took place, 'after a year's talk of marriage', on 5 October 1950. They quarrelled on their way to the register office and quarrelled again on the way back. Then they sat down to 'a cold lunch in sullen silence in Maidstone'. Alastair Forbes, who knows everything, claims that it's a mistake to make a song and dance of their squabbling. 'Lots of their friends,' he said, discussing Skelton's book in the *Spectator*, 'quarrelled as much as they did.' He knows, he was there. But it may be that in Connolly's case quarrelling was a natural extension of his endless capacity for self-pity. As for his wife, it was one of the things she did best, in life and in art. When Connolly was complaining about her to Edmund Wilson, he told him that she was busy turning her diary into a novel and that 'it was intolerable to have this typewriter going all the time, and somebody in the house who took all the paper and pencils.' Wilson listened sympathetically and suggested that 'he ought to get a different kind of woman, who would also take better care of him.' Someone, for instance, who didn't hog all the paper and pencils.

Book reviewed:

Tears Before Bedtime by Barbara Skelton

Promises

Almost every woman I know has at one time or another been to bed with a man she shouldn't have been to bed with—a married man, a friend's man, or, quite simply, a man who wasn't her man. It may be that some of them allowed themselves to be talked into it and afterwards wished they hadn't and it may be that someone (usually someone else) suffered for it, but to call these events 'seductions' would be to try to give them a status that they no longer enjoy. Seducers had victims, not partners in crime, and to seduce someone was to lead them astray, not merely to lead them to bed. 'I like to think I'm a sort of gay bachelor, Don Juan or Casanova,' Fiona Pitt-Kethley says at the beginning of her startling account of the sights she saw and the men she laid in the course of two journeys to Italy in search of the lairs of the sibyls and other poets and prophets of the ancient world. She doesn't, she adds, 'give the men anything to complain of', doesn't 'promise permanence' or 'leave them holding the baby'; and in that sense, however inviting or provocative her behaviour, what she describes isn't seduction but casual sex.

And later he caught a bus and she a train
And all there was between them then
                        was rain.

Brian Patten's perfunctory verse is included in Jenny Newman's anthology in order to make the same sort of point: seductions, which begin
with fine words and end with desperate recriminations, are a thing of
the past.

'You cannot seduce anyone when innocence is not a value,' Elizabeth
Hardwick said in 'Seduction and Betrayal', with the clear implication
that it is not a value now. In fact, the only innocence about which we
still obviously care is the innocence of children: and there is no doubt
that, unlike adults, children may be—and *pace* Freud often are—the
victims of seduction. Hardwick's essay was concerned with the fate
of literary heroines like Clarissa and Tess and with the penalties they
paid for their illicit engagements with men. It was written in 1972
and had first taken shape as a paper delivered to the students of Vassar when Vassar had just stopped being a women's college and the
pill had just begun to change women's lives. 'Technology,' Hardwick
said, meaning contraception, 'annihilates consequence.' If women have
nothing to lose and nothing to pay they can be loved and feted and
courted and bedded but they can't in the ordinary course of things be
seduced. Not in life or in literature. 'The old plot,' as Hardwick put it,
'is dead, fallen into obsolescence.'

It turns out, however, that technology has not annihilated consequence. Or, more precisely, that AIDS has reinstated it. Suppose
that a young man who knows he is carrying the HIV virus has some
sinister reason for sweet-talking the object of his desire into going to
bed with him while saying nothing about his medical condition. It
would be quite appropriate to call a case of this sort a seduction. (In
America it would also be a criminal offence.) It is an extreme case,

however, and there will presumably always be sexual encounters that carry less fateful penalties: penalties that have to be paid by men or women who may find themselves innocently caught in a sexual snare without being in the least innocent by nature. Suppose this time that the woman whose company cost Mike Gatting the captaincy of the English cricket team in the summer of 1988 was in the pay of John Emburey, who succeeded him in the post. A novel that featured an innocent Gatting, a conniving Emburey, and an unnamed temptress might be a pretty low-level novel, but its plot would hinge, however unseductively, on a seduction. In Newman's anthology there is a scene from *Rates of Exchange*, Malcolm Bradbury's satirical novel about a British academic on a visit to an imaginary Eastern European country. Set in the shower of a flat belonging to a woman who is both a witch and a Marxist, it describes her attempt to persuade the Englishman to engage with her in a 'dialectical synthesis'. 'Do you like me to soap you,' she asks, 'and we can talk also about your deviations?' Synthesis takes place; and as she herself, unhelpfully, tells him, it could have serious consequences—of a kind that might, quite plausibly, involve one or other of them spending a year or two in prison. Before Wolfenden, there were plenty of seductions (or deviations) in this country that began in lavatories and finished up in prison.

We may talk about seducing as if it were the same thing as making a pass but it works towards a darker and more distant goal. Nor is it the same as wooing, though wooing of course comes into it. When the Vicomte de Valmont, the smooth seducer of *Les Liaisons danger-euses*, sets out in pursuit of the Présidente de Tourvel it isn't sex that he has in mind but the less acceptable pleasure of corrupting a good woman. 'Let her believe in virtue,' he writes to his fellow conspirator, the Marquise de Merteuil, at the start of the novel, 'but let her sacri-fice it for my sake; let her be afraid of her sins, but let them not check her; and, when she is shaken by a thousand terrors, may it only be in my arms that she is able to overcome them and forget them.' There are pieces in Newman's anthology that a more pedantic editor might not have allowed, on the grounds that they only have bed in view when 'seduction' understands bed as a means to another, more subversive end. Similarly, saying 'No, I can't' is not the same thing as saying 'No, I don't want to' (though there may of course be occasions when the former is merely a polite excuse for the latter). At the very least, 'I can't' implies the existence of a larger issue than how to get through the next half-hour.

In the literature of seduction, it should be said, 'I can't' usually carries the further meaning of 'I would dearly love to.' Women have to be virtuous and at the same time susceptible: without this ambiguity there would be no uncertainty and no plot. Even Clarissa, seemingly the least tempted, most steadfast of heroines, almost acknowledges something of the kind when she writes in her last letter to Lovelace, 'To say I once respected you with a preference is what I ought to blush to own'; and this weakness must in part account for the difficulty she has in escaping his attentions.

Newman's anthology is an anthology of English seduction scenes that makes an exception for the biblical account of the tempting of Adam and Eve, the original seduction from which all others follow. But even there sex was only ambiguously the main issue. 'The Garden of Eden was lost for partaking of the fruit of the tree of knowledge of good and evil,' Nelson Goodman writes in *Of Mind and Other Matters*, 'lost not for lust but for curiosity, lost not for sex but for science.' Goodman's view is the view that now prevails, among feminists especially; and Eve, traditionally seen in the way the Church has seen her, as 'the weaker part of the human couple', the first member of her sex to deflect man from his noble purpose—or, in Adam's case, his noble lack of purpose—is now praised, as Gillian Beer has praised her, for being 'the first scientist'. (Pitt-Kethley, who, unlike most of her sisters, is a feminist in practice as well as in her reading, makes the somewhat sophistical point that 'it was only Adam who got kicked out of the Garden of Eden.') The Christian idea that she was weak because her flesh was weak—weaker even than Adam's—is something which, according to recent scholarship, we owe to the middle age of St. Augustine, who was the first to promote the idea of Original Sin on which the Christian interpretation of the Fall is based, or so Elaine Pagels argues in her study of the 'politics of paradise', *Adam, Eve and the Serpent*. But even St. Augustine took sexual desire to be the evidence for the Fall, not its cause or its chief consequence. One doesn't have to be a Freudian or, for that matter, a Christian to think that sex played some part in what happened, but for the biblical serpent, as for Milton's Satan, disobedience was the long-term objective. One way or another, a plot had to be devised to get Adam and Eve out of paradise, and in that sense the first agent of seduction was also the first agent of subversion.

Reading through this anthology in which every piece sings its subject's good looks ('fairer than the evening air/Clad in the beauty of a thousand stars'), I was reminded of Christopher Ricks saying 20 years ago, in an article about the sexual revolution of the 1960s, that he was against the whole thing on the grounds that the new free-for-all was unfair to plain women. (What about plain men? Are women pleased to get any old bugger? Not according to Pitt-Kethley, who complains so much—too big, too small, too fat—that you begin to wonder whether there are any good-looking men in Italy apart from Marcello Mastroianni.) If one were to judge English literature by this anthology one might wonder why plain women bothered to read books at all. That there can be no seduction without flattery is one thing (Moll Flanders speaks for all her ruined sisters when she says: 'that which I was too vain of, was my ruin, or rather my vanity was the cause of it'): the power that is ascribed to good looks quite another. The trick is that in order to be noticed women have to be beautiful and that, once noticed, their beauty is seen as something to be guarded against: as a threat to what Jane Miller in *Women Writing about Men* calls 'men's lifetime objectives', and beyond that, to the social order which is coincident with men's lifetime objectives. Newman hasn't arranged her anthology chronologically but if one takes the pieces in the order in which they were written, the Garden of Eden is followed by the court of King Arthur, where Eve's daughters prove no less dangerous than she herself had been. It's touch and go, for example, in the scene from *Sir Gawain* where the knight is visited in his bedchamber by Bertilak's wife:

He sees her so glorious, so gaily attired.
So faultless her features, so fair and so bright.
His heart swelled swiftly with surging joys.

It turns out, as we know, to be a ploy: Gawain is being tested and it's just as well that he is able to resist the lady's bright features because the court's honour depends on it. Nonetheless, it wasn't long before, as Malory has it, Camelot was undone by Lancelot's passion for Guinevere.

It is an Augustinian view of the world that represents men as unable to turn a blind eye to women and women, because they are the object and the embodiment of male desire, as instruments of disorder. Guinevere, unlike Eve, had no intention of causing trouble but Lancelot's infatuation was so powerful that it was rumoured she had cast a spell on him. The capacity to exercise magic, to bewitch, enchant, fascinate, or, literally, charm: this was something that only women possessed and it might or might not have a supernatural component according to the demands of the plot and the need to exonerate the men whose heads it turned and whose strength it sapped. It isn't the kind of power women approve of now (though it it isn't very different from flirtation and everyone likes that). Nor did the writers approve of it then, however much they enjoyed writing about it: at a time when desire had to be seen to be out of order bewitchment might be the only cover a writer had for speaking of sexual feeling.

Men endow women with the capacity to bewitch as a way of talking about themselves. Seduction, being largely a male prerogative, is largely a male subject. Of the 80 writers whom Newman anthologises 70 are men; and of the ten women only three—Angela Carter and two of her contemporaries—describe a woman attempting to get her way with a man. In the literature of seduction men have been allocated the words with which to propose—

And now she lets him whisper in her ear,
Flatter, entreat, promise, protest, and swear

—while women, if they want to be thought well of, are obliged to hold their tongues and find other ways of bringing themselves to a man's attention. They can put on their finery or they can take it off; they can, in the words of the incomparable Lady Wishfort in Congreve's *Way of the World*, affect a becoming 'sort of a dyingness' and 'a swimmingness in the eyes'; they can calculate their moves and decide whether they will appear to their best advantage in this chair or that. ('Nothing,' Lady Wishfort resolves, 'is more alluring than a levee from a couch in some confusion—it shews the foot to advantage, and furnishes with blushes, and re-composing airs beyond comparison.') They may in addition be winsome or witty, but their vocabulary is a vocabulary of looks and signs. They can't say what they want and they can't move directly to get it. Wilde's Salome is a repellent figure; and even in these more egalitarian times, there is something grim—as well as ideologically heartening—about Pitt-Kethley's pursuit of sexual pleasure. (It might have been different if she liked men, say, half as much as she likes sex.)

The first piece in Newman's anthology, a scene this time from Congreve's *Love for Love*, lays down the rules:

Tattle: De'e you think you can love me?
Miss Prue: Yes.
Tattle: Pooh, pox, you must not say yes already . . .
Miss Prue: What must I say then?
Tattle: Why you must say no, or you believe me not, or you can't tell.

It isn't that the women in Newman's anthology don't speak (far from it) but that with a few striking exceptions the only thing they are allowed to say is no. Men have one sort of story to tell, or line to spin, and it consists largely of promises, most of which turn out to be either empty (not meant) or out of order (unfulfillable). 'You shall to me at once/Be dukedom, health, wife, children, friends, and all,' Brachiano says to Vittoria Corombona in *The White Devil*, and they both die as a result. The story which women tell has to do with virtue and the impossibility of relinquishing it—and that, too, is a line, spun with varying degrees of eloquence and conviction. A few—the obvious case is the rebarbative Isabella in *Measure for Measure*—mean what they say, but the majority don't. 'You are a woman,' Tattle tells Miss Prue, 'you must never speak what you think. Your words must contradict your thoughts, but your actions may contradict your words.' That's what makes it all such fun—for the men and for the writers, who are also men.

It is usually said that what counts for the seducer is the joy of the chase and in that sense he is dependent on the woman's resistance. It is an activity less suited to life, where men at any rate have other things to get on with, than to literature, where completion can be almost indefinitely delayed. There are other ways of looking at it, however. One might, for instance, think in terms both of the satisfaction men derive from getting their own way and of the satisfaction women are said to derive from letting men think they are getting their own way. (I'm not saying that women wouldn't like to get their own way, but they don't, or they haven't, or not in this context.) Angelo isn't unusual in wanting Isabella because she is virtuous, and although he differs from, say, Lovelace or the Vicomte de Valmont in thinking badly of himself—

> Dost thou desire her foully for those things
> That make her good

—it doesn't hold him back. The lesson of the Garden of Eden was that women must be kept in line and the seducer's pleasure is the subversive one of getting them to step out of line—the pleasure, at its crudest, of committing an aggression on a prig. Maybe that's why the naughtiest items in Newman's anthology are two pieces by Rochester that feature a more amiable, less insistent version of Fiona Pitt-Kethley making sure that she gets what she wants:

> *Pricket*: Now I am in, and 't is as soft as wool.
> *Swivia*: Then move it up and down, you little fool.

Books reviewed:
The Faber Book of Seductions edited by Jenny Newman
Journeys to the Underworld by Fiona Pitt-Kethley

Christopher Ricks subsequently sent a letter to the editors:
Mary-Kay Wilmers's memory is as long as it is false. Reviewing

The Faber Book of Seductions, she 'was reminded of Christopher Ricks saying 20 years ago, in an article about the sexual revolution of the 1960s, that he was against the whole thing on the grounds that the new free-for-all was unfair to plain women. (What about plain men? Are women pleased to get any old bugger?)' My review of Richard Neville's *Play Power* in 1970 was not worth resurrecting, but since I don't like distortion and the smear of sexism, I want to quote the paragraph which she had in mind or somewhere:

> The emancipated young are right to think that prurience and envy play some part in middle-aged reproof; but the middle-aged are right to think that the emancipation has often been seen to promise less than it performs, and that bourgeois respectability does not entail one particular cruelty which lurks in emancipation's promiscuity: promiscuity's cruelty to those whom even promiscuity would reject. It is all very well for a Yippy pamphlet to proclaim that people should have 'all the time, anytime, whomever they wish'. But what about those whom nobody wishes? The world of *Play Power* is a fantasy world in which all men and women (but especially women, since it is a man's world) are beautiful people—or, to put it bleakly, where nobody is sexually unattractive. It will take more than freedom from inhibition plus weird clothes to turn this fantasy world into the world. Meanwhile the non-promiscuous respectable society does manage to convert some of its properties into a protective customariness: nobody is forced to face the iciest of tests, whether he or she would be wanted even if given away.

'He or she' does not say 'unfair to plain women'; nor do my words 'those whom even promiscuity would reject', 'people', 'those whom nobody wishes', 'men and women', and 'where nobody is sexually attractive'.

Granted, I wrote the words 'but especially all women', but I did so explicitly to deplore the male chauvinism of the deplorable book: 'The world of *Play Power* is a fantasy world in which all men and women (but especially women, since it is a man's world) are beautiful people.'

I hope that Ms. Wilmers the editor of the *LRB* is more scrupulous than Ms. Wilmers the insufficiently edited contributor to her pages.

Christopher Ricks
Boston, Massachussetts

Mary-Kay Wilmers writes: Christopher Ricks is right to chastise me for not looking up what he said, though I'm sorry he has taken the lapse so darkly to heart. I remembered the remark because I don't quite see the connection that Professor Ricks seems to see between good looks and good times; I misremembered it because I think of good looks as something that men have required of women but which women have required only of themselves. On the other hand, to go back to Professor Ricks's text, I'm not sure even now whether we are to understand 'it is a man's world' as a reference to the 'fantasy world' which Richard Neville describes or more generally. Either way, Professor Ricks's letter does nothing to disabuse me of the belief that it is a man's world that we live in, just as it is a man's world that most of the items in the Faber anthology address.

Nonchalance

It's a characteristic of all Sybille Bedford's fiction to tell the reader less than he wants to know. Ivy Compton-Burnett was a friend of hers and perhaps gave her lessons in leaving things out. She calls *Jigsaw*, which has to do with her own early life, 'a biographical novel'; and it may not be a coincidence that the book's most sympathetic reviewers have been those who seem already to know her life story. 'Truth,' one of the characters remarks, 'is such a feeble excuse for so many things.' Bedford, always inclined to look down her nose at the rest of the world, would probably consider it an excuse for being very boring. She was born in 1911 and doesn't think much of 'our tell-all age'.

Her mother, a daunting woman, had guessed that this book, or one like it, would eventually come to be written. When 'Billi', then 19 or 20, told her mother that she was writing a novel and that it was about a young man's adventures in the South of France, her mother had apparently said: 'I'm a much more interesting subject than your dreamt-up young man.' ('Billi' was what her family called the young

Sybille.) 'God forbid, mummy,' Billi replied. But Mummy was sure of her ground:

'One day. When you remember all this.'
'No,' I said. 'No, I don't think I ever could.'
She gave me a cynical smile.

Mummy was right. She is an interesting subject; and Bedford makes much more of her than she does of herself. Mummy was also right about the dreamt-up young man: his adventures were turned down by a succession of publishers. Since then, however, Sybille Bedford has published four novels, including the present one, which are all in some sense about her mother, though it is only here that Mummy's fatal addiction to morphine—'all this'—is described. 'As I was helping myself again from the carafe of wine, Oriane said in a velvet voice: "You know, *ma chérie*, I should be *careful* in your place—after all, *ta mère est une morphiniste.*"'

A Legacy, Bedford's first published novel, came out in 1956. Set in Germany at the turn of the century, it is about a minor aristocrat from the Catholic south of the country, Julius von Felden, and his complicated family history, which involves a great deal of money, much of it Jewish, and a scandal that comes close to unseating the Kaiser. Nancy Mitford said it was one of the very best novels she had ever read and Evelyn Waugh 'saluted a new artist'. Proustian in its preoccupation with money and rank, it has the charm of the dying Europe in which it is set: a world where the very rich, when they went to take the cure, travelled in a private railway carriage and took their own sheets.

It turns out, as Nancy Mitford maybe knew at the time, that the character of Julius von Felden is pretty much that of Bedford's father ('to say that Jules was my father would be as misleading as to say that he was not'); that his fate is to a large extent her father's fate; and that the family history which the novel describes is her legacy. 'I do not know a time when I was not imprinted with the experiences of others,' the narrator, who is also Felden's young daughter, remarks towards the end of the book. In other words, *A Legacy*, too, is a biographical novel, but unlike *Jigsaw*, it also reads like a novel. It is impossible, reading *Jigsaw*, not to think one is reading an autobiography; and one is continually pulled up short by the thought that what one has taken to be a memory might well be an invention.

It isn't Bedford's style to state the plain biographical facts: she doesn't say anything banal like 'I was born there on that date.' Similarly, if one wants to know her parents' names, one has to look them up in *Who's Who*. At least in *A Legacy* they have fictional names: here they have no names at all. Nor are we ever explicitly told that her mother was English. Had the story been narrated as if by Billi herself, this way of proceeding might have made sense, but Bedford has no time for this sort of formal pretence. Instead she gives the appearance of telling the story as she now remembers it; and *tant pis* for the reader, who has no way of knowing which bits are true and which aren't, or why some things are concealed and others spelled out. She speaks at one point of wanting, in the interests of tact, to confine her account to what she saw and heard at the time, which sounds reasonable, but it's something she does only intermittently, when it suits her, and it is hard not to think that this is yet another way of spiting the reader, of telling him to take his vulgar curiosity elsewhere. 'Loose ends can stimulate,' Peter Vansittart says in an introduction to the Virago edition of one of Bedford's earlier novels, 'and paying the readers the compliment of assuming they possess imagination, she creates gaps for that imagination to fill.' But gaps that are artful in other kinds of fiction can seem merely ill-natured in a novel that is at the same time a biography.

Jigsaw begins where *A Legacy* left off, at an unspecified time after the First World War, with the family scandal resolved and her parents' brief, unpromising marriage just about over. By 1919 her mother had bolted, leaving husband, daughter, and maid in the schloss she had bought for them a few years before. 'Now let no one think that I was missing my mother,' Bedford protests—and it's true that her mother in her own charming way could be quite a shrew. 'That I was her own made not a scrap of difference. When I was slow she called me slow, when I was quick she called me a parrot.' More to the point, perhaps, Mummy would have been annoyed to think that her daughter was missing her—and from an early age Billi had understood the importance of attending to her mother's requirements.

Of her mother's previous life, though she dominates the novel, the only thing we know for sure is that she has always been an object of avid attention. 'My mother captivated by her looks alone, yet what drew most men and women into her orbit at first meeting was her talk.' About her father Bedford is less secretive and some of the ground covered in *A Legacy* is rehearsed again here. He, too, had been good-looking (in this novel few people are plain) and was referred to in his youth as le beau Max—his real name was Maximilian von Schoenebeck. By the end of the war, however, he was a sombre, eccentric man in his sixties, with many objects—'we lived inside a museum, one that nobody came to see'—and no cash. He could have sold his objects, but chose instead not to spend any money. Billi had no new clothes, for example, but went about in a Red Indian outfit left over from earlier times. They grew their own crops, reared their own animals, made their own wine, and bartered these in the village for necessities they couldn't provide for themselves. Even so they ate well—instead of ham, which could only be bought at the grocer's, smoked mutton, made from their own sheep, killed and cured on the spot. I mention this because *Jigsaw* is, among other things, a tribute to *savoir-manger* as it used to be before egalitarianism entered the kitchen and killed it—the old diet, the ancien régime.

Le beau Max was resourceful but gloomy. 'What with the changes brought by the end of the war and the setting up of the Weimar Republic, he saw himself surrounded by an almost entirely hostile environment . . . My mother's defection did not help; nor did our poverty, our being ruined he called it.' In her mother's time, the house had been full of people: now they saw no one. In a fit of depression Billi in her turn defected, making a bid for freedom among the bright lights of Wiesbaden—an incident about which she still feels uncomfortable. It was her one lapse from filial loyalty. 'Are all young children unregenerate creatures?' Bedford now asks somewhat pointlessly. She must have had time to work that one out. On her return, she was briefly allowed to go to the village school, but taken away again when it became clear that she preferred the boys to the girls. After three years Mummy summoned her. She was neither glad to leave nor eager to stay, and had been gone only a few months when her father had an attack of appendicitis and died.

Her mother had promised her a new life: a home near Florence and a stepfather—a 'painter of some reputation' whose name we're not told. But within a few days of her daughter's arrival in Italy, Mummy went to a concert and fell in love with somebody else. Bedford's mother was a highly intelligent woman and interested in all kinds of things, but her good looks required that she should always have the man she wanted and off she now went in pursuit of her heart's new desire. Billi meanwhile stayed behind on her own—it could be for days, it could be for weeks—reading her books and looking for playmates in one Italian hotel after another. She was nine and it was the beginning of what Bedford calls her 'unsentimental education'. 'You will be all right, won't you?' her mother would say as she left her. If she wasn't, she didn't say so—Mummy would not have been pleased. Besides, for a young foodie consolation was always to hand: 'I ate at a table for one, attended by sweet waiters who brought the dishes for me to look at and gave me second and third helpings of anything I liked.' The man Mummy eventually settled with, in the novel he's called Alessandro, was closer in age to her daughter. He was beautiful, like Mummy; and rather grave. In a few years, her mother said, he would come to resemble Titian's Man with the Glove.

One of Bedford's (ambiguous) gifts is to make you feel that you missed a lot by not being her: by not knowing the people she knew or living the life that she led. About herself she's quite reticent: not only not self-important, but not in the least introspective—her way of indicating a bad moment is to say that she can't remember what she had for her supper that night. And in that sense she was right not to have described this as an autobiographical novel. As for calling her parents to account in the Freudian way, she's much too patrician for that; the sort of person who would say that what's wrong with the present-day world—apart from the food being less good and the beaches all spoiled—is that everyone whinges too much.

What we have instead is a novel written not exactly in praise of maternal nonchalance but in homage nonetheless to a very nonchalant mother. When Mummy decided that it was time for her and her young husband to push off to Africa, she sent Billi to England to stay with a couple she'd once met on a beach (or maybe not met at all), in the vague hope that they might be the sort of people to find her a school:

'They're both painters. You admire artists, I've noticed . . .'
'Where do they live in England?'
'How precise you're being. Actually they move about a good deal . . .'

'Mummy, when am I going?'
'As soon as I hear from them.'

Billi went off to England, as far as we know perfectly pleased with her lot; and in everything she does, seems so sure of herself, so self-reliant that one could find oneself wishing one's own childhood had been just like that. One might also, more shamefully, think it quite nice to be that kind of mother.

A school was not in fact found, though from time to time there were tutors; and most of Billi's adolescence was spent—or that's how it seems—thinking about the lives of the grown-ups around her. About her mother's rather haphazard life first of all. For the first few years of her new marriage Mummy was happy enough: winter in the Dolomites, summer on the Mediterranean, where Billi would join them ('oh, the clear water of those uncrowded bays') whenever her presence was asked for. When fascism made it dangerous to be seen reading the *New Statesman* ('my mother thought of herself as a socialist'), they decided to settle somewhere or other in France. 'Somewhere or other'—the place where the French train stopped when Mummy announced that she was tired of travelling—turned out to be a small fishing port on 'the unfashionable' (i.e., ultra-fashionable) 'part of the Côte d'Azur', between Toulon and Marseilles. It was called Sanary and they remained there—'Oh the Mediterranean addiction, how we fall for it'—until Alessandro's departure and her mother's final descent into morphine.

Sanary today is all car parks and concrete blocks, as Bedford isn't slow to point out, but in 1926 'the sea and sky were clear; living was cheap; there were few motor-cars, *there were few people.*' (Cyril Connolly hadn't yet got there.) And Elizabeth David herself couldn't have found fault with the food. Her mother for the time being was calm, a pleasure to be with. 'So there we sat Chez Schwob, my mother and I, sun-warmed, looking at the sea and tossing boats, drinking a modest apéritif . . .' It's obvious, however, that the peace will not last—obvious because Bedford writes with her mother's end always in mind. '*Have I changed?*' her mother asked Billi just back from London. Billi looked at her and 'saw what unasked I might not have seen: intimations of wear . . . I can still hear the answer I gave . . . an answer to the effect that for me she was, she would be, always the same. I remember the exact words but cannot bear to write them down in their shameful inadequacy.' It was, she says now, 'a most painful moment of my early life'.

The local people were civilised (Schwob, the café owner, who came from Alsace, 'spouted Heine and Descartes'); the expatriates everything that a sophisticated young girl might have wished for. Taken to meet Aldous Huxley ('a writer whose work I idolised'—hence the later biography), Billi 'felt like some girls are said to feel when taken to their first dance before they are allowed to wear the clothes that they like'. (Her mother, incidentally, resurfaces as Mrs. Amberley in *Eyeless in Gaza*, once 'the very embodiment of desirability', now a taker of morphine.) Almost everyone was artistic, bohemian, unconventional, wise in the ways of having a good time. They had affairs, sometimes with members of their own sex, and Billi, a few years on, fell in love with a very superior French woman. Her mother, always a little short with her daughter, called her 'a goose'; told her above all not to think of herself as a 'doomed Baudelairean pervert'; and sent her back to London where she might have a chance to come to her senses. Billi, for all her swooning, complied. The events of her own life, it seems, never troubled her.

In London as in the South of France, it was other people's affairs that concerned her—how they managed their lives and their feelings. She had a room in a North London boarding house (a fact that she had no difficulty in keeping from her mother) and spent most of her time with one or other of two German sisters, both much older than she was, one married to—then divorced from—an English bookseller, the other the mistress of a well-known (and unnamed) English judge. Things didn't go well for them: the bookseller was unfaithful; the judge, who gambled away his own money and that of several distinguished friends, committed suicide. Billi listened to their stories, observed their reactions, and—it sometimes seems—made notes to add to an imaginary dossier on the harm women (her mother especially) can do themselves as a result of their feelings for men.

Bedford isn't a feminist; she doesn't think women are done down by men, or better or nicer than them. Most of Billi's friends are women and she feels for them in their difficulties, but she speaks of her mother's appalling 'feminine' habits and seems to find men rather more sensible. Bedford describes herself as having 'a tendency to side with lovers'—which makes sense when one considers the life Billi led with her mother. But one could instead see it as the only child's tendency to take charge of his parents, to shoulder their grief ('a most painful moment of my early life') and work for their happiness. Billi was, for example, very fond of Alessandro, her young and at the end much abused stepfather: they were, she said, 'like two brothers serving, in different ranks, in the same regiment'. Her mother may have educated them both, taught them that most questions have more than one answer, but it was the two of them who looked after her, who made excuses for her derelictions of duty, her scattiness, her habit of not doing the right thing, while she taunted them for their old-fashioned virtues, telling Billi that she was 'pompous and bourgeois' and had boring 'clubmanly' ways. And when the loss of her looks and her jealousy drove her to morphine it was Billi, now living alone with her, who had to see to her needs:

There was one brutish occasion when I dropped the syringe, a glass syringe already primed with the precious contents of an ampoule, on the tiled floor. It shattered. My mother crouched down trying to retrieve fragments with her fingers. Then she flew at me, pulling my hair. I did the most sensible thing I could, ran out of the house, started the car and drove down to the chemist, our friendly chemist. Fortunately it was neither siesta hours nor night. From then on we kept two syringes in the house.

For a literal-minded reader it is hard not to regret that Bedford should have written her terrifying story in semi-fictional form and at the same time hard to imagine her writing a straightforward, confessional memoir. The consequence is that *Jigsaw* is as irritating to think about as it is engrossing to read.

Book reviewed:
Jigsaw: An Unsentimental Education by Sybille Bedford

Attraction Duty

I have complained a lot about men in my time. In fact, I do it more and more. But I have never been part of what used to be called the women's movement and those who have or who are, or who have never wanted to be, would probably consider me some sort of moron. I didn't do consciousness-raising with my sisters in the late 1960s. I was married at the time and it seemed to me that if my consciousness were raised another millimetre I would go out of my mind. I used to think then that had I had the chance to marry Charles Darwin (or Einstein or Metternich) I might have been able to accept the arrangements that marriage entails a little more gracefully. In the 1980s, long since divorced, I decided that marriage to Nelson Mandela (or Terry Waite) would have suited me fine.

When *The Female Eunuch* came out in 1970 the man I was married to bought me a copy (clearly *he* can't have been the cause of all my troubles). But it was the same with the book as it had been with the sisters—I couldn't get on with it. In the first place, I knew it all. Secondly, I couldn't bear to think about my condition any more than

I already did—which was, roughly speaking, all the time that was left from thinking about what to wear, what to cook, and what colour to paint the downstairs lavatory. That's an exaggeration, of course, but not nearly as much of one as I would like it to be.

I am the same age as Germaine Greer and therefore in much the same relation to the subject of her new book, *The Change: Women, Ageing and the Menopause*, as I was to *The Female Eunuch*. It's my story. At least that's how I see it. ('Oh God,' my ex-husband said when I told him what I was writing about.) There are those—i.e., men—who say that a 'male menopause' deserves consideration, and it's true that even men get old and fat and die. But the admirable Greer has no time for their menopauses. 'This book will not devote any of its limited space to the "male menopause".' Later, and more bluntly, it's 'a phenomenon that doesn't exist'.

Would a more fair-minded woman have given the men a hearing? I don't see why, but then I wouldn't. 'Me, me, me,' the men shout and I hear them very clearly. 'Me, me, me,' I growl under my breath. Here I am, four paragraphs into my musings, or ravings, and beginning to doubt whether I will find anything to say about the menopause that isn't a way of saying something about men. I look out of the window and see a roly-poly middle-aged man about the same age as me walking along arm in arm with his eight-year-old daughter. His first wife, assuming he had one and she was the same sort of age, may now be a millionaire, she may own a chain of shops or be a top civil servant or the wife of a duke: but her womb, according to Greer, will be the size of an almond and one thing she won't have is an eight-year-old daughter. The menopause isn't some sort of metaphor and it doesn't make you believe in the even-handedness of God, or of human biology.

On the other hand, even I don't think it's the invention of a mean-minded Creator wanting to give women a bad time. Or do I? Other female animals, we learn from zoology, don't have a menopause; for better or worse, they carry on reproducing all their adult lives. Human animals take such a long time to get going, however, that they can't afford to have mothers who are reaching the end of the line. I remember wailing in the days of my marriage that if anyone could suggest one good reason why I should do it I wouldn't mind being the person who always washed up. Unfortunately I can't see myself zenning out on thoughts of the species when I next catch sight of that roly-poly man and his daughter. There we are, however. At some point between the ages of 45 and 55 women dip out of the race while men carry on booming and fathering until the very brink of the grave.

An old man I used to know, a painter well into his eighties, was so confident and so predatory that at night you couldn't walk down the street with him unchaperoned. If it is part of the great scheme of things that men should go on contributing to the world's population (and the planet's decline) till they drop, then it follows that they will go on strutting and preening and considering themselves eligible for what Clive James used to call 'the grade A crumpet' until at last senility takes hold. (In James's phrase, Ford Madox Ford, himself neither young nor pretty, had the grade A crumpet 'coming at him like kamikazes'.) Germaine Greer may say, uncontroversially, that 'many a man who was attractive and amusing at twenty is a pompous old bore at fifty,' and Melvyn Bragg got a lot of stick for the novel he wrote about an icky romance between a nice enough man in his fifties and an even nicer 18-year-old whose looks were out of this world, but women (for whatever reason) never seem to tire of telling stories about young ladies and older men and living happily ever after. It doesn't happen very much or very plausibly the other way round, not in life or in books. Even Colette, who pioneered the notion of the young man and the older woman, makes Léa give Chéri up for a biologically appropriate wife.

'Men,' man-in-the-news *Iron John* Bly reports, 'are more lonesome in every generation.' In the last few days, as I've been getting more and more inflamed in my thoughts about the human (i.e., female, i.e., menopausal) condition, I've been hearing a lot about how hard it is being a man and having to stake your claim and prove your wonderfulness at every turn. Robert Bly says men need a male mother, and that's fine by me. But I won't believe it isn't harder to be a woman until the day, should it ever come, when the balance of power is so drastically reversed that women can get into serious trouble, lose their jobs or be despatched to the gulag, for making jokes about men. However strongly I feel about the things I've been saying, I doubt whether anyone—i.e., any man—will find them upsetting. In fact, I wonder whether all my ironies aren't simply one more way of sucking up to the ruling class. Is it just me, or do men care what women say provided they don't look like Andrea Dworkin?

On the other hand, I can't say I think it's entirely men's fault that women live as if under their spell. Looking back at what I've written so far, it seems clear that I made a mistake in skipping those consciousness-raising sessions. The menopause isn't simply something that happens to women that doesn't happen to men. Nor is the big question—the really big question—why men, all men, whatever they have or haven't got going for them, can always find a woman to sew on their buttons or proof-read their books. What we need to know is whether women are going to go on forever dreaming about men: dreaming of finding one if they haven't got one, of winning him back if he is slipping away, of killing themselves should he finally bolt. Greer, who, unlike almost every other woman in the world, has never seemed to share this obsessive interest in the opposite sex, is pretty clear: time to get out. 'I never have to think any more, oh a party,' she said in an interview in the *Independent on Sunday*, 'what clothes shall I wear, what men will be there, what am I going to do?' And even if, as I've heard suggested, she doesn't wholly mean it, it's good enough for me if she half-does.

'Unless you have a really decent guy, talking to him about the menopause is like taking hemlock,' a (married) Californian woman remarks in *Vanity Fair*. I don't know about hemlock, but I've always kept my cardy on through the most equatorial flushes for fear that some male bystander (or colleague) would understand what was happening and laugh. Greer, you could say, is vigorously alert to the ways in which women let themselves be enslaved by men—or rather the idea of a man:

> The very notion of *remaining attractive* is replete with the contradictions that break women's hearts. A woman cannot make herself attractive; she can only be *found* attractive. She can only remain attractive if someone remains attracted to her. Do what she will she cannot influence that outcome. Her desperate attempts to do the impossible, to guide the whim of another, are the basis of a billion-dollar beauty industry. All their lives women have never felt attractive enough. They have struggled through their thirties and forties to remain attractively slim, firm-bodied, glossy-haired and bright-eyed. Now in their fifties 'remaining attractive' becomes a full-time job . . . Jane Fonda's body may look terrific, what there is of it, but has anyone looked at the strain taken up by her face and neck muscles? . . . Is a middle-aged woman supposed to have the buttocks of a twenty-year-old? Such buttocks are displayed on advertising hoardings all over town. The man who is still making love to the wife of his youth may be thinking of other breasts than his wife's. There is no lack of spectacular publications to furnish such imagery. The middle-aged woman who tries to compete with her husband's fantasy sex partners hasn't a hope.

She's the Norman Tebbit of feminism, a founder member of the on-yer-bike branch of the women's movement; and I don't imagine she'll be sorry to think that it's all over for her contemporaries; that for us what she memorably calls 'the white-slavery of attraction duty' is a thing of the past. 'To be unwanted,' she says in her introduction, 'is also to be free.' Which sounds good. But women, as men always say, are so unreliable; and no sooner has Greer got us off the hook than she's talking in a most un-Tebbit-like way about 'the older woman's love' being a 'feeling of tenderness so still and deep and warm that it gilds every grassblade and blesses every fly'.

So what do we do now, my ageing sisters and I? If we can't line up behind the new-order Greer, who do we take as our role model—Joan Collins or Alan Bennett's lady in the van? Or, to put it differently, do we or don't we put in a bid for hormone replacement therapy? (I don't want to get into difficulties here: Joan Collins swears she's never had it—she only looks as if she has.) There are reasons for taking it, and reasons for not taking it, and reasons for getting angry with your doctor either way, but if you do and it works, you feel better, you look better and you *are* better. (I speak from envy, not experience.) Then the question arises: what does 'better' mean? And is that sort of 'better' appropriate? Or, to quote Germaine Greer: 'We hear that Mrs Thatcher uses hormone replacement but do not know whether to be encouraged or disheartened by the result.'

Years and years ago I remember some poor woman being lambasted in the *Guardian* for liking a certain sort of maternity dress because in it she didn't look pregnant ('misses the point of *being* pregnant', she was told). There are people on whom talk of hormone replacement therapy has a similar effect, as if it were to be blamed for overlooking or deferring the pleasure of being known and knowing yourself to be past it. No doubt in five or ten minutes' time it will be really chic to be menopausal. Perhaps thanks to Greer and others it's happened already. The only trouble is I'd rather go back on attraction duty than sit in my garden saying hello to the grass.

My Distant Relative

A distant relative of mine was a general in the KGB. 'As long as I live,' Stalin said of him, 'not a hair of his head shall be touched.' Stalin didn't keep his word—which can't have been wholly surprising even then. Unlike many of his colleagues, however, my relative wasn't shot: he was beaten and tortured and kept in prison for 12 years. He died in 1981 with—I've been told—a portrait of Stalin by his bed.

I am intrigued by his story and by his connection with the rest of my family, the last of whom left Russia in the first years of the Revolution. (My mother and her sisters were in Moscow in 1917: when I asked them what they did during that time they said they played cards—children in one room, grown-ups in the other.) None of those who are alive now—about the previous generation, who can say?—had ever heard of this KGB relative until an article in *Life* magazine revealed the identity of Trotsky's assassin, a Spanish communist called Ramon Mercader, and that of his mentor, my relative, Leonid Eitingon.

For the fact of his being a relative the evidence, despite my efforts, is only circumstantial. I have sent my agents to the archives in Minsk, but there is nothing in writing to prove that the various sets of Eitin-gons living in a cluster of small towns on the banks of the Dnepr in the late 1890s belonged to the same family—though I would be amazed if they didn't. A Soviet intelligence officer could be shot merely for hav-ing family in the West and when, in 1991, I went to Moscow for the first time to visit my putative relatives, Leonid's children and grand-children, they were willing enough to see me but reluctant to accept that I was anything other than an Englishwoman with a bee in her bonnet.

The first indication that we might belong to the same family and that some of his relatives might have known some of mine came in 1993 from a cousin of Leonid's, an old lady called Revekka who remembers meeting one of my great-uncles in Moscow in the late 1920s. My great-uncle was by then an American and very rich. Re-vekka's mother, who was very poor, hoped that if the rich Ameri-can saw her young daughter, he would give her some money—which he did. He called Revekka a little flower and gave her 100 dollars. But Revekka wasn't pleased. Not only did she feel that her mother had tricked her, she didn't like the compliment either. By the time she got home, the money had gone, been lost or mislaid. A month or so later, when she and her mother moved flats, it turned up. She doesn't remember how it was spent, except that she got something she'd always wanted: a raspberry-coloured beret like the one Tatiana has in *Eugene Onegin*.

I was in Moscow again ten days ago, for reasons I'll come to. It was looking very beautiful, though it's not a place that I generally like. In fact, I quite often hate it. The city is too big (you are forever travelling, as it were, from Norwood to Highgate), the roads are too wide (wher-ever you go an eight-lane highway to cross), the drivers unbelievably heedless. Most people, you feel, would just as soon you weren't there. Not because they see you as the enemy or even the former enemy: they simply have no interest in you at all. No one in the street ever smiles. If you buy something they bark, if you ask the way they don't answer or answer over their shoulder, walking away. At first 'our victory' was an embarrassment. Now it's more straightforwardly a nightmare, or *cauchmar*, as the Russians say—odd that they don't have their own word, only their own pronunciation. It may seem in order to Milton Friedman that Russian citizens trade in dollars as much as in roubles, that the road from the airport into town is marked by a procession of billboards advertising ventures with fly-by-night names like Inkombank and Discountbank, that most of the ads on the Metro—ads on the Metro!—invite you to get rich as fast as you can, but not even Friedman would say this is capitalism with a human face.

In the cause of getting rich quick 63 foreigners were murdered in Moscow in the first six months of 1994. (Moscow is the only place I've ever heard shots being fired—quite a few.) Under the ancien régime it was the rough-handedness of the state that you had to watch out for: now it's scary wherever you look. (My distant relative, I should explain, worked abroad: it wasn't he who sent men at night to knock on your door.) In summer the sky is still a luminous blue at one or two o'clock in the morning, but the streets are scarcely lit; the Metro is thought not to be safe, taxis even less so. A few days ago the *LRB* contributor R. W. Johnson, a big man but in Moscow an obvious foreigner, was set upon by a gang of ten-year-olds on Gorky Street at midday. His clothes were ripped; he was lucky, he said, to have escaped with his life.

In the block of flats where I was staying there were two families sharing a two-room flat. Nothing unusual about that. (When my distant relative first lived in Moscow he had a large room in the centre of town. His mother came to live with him there and when he was sent abroad in the 1920s, the old lady, her two daughters, their husbands, and eventually their children all lived in that room and went on doing so for the next 30 years.) In the present case, however, one room was bigger than the other and in the larger of the two an old man lived on his own while a young couple with a child had to make do with the smaller one. The young man asked the old man if he would swap: in fact, he asked so often that in April the old man shot him. Now the old man is still living in the big room and the woman and her child are on their own in the smaller one.

Komunalkas, as such flats are called, won't disappear immediately thanks to capitalism, but more is in hand than one might have expected. Cranes no longer stand still on building sites; in one neighbourhood all the pipes were being replaced, in another the telephone cables. There is more food than there was, and however extreme the rate of inflation, pensions too have increased. So when you look out of your window in the early morning you don't see what used to be the first familiar sight of the day: large women in padded clothes shuffling towards the neighbourhood bread queue. And if you're a visitor about your business in the middle of Moscow, and you'd like to sit down, you no longer have to take a trip on the Metro: there are places to sit, even cafés, in the centre of town. There is, for example, in addition to the flagship of capitalism in Pushkin Square, a new kind of McDonald's, a pseudo-modish café on the modish Arbat (the street where in pre-revolutionary times my great-aunt Bertha had her dental practice). Prospective travellers to Moscow might like to think of arranging their visit before there's a Dunkin' Donuts next to the new McDonald's and every neighbourhood has its own Body Shop.

It's all part of the Eurofication of the Soviet Union. (What happened to the cafés that must have existed in tsarist times: was it policy to close them down?) Trams rattle late into the night along the street I stay on: a reminder of the end of Mikhail Alexandrovich Berlioz, the literary editor in *The Master and Margarita* who thought he knew it all. The trams used to be white and red and a little dishevelled: now some are a spanking bright blue and have 'Panasonic' written on the front in large letters. Like much else in Moscow, they're being taken over, Eurofied. It struck me this time that the rebarbative Stalinist skyscrapers had retreated into the background, as if in the new capitalist Russia they had given way to the pre-revolutionary buildings they themselves replaced. From my room, I see a group of dusty buildings, dressed in a rough compound with trees and a square of parched grass at the centre, framing a couple of rusty swings. In the next street along, a main road, there are large ramshackle apartment houses, reminiscent of Rome in their weight and their colour, irregular, dilapidated, stagey. In the event of a thunderstorm the heavy stone balconies are liable to break away from their moorings and tumble into the street. At one point my distant relative lived not far from here, in a handsome, pre-revolutionary block. In other parts of the city, the neoclassical centre especially, restored thanks to JVs (joint ventures) with the Germans, the Finns or the Italians, there's a distinct whiff of Covent Garden—the Euro-heritage that one day will stretch from the Atlantic to the Urals.

Sometimes as I walk past some newly manicured bit of Moscow I wonder what my distant relative Leonid would make of these changes. But I only know—or think I know—what he would have said, because it's what most former party members say when you ask them: 'times change and one has to change with them.' (You can always recognise a party member by his reluctance to say anything of interest.) A couple of years ago I went, as I then thought very bravely, to interview Leonid's former KGB boss, Pavel Sudoplatov, a very old and once a very powerful man; in the words of the *New York Times*, 'the last of Stalin's wolves'. As Stalin's wolf, he fell from favour when Stalin died, spent 15 years in prison and emerged in 1968, unrepentant and disgraced. He'd been 'a spy', he said, 'a professional since 1921', when he was 'still a teenager'. As a professional he told me nothing. Now he has published his memoirs in English, French, and German. ('I don't like to see my name in print,' he said when I first met him.) The book, *Special Tasks: The Memoirs of an Unwanted Witness*, was written with his son Anatoli and—I would have thought uniquely in the annals of war and its aftermath—two Americans, Jerrold and Leona Schecter, who not only translated the material but effectively made of it a book Americans would want to read.*

Americans may or may not be reading it: they have certainly been reading about it. In the mid-1940s General Sudoplatov was in charge of atomic espionage—of the flow of information from Los Alamos to Moscow. In 1992 when I asked him about this part of his working life (my distant relative was at this point his deputy) he was outraged: 'The American bomb,' he screeched, 'was made by foreigners, by immigrants . . . *We* did it all by ourselves, with our own scientists, our *atomshiki*.' Since then he has evidently changed his mind about what to say, because in *Special Tasks* he makes what has come to be seen as the electrifying claim that the parents of the American bomb, Oppenheimer, Fermi, Bohr, and Szilard, were not only keen that their knowledge be shared with the Soviets, but one way or another made sure that it was. In America the response has been unanimous: as far as I know, there is no one who has written on the subject who hasn't been outraged. Many people in Russia, too, are outraged, the scientists especially, who don't want to hear what General Sudoplatov pretended not to want to hear when I talked to him: that Kurchatov and Co. were merely following a recipe. One of the peculiarities of the new Russia is that in a newspaper still named in honour of the Komsomol movement it's possible to treat the whole business with even-handed irony:

> American and Soviet physicists have been disturbed by the memoirs
> of Pavel Sudoplatov . . . The American people are disturbed and
> saddened. Sudoplatov's book came out there and they discovered
> damaging facts about their heroes. The Russian people are quiet . . .

We have more pressing reasons to be sad. But our physicists are very upset. If we are to believe Sudoplatov we stole the atom bomb. The American physicists blurted the secret out to Soviet spies, the Soviet spies transmitted the information to Beria, Beria gave it to Kurchatov and Kurchatov made the bomb. No one wants to believe Sudoplatov. It could be that the American physicists were traitors and ours . . . mmm. Shaming.

Moskovsky Komsomalets, 29 June

General Sudoplatov's book was the reason for my visit to Moscow. The Russians have only read extracts from it, and may not be allowed to read more, though a translation is due at the end of the year. At present the two Sudoplatovs are under interrogation—the general, because he is old and unwell, at home, his son at the offices of the military procurator. Neither is being tortured, no one is pulling out their teeth as they did Leonid's, but there is a chance that they will have to stand trial for betraying state secrets. Or they may be stripped of their honours: the son, who teaches at Moscow University, would no longer have the title of Academician, the father would be un-rehabilitated and with that lose his pension.

Many people besides the physicists wouldn't be shocked if that happened: the children of the general's former colleagues and employees, for example, who don't like the way he has spoken about their fathers—truthfully or untruthfully, I can't always judge, but more informatively than they are used to and more self-servingly than he should have. There are those, too, who say that it is inappropriate to receive a pension from the KGB and then spill its beans and those who believe that in speaking of the past one should respect the traditions of the past; that one should not disclose people's names or say in the manner of today, 'I was responsible for X's assassination,' but instead: 'I fulfilled a very important party task.'

I was with Nikolai Khokhlov, one of the general's former intelligence officers, who now lives in the West, when he bought a copy of the book. He looked his own name up in the index and discovered something he'd never known: that in 1952 he'd been on the point of murdering Kerensky. Khokhlov's account of the incident is not quite the same as the Sudoplatovs', however. In his own book, *In the Name of Conscience* (1959), he describes himself as having had enough of killing and refusing to go to Paris to liquidate the unnamed enemy; he even praises Sudoplatov for letting him get away with it when it would have been more normal to have him shot. As the general now tells it, Khokhlov had simply shown himself to be an incompetent agent and, in any case, the operation was called off. Who knows the real reason—if there was a real reason—Kerensky wasn't shot? But it's unlikely that Khokhlov was incompetent if, of all their agents, the KGB had chosen him for the job. There was certainly a look of triumph on his face after he'd read the book: he may not have wanted to be an agent but pride, too, was at stake. A few days later he said: 'You know, I saved Kerensky's life.'

Special Tasks: The Memoirs of an Unwanted Witness—A Soviet Spymaster by Pavel Sudoplatov and Anatoli Sudoplatov, with Jerrold and Leona Schecter.

Brussels

'Adjustment, no matter how comfortable it appears to be, is never freedom.' David Reisman said that in *The Lonely Crowd*, a work of academic/pop sociology, published in the US in the late 1940s; much read and remarked on at the time, and now forgotten. I looked it up the other day when I was due to say something at the South Bank Centre in connection with an exhibition on cities at the Hayward. Reisman divided social behaviour into three categories: 'anomic', 'adjusted' and 'autonomous'. 'Anomie' is bad—everyone knows that—and something that has long been associated with urban life. But who could be sure, as David Reisman was, that an 'autonomous' citizen, no matter how uncomfortable, was better off than one who had taken the trouble to adjust—unless they'd told themselves that adjustment was un-American, the sort of feebleness Charlton Heston might despise? And if you could choose one or other way of being which would you go for? And where would you live?

I had been asked, specifically, to say something about cities I'd lived in and those questions are ones that I find troubling. I was born, not long before the Second World War, in the United States, where until the age of nine I lived in a succession of different towns and states, of which New York was the last, the place from which I left the country for good. I didn't know at the time that we weren't going back; and it was only later that it occurred to me that I'd spent the rest of my childhood in some sort of exile.

We were moving—it was now the late 1940s—to Europe. More particularly, we moved to Brussels: a dark, rainy, unfriendly, unseductive, unappealing, charmless city. At the time I wouldn't have been able to say any of that. For one thing, I wouldn't have been allowed to: Brussels was where we had to be and if I didn't like it, it was because, my mother said, I was unwilling to make the effort. David Reisman perhaps would have been pleased with me. I found it all very difficult. Again, we moved often. Not that it mattered: I don't remember knowing the neighbours or playing with the children next door or downstairs, as everyone did in the States. There was a tennis club to which families like mine belonged but very few places where one could detach oneself from one's family. I missed the comic books (missed them all the more for not having been allowed to read them), the roller-skating rink in Central Park, the Lexington Avenue drugstores, the Hershey bars and Hamburger Heaven: all important markers of a New York child's place in the world and signifiers, too, of a world in which there was much to desire. Belgian children ate the same serious chocolate as their mothers and fathers ate and didn't have places of their own to go to: they stayed close to their parents and wherever they went walked behind them like the Duke of Edinburgh behind the queen.

What I remember most clearly, besides the gloom and the rain, is the formality: having to shake hands with my classmates three or four times a day—schoolchildren and office workers always went home for lunch—and being told off for all kinds of things that were nobody else's business, like eating in the street, or sticking my tongue out at children

I didn't like the look of. My father was quite a prominent figure in what was, in the days before the EU, a very small world and I was known as 'the little Wilmers girl', whose misdeeds were inevitably seen by someone who knew who I was and considered themselves obliged to tell tales. 'In the devious world of *Villette*,' Tony Tanner said of Charlotte Brontë's novel, most of which is set in Brussels, 'everyone spies on everyone else, the watcher is watched with a minimum of eye-to-eye contact. It is a very voyeuristic world.' Baudelaire, who also noted the spying, said it was boredom that led to it.

When I was 14, in the early 1950s, I was allowed to leave. My father was English and I was sent to an English boarding school. Which is how, eventually, I came to live here. Wondering what to do with myself after I left university, I took up some unwelcome advice I'd been given and went every day to a place in Kensington High Street where young women were taught a few secretarial skills. On my first morning, as I came out of the Tube, I was alarmed to hear someone shouting a bit further up the road. 'Alarmed' because I thought something might be required of me. A minute later a mad woman stormed into view: she was quite well dressed, not a tramp or a beggar, but a straightforward middle-class mad woman, addressing the world. That sort of thing seemed to happen quite regularly around there, with women of different ages but similar habits. And no one ever paid any attention. Without doubt, London was the right place to live.

My family left Brussels in 1960 and several decades went by before I thought to go back to have a look and found that I hadn't imagined its dreariness: Brussels, it turned out, wasn't a metaphor for my forced separation from the neighbourhood drugstore, or a virtual city thought up to express my pre-adolescent or late childhood gloom. It was in actual fact much as I'd remembered it. The difficulty is to know who or what to blame. You could say that a place that worships an undistinguished statue of a little boy urinating deserves to be held in contempt. But that statue is just around the corner from the medieval Grand-Place, which the Blue Guide describes as the most beautiful square in Europe. There are plenty of old streets of the kind that are admired in Paris or Bordeaux and some exceptionally nice old buildings; there are trees; the streets aren't lit with sodium lights; there are shops, there are cafés; the roads aren't too wide or the pavements too narrow; the art galleries have wonderful things in them, there's an opera house and an orchestra and all that sort of thing: what's wrong with it? As a child I might have said food was what was wrong with it. Too much food, too many long meals, too many restaurants, too many fat bellies. I might still say that now but it wouldn't explain why it's a city that seems to interest no one, not even Belgians. There are three Belgian writers whose names are known outside Belgium. None of them wrote about his own country. Simenon went to France, Hergé to Tintin-land and Maeterlinck took flight with his bird. And of English novelists, only Charlotte Brontë wrote about Brussels, that 'great selfish city', as she called it.

The narrator of *Heart of Darkness* is obliged to make a stopover in Brussels to collect the documents he needs for his journey. He arrives to find two crones 'guarding the door of Darkness', two tricoteuses whom he describes 'knitting black wool as for a warm pall, one introducing, introducing continuously to the unknown, the other scrutinising the cheery and foolish faces with unconcerned old eyes. *Ave!* Old knitter of black wool,' he continues. 'Morituri te salutant. Not many of those she looked at ever saw her again—not half, by a long way.' Door of Darkness, gateway to the Congo: the association says much of what needs, or needed, to be said about Brussels. I wonder whether the Union Minière, which in my time owned the Congo in much the same way as United Fruit owned Guatemala, still exists. It was one of the few enterprises my parents talked about whose activities I could imagine. The most often mentioned, and most perplexing, was the ominously unparticularised Société Générale, which in fact owned the

Union Minière (and thus the Congo) and a great deal besides. Reading Conrad might have done more to alleviate my discontent ('divine discontent', my father called it, but I wasn't so sure) than the many Angela Brazil–type school stories through which I plotted my escape.

Marx and Engels worked on *The Communist Manifesto* in a house—now inevitably a restaurant—on the Grand-Place. A few French writers—Baudelaire, Rimbaud and Verlaine, Victor Hugo—spent time in Brussels when for one reason or another they had to leave France. Edith Cavell, the English nurse who said 'Patriotism is not enough,' was executed by the Germans in 1915 for helping fugitive soldiers escape to Holland. I was about to say that nothing else happened in Brussels, nothing at any rate to catch the imagination, when I remembered the Duchess of Richmond's ball and the battle that followed ('who would guess . . . upon night so sweet such awful morn could rise'). But I don't suppose Byron ever went to Brussels, and the Battle of Waterloo apart, it's a city without associations. What you see is what there is to see. Geneva, where my family moved after Brussels, is quite a bit duller still, but in my mind it is buoyed up by its past and its connection with larger things. There isn't even a river passing through Brussels on its way from one place to another: there was one once but it got cemented over. What can be said in its favour is that, unlike London, it names its streets after people who have done something more useful or more glamorous than acquired the land on which the houses were subsequently built. I live near Primrose Hill. What are the streets around there called? Oppidans Road, King Henry's Road—in honour of Eton College, of course, from which the land was bought.

In my eyes, Brussels would have been more interesting had it at least been bombed. The one thing I wanted to see, arriving in Europe in 1947 or 1948, were signs of the war: but Brussels had been occupied by the Germans and there was nothing to see—only whispers and rumours about fat-cat collaborators. One fat cat had a daughter in my class: he wore a camel-hair coat and before long his children were known by their mother's name. The king, too, was in trouble for having been too close to the Germans. On that matter feelings ran high, and there were stickers everywhere, including my bedroom, in the form of a one-way sign with the word 'non' written across it. A referendum took place; the no-sayers won; and the king's son, the unhappy Baudouin, was invited to reign in his place. In the 25 years between the end of the war and the debacle in the Congo it was the one exciting moment in that city where, Baudelaire said, 'only the dogs are alive.'

I hadn't intended to go on like that about Brussels, so I had to tell myself it had some significance as a dystopia of a mild and unthreatening kind. What I'd wanted to talk about was urban oppression more generally and the sense cities can give you of being in the wrong novel or, worse, magazine. New York, for example, was a great children's book. Now when I go there I feel as if everything I look at or walk past has a frame around it—the seedy parts as much as the affluent. A frame of the kind that is provided by the edge of the page in a glossy— or too chic to be glossy—magazine. From the uptown stoops and the families sitting on them to the ubiquitous fire escapes, everything that remains of what once made New York so likeable has been appropriated by fashion editors; one thing only is still untouched and unglamorised: the steam from the subway that comes up through the grates in the sidewalk. Otherwise, in the parts of Manhattan that I know, from Riverside Drive to the Meat District, it's all style. Even if I were to walk up and down in front of the Plaza yelling and railing like the former habituées of Kensington High Street—by this stage in my life a dangerously real temptation—I'd probably be thought to be making a fashion statement. I won't do it, though. Adjustment and freedom may have trouble getting on with each other: what David Reisman seems not to have known is that autonomy can be quite pointless as well as quite painful.

What If You Hadn't
Been Home

This is how it begins: 'July 26 2010. Today would be her wedding anniversary.' Joan Didion's daughter, Quintana Roo, was married at the Cathedral of St. John the Divine on Amsterdam Avenue in New York in 2003. Dates are important. In a writer as fastidious as Didion they carry a lot of weight. Detail matters too, sometimes more than the main thing, or instead of it:

> Seven years ago today we took the leis from the florist's boxes and shook the water in which they were packed onto the grass . . . The white peacock spread his fan. The organ sounded. She wove white stephanotis into the thick braid that hung down her back. She dropped a tulle veil over her head and the stephanotis loosened and fell. The plumeria blossom . . .

What Didion doesn't say, here or elsewhere, is what Quintana looked like: was she tall or short, plump or skinny—who knows?

Blue Nights is dedicated to Quintana. The reference in the title is to a colour of evening light—'the French called this time of day "l'heure bleue".' You see it first in late April when 'suddenly summer seems near, a possibility, even a promise,' but only in certain latitudes: in New York, for example, where Didion now lives, but not in California, where she is from and where much of the book is set. When the days begin to shorten it fades: 'as the blue nights draw to a close (and they will, and they do) you experience an actual chill, an apprehension of illness.' Between Quintana's wedding and the writing of *Blue Nights*, first Didion's husband, the writer John Gregory Dunne, then Quintana died: the meaning of the title is obvious.

Dunne died of a heart attack in 2003: 'My attention was on mixing the salad. John was talking, then he wasn't.' His death and Didion's response to it—her grief with all its complexities, her uncertain state of mind, her lingering fantasy that he might be back (he would need his shoes), her guilt that she hadn't believed him when he said he was dying—is the principal subject of *The Year of Magical Thinking*, published in 2005, and not long afterwards made into a Broadway play starring Vanessa Redgrave. Dunne died on 30 December. *'You sit down to dinner and life as you know it ends.'* Eight days earlier, Quintana, with a temperature of 103 and 'feeling terrible', had gone to the emergency room at Beth Israel North on the Upper East Side and been told she had flu; on Christmas Day the hospital admitted her and by the evening she was in intensive care. X-rays showed double pneumonia; her blood pressure indicated septic shock. *'I don't think I'm up for this,'* Dunne had said in the taxi on the way back from visiting her. *'You don't get a choice,'* Didion replied. Later she wondered if she'd been wrong. At that point it wasn't clear whether Quintana would live. Her illness is *The Year of Magical Thinking*'s second subject. *'When we talk about mortality we are talking about our children.'*

In the middle of January Quintana's sedation was reduced and she was told her father had died. At his funeral, 'in the same cathedral where she had eight months before been married', she read a poem she had written in his memory. Two days later, ready to start her life again, she set off for Los Angeles with her husband. That was in March, three months after she was first taken ill. 'Do you think I'll be okay in California, she said. I said yes.' As she was walking out of the airport towards the car hire she collapsed:

They had gotten off the plane.
They had picked up their shared bag.

'When I'm working on a book,' Didion told Hilton Als in a *Paris Review* interview, 'I constantly retype my own sentences. Every day I go back to page one and just retype what I have. It gets me into a rhythm.' Had she done that for *The Year of Magical Thinking*? 'It was especially important with this book,' Didion replied, 'because so much of it depended on echo.' There and in *Blue Nights*, its companion, the rhythm, with its two or three one-line paragraphs coming at the end of a longer paragraph, its dates, its italicised tags, its almost liturgical repetitions, can feel like a snare, something one can't escape from, a spell, a seduction. You think you are writing your own sentences: you find you are imitating hers.

Quintana was now in the neurosurgery unit at UCLA Medical Centre. Either her fall had led to a brain haemorrhage or a haemorrhage had caused the fall. It didn't seem to matter which. ('There were two possibilities, both of them, I came to see, irrelevant.') The question again was whether she would live. Didion flew out to LA and resumed her vigil. 'She's a pretty cool customer,' they'd said of her in the hospital in New York when they told her John Gregory Dunne was dead. Didion hadn't found the remark unwarranted, merely wondered what an uncool customer would be 'allowed' to do. Would they scream?

She didn't scream or break down or require sedation. And she didn't keep asking the doctors for 'the prognosis', as other relatives in the neurosurgery unit did. Instead, she found herself 'pointing out oedema to one intern, reminding another to obtain a urine culture to check out the blood in the Foley catheter line, insisting on a Doppler ultrasound to see if the reason for the leg pain could be emboli'. If this didn't endear her 'to the young men and women who made up the house staff' so be it. Didion is a spellbinding writer: she isn't necessarily likeable, or un-scary.

'In time of trouble, I had been trained since childhood, read, learn, work it up, go to the literature. Information was control.' She knew the names of the neurological tests the doctors had ordered ('The Kimura Box Test. The Two-Point Discrimination Test') and the scales on which Quintana's coma was measured ('The Glasgow Coma Scale, the Glasgow Outcome Scale'), just as she knew the names of the antibiotics Quintana had been given in Beth Israel North. Azithromycin, gentamicin, clindamycin, vancomycin: it's all part of the rhythm. And if she didn't need 'the prognosis' it's because she was well aware that there couldn't be one—'I recall being told that it would be a minimum of three days before anyone could begin to know what shape her brain was in'—and knew better than to ask pointless questions.

Five weeks later, at the end of April, Quintana was well enough to be flown back to New York in an air ambulance. The next phase was a rehabilitation unit at a different New York hospital. The feeding tube was still in place but no longer necessary. She was recovering the use of her right arm and leg and the mobility in her right eye without which she couldn't read. At weekends her husband took her to lunch in the neighbourhood. Her husband, incidentally, is called Gerry. He has his bit part in Didion's story; he isn't left out.

Didion finished *The Year of Magical Thinking* on 31 December 2004: the year was over. 'John did not see this day a year ago. John was dead.'

She no longer disputed it. She would no longer hold on to his shoes. Or see herself through his eyes: 'this year for the first time since I was 29 I saw myself through the eyes of others.' On 31 December 2004 Quintana was still alive. The previous year, when she'd been in intensive care in Beth Israel North, her Christmas presents were stacked in her old bedroom, waiting for her to get better, but now there is no mention of presents; is that a bad sign?

She died eight months later, on 26 August 2005, two months before *The Year of Magical Thinking* was published. She had been ill in all 20 months: 'twenty months', Didion tells us in *Blue Nights*, 'during which she would be strong enough to walk unsupported for possibly a month in all'.

Blue Nights, a more anxious, self-questioning book than *The Year of Magical Thinking*, is about fear, Didion's and Quintana's principally: fear of being abandoned, of time passing, of losing control, of dying; and about the memory of a time between the mid-1960s and the late 1980s when Didion and Dunne lived in California and Quintana was growing up; a charmed time when 'there had been agapanthus, lilies of the Nile, intensely blue starbursts that floated on long stalks'; when children might develop a liking for caviar; and there were birthdays at which rafts of balloons were released to drift over Hollywood Hills; a time when fear was glossed over or unrecognised and Didion was a mother who wrote books:

> The oleander branch on which she swings is familiar, the curve of the beach on which she kicks through the wash is familiar.
>
> The clothes of course are familiar.
>
> I had for a while seen them every day, washed them, hung them to blow in the wind on the clotheslines outside my office window.
>
> I wrote two books watching her clothes blow on those lines.

It sounds good. Who, on paper, wouldn't like to have children and write books? But what about the children? Quintana was born in March 1966. She wasn't Didion and Dunne's biological child. Didion had first wanted a baby when she was in her mid-twenties, living in New York and working for *Vogue*. She was now 31. Had she gone on thinking about babies and then despaired? Or had other thoughts taken their place? In *The Year of Magical Thinking*, remarking on how easy everything had been in the past, Didion describes 'a time in our life when most things we did seemed without consequence, no-hands'. Was that true of the decision to adopt? A moment—there are several—of 1960s heedlessness? It's New Year 1966, she and Dunne are on a boat with friends: they're thinking of the next drink. 'Maybe because the Erskines were there'—the Erskines, friends of friends, had an adopted daughter—

> or maybe because I had mentioned wanting a baby or maybe because we had all had the drink we were thinking about having, the topic of adoption had entered the ether . . .
>
> That was all.
>
> Yet the next week I was meeting Blake Watson.

Blake Watson was the obstetrician who'd delivered the Erskines' adopted daughter.

Three months later he rang Didion and her husband to say he'd just delivered 'a beautiful baby girl' to a mother who was unable to keep her: were they interested? After they'd been to the hospital and looked at the baby and made up their minds to have her they called on Dunne's brother and his wife in Beverly Hills for a celebratory drink ('only when I read my early fiction, in which someone was always downstairs making a drink and singing "Big noise blew in from Winnetka", did I realise how much we all drank and how little thought we gave to it'). Lenny, Didion's sister-in-law, offered to meet her at Saks the next morning to buy a layette (in the 1960s people still talked about 'layettes'); if she spent 80 dollars Saks would throw in a cot—a 'bassinette':

> I took the glass and put it down.
> I had not considered the need for a bassinette.
> I had not considered the need for a layette.

It's hard to imagine that happening now, when having a baby and having the stuff seem to be inseparable parts of the same enterprise.

Not that Didion isn't interested in stuff—clothes and their provenance most of all. Like dates, clothes are freighted; they signal the passing of time ('When I bought that black wool challis dress Bendel's was still on West 57th Street'), the good times especially ('She was wearing Christian Louboutin shoes': 'you saw the red soles when she kneeled at the altar') and they distinguish one era from the next ('I look at those photographs now and am struck by how many of the women present were wearing Chanel suits and David Webb bracelets'), one mood from another. The bassinette was a turning point: 'Until the bassinette it had all seemed casual, even blithe, not different in spirit from the Jax jerseys and printed cotton Lilly Pulitzer shifts we were all wearing that year.'

Before the bassinette there had been a plan to go to Saigon: 'we had assignments from magazines, we had credentials, we had everything we needed. Including, suddenly, a baby.' It was a particularly bad year for that sort of tourism—US planes had started bombing the North— yet it didn't occur to her to alter or give up the plan: 'I even went so far as to shop for what I imagined we would need: Donald Brooks pastel linen dresses for myself, a flowered Porthault parasol to shade the baby, as if she and I were about to board a Pan Am flight and disembark at

Le Cercle Sportif.' In the event the trip didn't take place but not for 'the obvious reason'. Dunne, it turned out, had to finish a book.

With Quintana and the Lilly Pulitzer shifts soon enough came fearfulness: 'Once she was born I was never not afraid': 'afraid of swimming-pools, high-tension wires, lye under the sink, aspirin in the medicine cabinet . . . rattlesnakes, riptides, landslides, strangers who appeared at the door, unexplained fevers, elevators without operators and empty hotel corridors'. It's a bewitching list: 'riptides', 'landslides'—the words sound so nice side by side. Until Quintana was six months old and her adoption became legal Didion had also worried that the baby might somehow be reclaimed, removed, taken away from them. A few years later she realised that she 'had never been the only person in the house' to have fears of that sort: *'What if you hadn't answered the phone when Dr. Watson called,'* Quintana would say. *'What if you hadn't been home, what if you couldn't meet him at the hospital, what if there'd been an accident on the freeway, what would happen to me then?'* Didion's response was brisk: 'Since I had no adequate answer to these questions, I refused to consider them.' Fair enough, I suppose, if literal-minded. Didion is more interested in what people say than the reasons they say it, in what they feel than the reasons they feel it: Freud & Co.—they don't do much for her. She has her own sentences to deal with these things.

When should Didion have realised that all was not well with Quintana, that her mood changed too quickly, that she would grow up to be depressed and anxious ('we went through many diagnoses, many conditions that got called by many names')? Was it when she nailed a list of 'Mom's Sayings' to the garage door that read: 'Brush your teeth, brush your hair, shush I'm working'? Or earlier, when, aged no more than five, she told her parents that she had rung the local psychiatric hospital while they were out 'to find out what she needed to do if she was going crazy'? Or when she rang Twentieth Century–Fox 'to find out what she needed to do to be a star'? Or when, some years after that, she told her parents that she was writing a novel 'just to show you': a novel, Didion discovered after Quintana's death, whose heroine, called Quintana, dies and her parents 'didn't even care any more'.

Looking now at photographs of Quintana as a child, Didion wonders how she could have missed 'the startling depths and shallows of her expressions, the quicksilver changes of mood'. But what's the standard here? How alert do parents have to be not to find themselves looking back with dismay? Or how lucky? 'When we talk about our children . . . are we talking about . . . the whole puzzle of being a parent?' Didion asks. When she talks about Quintana is she always thinking about herself?

'Was I the problem? Was I always the problem?' she asks when she fails to find a way to pull out the five-year-old Quintana's tooth:

> My most coherent memory involved my mother tying a piece of thread around the loose tooth, attaching the thread to a doorknob, and slamming the door. I tried this. The tooth stayed fixed in place. She cried. I grabbed the car keys: tying the thread to the doorknob had so exhausted my aptitude for improvisational caretaking that my sole remaining thought was to get her to the emergency room at UCLA Medical Centre, thirty-some miles into town . . .
>
> The next time a tooth got loose she pulled it herself. I had lost my authority.

'I do not know many people who think they have succeeded as parents,' Didion says sniffily. 'Those who do tend to cite the markers that indicate (their own) status in the world: the Stanford degree, the Harvard MBA, the summer with the white-shoe law firm.' These aren't markers likely to impress Didion—that's why she chose them. And in any case she was OK: she didn't need Quintana to shine on her behalf. But the markers of success her parents no longer had any need for were precisely the ones that preoccupied Quintana. As well as writing novels Didion and Dunne wrote for the movies, they had Hollywood connections and, to the extent that they wanted them, Hollywood lives. Hence Quintana's novel, hence her call to Twentieth Century–Fox. When she was four or five Didion took her to see *Nicholas and Alexandra* and when Didion asked her how she had liked it she said: 'I think it's going to be a big hit.' 'Was this confusion about where she stood in the chronological scheme of things our doing?' Didion asks, and I suppose one might wonder why Quintana had been taken to see *Nicholas and Alexandra* when she wasn't yet six, maybe not even five. 'Did we ask her to assume responsibility before she had any way of doing so? Did our expectations prevent her from responding as a child?'

In one form or another and in different contexts the questions recur. They don't expect an answer. Reassurance too is something Didion doesn't need. She is talking to herself, weighing up the past, going over old stories, keeping herself company. Staging herself. 'Was I the problem?' she asked after describing the tooth-pulling fiasco and maybe she was, but her decision to drive 30 miles to UCLA Medical Centre to get a doctor to pull the tooth out doesn't answer the question, funny and revealing though her account of it is. Like the trip to Saigon that didn't happen it's the sort of comic story we—by 'we' I mean women—like to tell against ourselves. Usually we tell the stories winsomely, self-deprecatingly, but Didion, even down in the dumps, is more ruthless.

Take Quintana's troubles—the 'quicksilver changes of mood', etc. 'How could I have missed what was so clearly there to be seen?' Didion asks herself—another question that has no answer. Later on, there are names—'manic depression . . . became OCD and OCD was short for obsessive-compulsive disorder and obsessive-compulsive disorder became something else, I could never remember just what'—and as one diagnosis succeeds another Didion becomes increasingly intemperate: 'I have not yet seen that case in which a "diagnosis" led to a "cure", or in fact to any outcome other than a confirmed, and therefore enforced, debility.' Eventually borderline personality disorder is settled on: 'Such patients,' the manual says, 'may seem charming, composed and psychologically intact one day and collapse into suicidal despair the next.' At last an account Didion is willing to accept: 'I had seen the charm, I had seen the composure, I had seen the suicidal despair':

> I had seen her wishing for death as she lay on the floor of her sitting room in Brentwood Park, the sitting room from which she had been able to look into the pink magnolia. *Let me just be in the ground*, she had kept sobbing. *Let me just be in the ground and go to sleep.*

Note the pink magnolia: however painful the moment, Didion never lets go of the rhythm and the décor. There are intervals in the book, one or two moments when people come in from outside. Quintana's biological mother is one and the episode gets short shrift: Didion is slightly appalled and not very interested. Another, more vexed, concerns Vanessa Redgrave's daughter Natasha Richardson who, like her parents, was a friend of Didion's and who died as a result of a skiing accident at the beginning of 2009. Three or four years older than Quintana, she appears to be many things Quintana is not (Le Nid du Duc was her father's estate above Saint-Tropez):

> by the time John and I arrived . . . Tasha was running Le Nid du Duc, the 17-year-old chatelaine of what amounted to a summer-long house party for a floating thirty people. Tasha was managing the provisioning of the several houses that made up the compound. Tasha was cooking and serving, entirely unaided, three meals a day

for the basic thirty as well as for anyone else who happened up the hill . . . Tasha made certain that Quintana and Roxana got to the correct spot on the beach . . . Tasha made certain that Quintana and Roxana got a proper introduction to the Italian boys . . . Tasha did a perfect beurre blanc . . . Tasha devised the fables, Tasha wrote the romance.

Poor Quintana. While Tasha is rustling up the beurre blanc she is lying on the carpet wishing she were dead. There are several reasons why Didion might write differently about her friends' daughter from the way she writes about her own. Tasha is an outsider, however fulsomely praised, or fulsomely praised because she is an outsider (and there's no reason to think she doesn't deserve the praise). Unlike Quintana, she isn't folded into the rhythm of Didion's sentences; hasn't been allocated any lines/allowed any interruptions in Didion's conversation with herself. And given the painful contrast with Quintana it's hard to know what part Tasha is playing here unless as another loss that Didion suffered in the timespan covered by the book.

Blue Nights has been billed as a book about Quintana, it is dedicated to her, there is an enchanting photograph of her on the back cover looking as if Twentieth Century–Fox had already made her a star; she is the focus of the book, or more precisely of Didion's memories, as well as being the object of her loss, but Didion herself is its subject, its best subject. That doesn't mean that she doesn't miss Quintana, far from it; or that she hogs the limelight or lets herself off the hook or appears to be more than normally self-obsessed; her writing is measured and has its own kind of narcissistic grace.

Towards the end, as Quintana fades out of the picture Didion writes about herself as she is now: frail, uncertain, unsteady, childless; afraid to get up from a folding chair; afraid to admit she might not know how to start a strange car; afraid that she is no longer able to tell a story, that she will 'never again locate the words that work'; afraid to die and afraid not to die; she tells herself not to whine, to get used to being alone; faints and wakes up on her bedroom floor unable to move and not within reach of any of the apartment's 13 phones. In short, finds herself not growing old but old already:

> One day we are looking at the Magnum photograph of Sophia Loren at the Christian Dior show in Paris in 1968 and thinking yes, it could be me, I could wear that dress, I was in Paris that year; a blink of the eye later we are in one or another doctor's office being told what has already gone wrong, why we will never again wear the red suede sandals with the four-inch heels, never again wear the gold hoop earrings, the enamelled beads, never now wear the dress Sophia Loren is wearing.

'When I began writing these pages,' Didion says quite early on in the book, 'I believed their subject to be children, the ones we have and the ones we wish we had, the ways in which we depend on our children to depend on us . . . The ways in which neither we nor they can bear to contemplate the death or the illness or even the ageing of the other.' Then, 'as the pages progressed it occurred to me that their actual subject was this failure to confront the certainties of ageing, illness, death . . . Only as the pages progressed further did I understand that the two subjects were the same. *When we talk about mortality we are talking about our children.*' The children who won't be there to mourn us when we die.

Book reviewed:
Blue Nights by Joan Didion

Peter Campbell

The fox on the cover of the *LRB* of 17 November 2011 is walking past Peter Campbell's house in South London, the house where he and his wife had lived since 1963. Peter died—in that house—on 25 October and the picture on that cover is the last one he painted.

Peter was always at the heart of the *LRB*. He designed the first issue in October 1979—a 28-page insert inside European editions of the *New York Review*; redesigned it six months later after the papers' divorce; and in 1997 re-redesigned it. But saying that gives no sense of his importance to the paper. As much as the original editors and the founder, Karl Miller, Peter shaped the *LRB*. Unlike us, he never lost his temper. More adjusted than most to his own wants and necessities, and so better able to accommodate other people's, he was an exemplary person to work with.

He was born in New Zealand in 1937 (in a taxi in a tunnel: he never told us that) and had two sisters—often a help to a boy. At university in Wellington, he did 'the kind of degree in which you are allowed to mix subjects' and spent his first year reading philosophy, geology, and English: 'I never quite got a grip on these subjects,' he said in a review of George Landow's *Hypertext* in 1992, 'but the memory of what it is like to do philosophy or geology remains; and when I read about debates that are going on in these areas I believe I know, even if I cannot follow it all, what kind of row or celebration is taking place.' There are people whom getting a grip doesn't suit, who don't want to be confined. One can honour the world in depth or across a wide range and there were few aspects of the world that Peter didn't wish to honour.

Dandelions: 'Weeds have only a passing hegemony and must expect a modest future role.' Rainbows: 'If the rainbow is something you assumed you understood, humility follows on the unsurprising discovery that things which gave Aristotle . . . serious problems are lying about in your own head, like unopened mail waiting to be dealt with.' Bodies and clothes: 'Bodies differ from place to place and race to race, from person to person and from fat times to lean. Clothes battle against these differences. They help bodies to conform to norms of what is decent, impressive, dignified, lovely, erotic or charming.' Cycling: 'Asker Jukendrup, a Dutch expert on carbohydrate and fat metabolism, uses the cheeseburger as a unit to describe calorific intake. Inputs equivalent to 28 cheeseburgers a day fuel the rider during a mountain stage.' Ducks: 'It seemed that the drake was struggling with a long pink worm; I remembered a piece of research that was in the press a year or so ago: not many birds have a penis but the stifftail duck does.' Doors: 'The door to Number 10 domesticates politics because it is commonplace in its look and scale: we know what it is like to stand on such a threshold, we too do things behind closed doors.' Horses: 'Equestrian monuments give short generals dignity. Once mounted, Frederic Remington's scruffy cowboys and Indians become brothers to the riders on the Parthenon frieze.' Port Sunlight: 'I know of no other place where I feel such a snob and where snobbishness feels such a thin emotion.' Finally, a lament: 'We know (roughly) what Maisie knew, but not what Maisie wore.'

He graduated in 1958 with a philosophy degree, but a couple of years into his course he'd already become a compositor's apprentice: 'I was an inveterate picker-up and putter-down of books,' he recalled in the review of *Hypertext*, 'because I was interested in how they looked. I got to care more about how they were put together and organised than about their content.' He paid for the month-long sea voyage from Wellington with money he'd earned as a typographer and illustrator, and arrived in London in 1960. He found work at BBC Publications designing pamphlets for schools. The ship he'd travelled on, MS *Willem Ruys*, was later renamed *Achille Lauro*—that was another thing he didn't tell us.

Karl Miller and I got to know him a few years later when he'd begun to design the BBC books that accompanied the famous television series of the late 1960s and early 1970s—Kenneth Clark's *Civilisation*, *The Ascent of Man*, *Life on Earth*—and we were working on the *Listener*, which published the scripts. (The *Listener*'s circulation rose by 16,000 with the first Clark lecture and dipped by 16,000 after the last.) BBC Publications was based in Marylebone High Street and the *Listener* in what is now the Langham Hotel. Peter must have walked over to see Karl about the pictures we might reproduce in the text of Clark's first lecture. He had no great liking for corporate life; he preferred to get around, talk to people, find out what they did and how they did it. He got on well too with the grandee lecturers and pontificators—even the supercilious Clark, who was won over when Peter went to see him in his flat in the Albany and recognised an oil painting by the *Punch* illustrator Charles Keene. He confirmed Clark in his new regard for him when he pointed out—had Clark not known or was he just impressed that a man from New Zealand might know too?—that St. Paul's was built on a Gothic plan and went on to describe the figures in a photograph of Roman ruins as 'Piranesi people'.

It wasn't long before Karl asked Peter to write for the paper and in the late 1960s he wrote his first piece, about Claes Oldenburg. Looking for but failing to find that issue in an untidy stack of old *Listeners*, I found three from 1972, fairly late in Karl's reign. Like all Peter's pieces about exhibitions they take you with him into the gallery. The first is about an exhibition of photographs at the Whitechapel ('When a glum, derisive, sulky or tired face looks out at you, remember it is the photographer he is seeing—not you'); the second about a print-making show at Colnaghi's ('Whistler . . . produced simpler and simpler etchings until his colleagues in the Etching Club thought that an adjustment should be made to prices to allow for the lack of labour in his plates'); the third about painting in the age of Charles I, an exhibition at the Tate: 'These portraits,' Peter wrote, 'are triumphs of an international style: a reminder that artists could be contracted to courts as film stars once were to their studios—and as jealously guarded.'

Peter didn't like everything he saw, but mostly he avoided writing about work that didn't accord with his taste or his sense of things; if he couldn't find a reason to be interested he wrote about something else—another exhibition or the trees on the street. A comprehensive show of 1930s art was the first exhibition he wrote about in the *LRB*; it was, he felt, misconceived: 'an attempt at total recall' that reduced the works on display 'to the status of evidence'. But once the point had been made there was no further reason to mope:

> One could say that the time has come . . . honestly to enjoy the shine on the rump of a Munnings horse, the discretion of a Nicholson relief, the fresh-as-paint prettiness of a Susie Cooper teapot, the housewifely amateurishness of an Omega Workshops painted table,

the wit of a Shell poster: to chuck exclusive theories overboard. The makers could not; perhaps historians now can. Fifty years should be about the time it takes for the intellectual scaffolding around art to decay, fall away, be dismantled.

He tells you things about painting and how it's done that no one else thinks to tell you—of an Alice Neel nude self-portrait, for example: 'Her face is rather tight around the mouth, as a painter's face can be when reaching a decision about just how a detail seen in the mirror can be put down with the next stroke'—or maybe has noticed: 'It comes to you that when you can see a sitter's feet . . . the view is wide enough to let you in.' And why sometimes you don't want to be let in: 'Looking at her work in displays like these at the Tate,' he says of Louise Bourgeois, 'one feels to a degree excluded from what made her own work important to her. At times you are grateful. Some of the objects would like to enter your imagination by a back door that you might think it better to keep shut.'

He has his own ways too of making sense of artists' trajectories, the contexts and constraints of their careers—Bourgeois's or Titian's:

Bourgeois at one time or another met, often knew well, the great artists of her time . . . While they pursued single ways of making art—and were told that they stood on the threshold of a future in which modernism would advance with an assurance to match that of the thousand years of art that lay behind them—Bourgeois was playing Martha in the kitchen, cooking up art that seemed to be the work of a not-quite-in-tune follower of a whole string of them, but which now looks much more contrary.

On the one hand, Martha; on the other, the doge:

It is hard now to imagine the relationship between a painter made independent by great men competing for his services, and a ruler entranced by the artist's ability to give substance to the notion of embodied power—in images, moreover, which are from the same hand as those which show Mary assumed into the vault of heaven and the adventures of mythical heroes. Whatever the reality of these relationships, the fact that the painter had something of great value in his gift makes sense of anecdotes in which king and painter treat each other as equals—the one a real ruler, the other a ruler in the kingdom of representation.

'The finish is smooth, precise and brilliant,' he wrote of Ingres's portraits. 'The brush-strokes are hardly visible and you have to look closely to see how the paint was applied. It is as though these people had been expensively transformed by some cosmetic process into Ingres-flesh.' He was unusual in getting equal pleasure from the world and from its representation; from understanding Ingres-flesh and the anatomy of the stifftail duck. In the same way I imagine that he got equal pleasure from writing about pictures and from looking at them.

It is hard to believe that soon there will be paintings that aren't by Peter on the cover. It's only now when we explain to other people how the covers worked that we realise how spoiled we were. From time to time Peter would come into the office with a batch of watercolours under his arm, three or four in a big folder—'I've got some covers for you'—and go away before we looked at them. Usually there was one in the batch that Peter knew we wouldn't like: a figure, often a woman, often blonde with an air of the 1950s about her, almost always half-asleep. Sometimes it wasn't a woman but a man, say, with a flower in his hand, and those too we had trouble with. Peter would bring in the original drawing and a mock-up with words from a previous issue to show where the new words should go. Understandably, he didn't like the words—not the words we had chosen: any words at all—and there was an unstated war between covers that couldn't accommodate words and covers that were all words, as sometimes they had to be. Every other Thursday afternoon we would choose the cover for the next issue. The considerations were simple: season (no beaches in winter, no bare trees in summer); general appropriateness (no ice-cream sundaes in wartime); and how many pieces had to be signalled on the cover. Sometimes a cover would hang around for a year and suddenly find favour. There's one in the drawer now: a yellow coach parked at night beside a dark forest. I find it scary and keep taking it out and putting it back. The only literal connection I remember between a cover and the content was in an issue with the piece by Jenny Diski that eventually became her book *Skating to Antarctica*: Peter did a wonderful painting of the moon in its successive movements, rising and falling over a polar landscape. That may have been a pure coincidence (nobody can remember) and in any case the piece advertised on the rubric—it was the first issue of 1997—was Alan Bennett's 'What I did in 1996.' One thing Bennett didn't do was skate to Antarctica.

Flirting Is Nice

Amativeness was the cause of Isabella Robinson's disgrace:

Soon after they met in Edinburgh, Combe examined Isabella's skull. He informed her that she had an unusually large cerebellum, an organ found just above the hollow at the nape of the neck. The cerebellum, he explained, was the seat of Amativeness, or sexual love.

George Combe, natural philosopher and Edinburgh sage, was Scotland's—possibly Britain's—leading phrenologist. Men, he noted, had larger cerebella than women, 'discernible in their thicker necks, just as highly sexed animals such as rams, bulls and pigeons had fatter necks than other creatures'. And in men too a more than usually thick neck could lead to problems:

Another of Combe's subjects, the nine-year-old Prince of Wales, had a similarly shaped skull: when Queen Victoria and Prince Albert consulted the phrenologist about the upbringing of their children, he observed that the young prince's 'Amativeness is large and I suspect will soon give trouble'. Combe's own amative region, he said, was small—he had not known the 'wild freshness of morning', even in his youth.

Isabella's bumps were against her: Love of Approbation and Adhesiveness were too big; Cautiousness and Veneration too small. For her too, there was trouble in store. Few people would have noticed, however, and we would probably never have heard of her, were it not for the fact that she kept a diary and that her husband was one of the first people in England to petition the new, secular divorce court for the dissolution of their marriage.

She was born in London in 1813. Her grandfather had been accountant general to George III, her grandmother a coal-mining heiress: the family had cash. In 1837, when she was 24, she married a naval lieutenant in his forties, who died a few years later. That was her first unwise marriage. Henry Robinson, a Protestant from Northern Ireland, proposed twice before she accepted him—with 'almost open' eyes. By then her chances of finding a husband more to her liking were not good: she was 31, not pretty (we don't know what she looked like but she herself said 'plain'), and already had a child. She took what she could get and so too did Henry, who almost as soon as they were married asked Isabella to sign all her cheques and hand them over to him. She had two more children, lived comfortably in large houses in different parts of the country, spent time in Boulogne, read books, lost her faith, attended to her children's education, and flirted with their tutors (on some occasions 'seduced' would have been the right word). Kate Summerscale sees Isabella as an 'English Madame Bovary'. Henry, had he read Flaubert's novel, would have agreed and used it as he used her diary as proof of her unfitness to be his wife.

Almost everything we know about her comes from the diary. Not the diary as she wrote it, which Henry probably destroyed, but the extracts he chose to show her friends and have read out in court in evidence against her and that were quoted at length in the press and subsequently published in the official trial report: the material that was intended to bring about her disgrace—and on which Summerscale has based her book.

Edward Lane was 27 and three years married when Isabella fell for him: she was ten years older. Where Henry, in her account, was 'uneducated, narrow-minded, harsh-tempered, selfish, proud', Edward was 'handsome, lively and good-humoured'—in short, 'fascinating'. He talked about the things that interested her—literature, politics, philosophy, the latest this and the latest that. Henry 'had only a commercial life'. Boring middle-aged husband or good-looking young man: who would choose differently, given the nerve? Or the bump? 'A wish had taken hold of her,' Summerscale writes, 'and she was to find it hard to shake.' What makes her story unusual—or less familiar than it would otherwise be—is that she tells it herself; that it doesn't come in the form of a novel written by someone else, someone who would have felt for her, even claim to have identified with her, but punished her all the same.

In 1849, when they'd been married five years, the Robinsons moved to Edinburgh. By now, Summerscale tells us, Isabella knew that Henry had married her for her money, just as she knew he had a mistress and two illegitimate daughters. She despised him. She met Edward Lane not long after her arrival in Scotland, at the house—an open-house sort of house—of his widowed mother-in-law, Lady Drysdale, with whom he and his wife were living. Within a week or two of the encounter Isabella took a trip to the coast, and sitting on the beach, drew up an inventory of her defects:

my errors of youth, my provocations to my brothers and my sisters, my headstrong conduct to my governess, my disobedience and want of duty to my parents, my want of steady principle in life, the mode of my marriage and my conduct during that marriage, my partial and often violent conduct to my children, my giddy behaviour as a widow, my second marriage and all that had followed it.

The wish had taken hold and nothing she says suggests that Henry's infidelity had much to do with it. She liked to be in love; she also liked writing about it.

Lady Drysdale's guests, Isabella's new Edinburgh friends, were writers and intellectuals, artists and actresses. 'Progressive types', Summerscale calls them. Several were free-thinkers, proto-Darwinians—the publisher Robert Chambers, for example, secret author of *Vestiges of the Natural History of Creation*, and George Combe himself—though, like Darwin, they hesitated to spell it out. The Drysdales too saw the universe in largely materialist terms, finding it hard to believe in God—and painful, as well as inconvenient, not to. Edward Lane was training to be a doctor at the Edinburgh Royal Infirmary when Isabella met him. Convinced that the infirmary's gloomy surroundings made it difficult for patients to get better, he was drawn to what would now be seen as holistic medicine—the kind that involved clean air and exercise in nice surroundings—and a few years later found and acquired the perfect place in which to practise it: Moor Park, a water-cure establishment in large grounds near Farnham in Surrey. Hydropathy was fashionable, among intellectuals especially, and Darwin himself was briefly Edward's patient there; 'I am well convinced that the only thing for Chronic cases is the water cure,' he told his cousin.

Edward's three brothers-in-law, Lady Drysdale's sons, also studied medicine and became doctors; and like Edward, were not strictly orthodox in the manner of their practice. They were also in varying degrees social reformers, concerned to ease constraints on the mind as well as the body, to make things easier for women, and to acknowledge sexual desire. As a young man George Drysdale, the middle son, had been driven close to insanity by an urge to masturbate so overwhelming, and to him so shameful, that he staged his own disappearance in the course of a European walking tour, leaving his clothes on the banks of the Danube to suggest that he'd drowned. (Lord Cockburn, a family friend, feared the influence of *Young Werther* and 'a sudden Germanising of the noddle'.)

He reappeared in Edinburgh two years later, still not cured despite the excruciating interventions of a Hungarian surgeon; eventually a French physician suggested sexual intercourse and a Paris street-walker provided the cure. The good that came of his experience was a book about sex written in time taken off from his medical studies. Welcomed in the *People's Paper* as a 'Bible of the Body' and in the mainstream press as a 'Bible of the Brothel', it provided a guide to contraception, celebrated the relationship between free thought and free love, argued that sexual desire was as natural in women as in men, and marriage 'one of the chief instruments for the degradation of women'. Like many of these 'progressive types', George wrote his book in secret; his identity as its author wasn't revealed until his death in 1904. It was then in its 35th edition.

Isabella was not out of place in the company of the Lanes, the Combes, and the Drysdales. She was more radical than they were on the subjects that concerned her most—religion and marriage principally—but she was also more circumspect than everything that was said about her lack of self-control suggests. An essay about marriage in *Chambers's Edinburgh Journal*, entitled 'A Woman and Her Master', was most probably written by her, but prudently signed 'A Woman'. And when she wanted to publish her views about religion, she accepted Combe's advice and held back. 'You are clear-headed, forcible, & intellectually comprehensive in the power of penetrating into the relations of cause & effect, far beyond the average even of educated women,' he wrote to her, while advising her to remain silent. Later, when he decided to set down his own, more guarded opinions on the subject, phrenology somehow staving off the need for a complete rejection of God, she was one of the 'very, very few' whom he allowed to read the manuscript. (Another was George Eliot.) Were the essay's contents to be known, Combe warned, he would 'find it necessary to leave Edinburgh'. Isabella was not impressed by what she read, pointing out that unlike him she was 'obliged to . . . live without the cheering belief that a great and Beneficent Ruler exists whose mind is in relation with ours', but then added, as if to say 'I know my place': 'I fear, it is my own fault that I do not see with you on this point.' The great man had to be right even when he was wrong.

It is clear from her diary that she and Edward had many interests in common, that the relationship, whatever was later said, wasn't all kisses and impropriety; and clear, too, that in the right company any subject is grounds for a flirtation. The Lanes come to stay and at teatime Edward and she 'talked for an hour on politics, hereditary descent, funds, paupers, emigration etc'. In the evening they talk 'of Lord Byron, of riding, of courage, of balloons and of coolness'. As night falls and the moon comes up, they talk about 'man's spirit, his life, the grave, immortality, God, the universe, man's reason and his short fleeting nature'. She tells Edward that she is alone among her friends in not believing in 'all the illusions of the Christian's creed' and he confides his own doubts, telling her that 'he longed to pray, longed to believe.'

That day, Whit Sunday 1852, had been one of the best: in the morning, as Summerscale reports, 'they talked about "great men" such as Samuel Taylor Coleridge and George Combe.' Later Edward read her a passage from an essay on the imagination by Shelley; after lunch ('plucked pigeons laid on a bed of beef steak and baked in puff pastry') they went out for a walk and stopped 'a good while' by a swing—'Mr. L sent me very high; Mrs. L looking on.' Mrs. L was then called away and Edward and Isabella rested a while in the shelter of a steep bank: 'F, the spaniel, was on my lap, and Mr. L next me. It was the very scene I had often longed for and pictured to myself; but now it was realised.' At tea he sat next to her. In the evening Mrs. L went inside to sit by the fire while Isabella and Mr. L talked about God and his absence and Edward, 'entranced by the beauty of the scene', told her that he wished to stay out all night.

But he didn't. 'Soon after eleven', fearing that 'Mrs. L would think us unkind to leave her,' they went inside. When Henry's petition came to trial some years later his case against Isabella rested on two entries for October 1854. On the morning of 7 October, a Sunday, Edward asked her to walk with him in the grounds of Moor Park. They walked for a while, then sat down 'on a plaid' to talk and read: 'There was something unusual in his manner,' she wrote, 'something softer than usual in his tone and eye', but she didn't know 'what it proceeded from' and 'chatted gaily' about 'Goethe, women's dress and of what was becoming and suitable'. At the next stop a momentous thing happened: 'what followed I hardly remember –' she wrote. 'Passionate kisses, whispered words, confessions of the past. Oh, God! I had never hoped to see this hour, or to have my part of love returned. But so it was.' In the evening he came to find her in the library and there were more kisses, 'not unaccompanied with dread of intrusion. Yet bliss predominated' and when they parted for the night he gave her hand a shake 'so warm' that it crushed her fingers with the rings so that she 'felt it for an hour'.

The following day, another walk, another pause, and then something so tremendous it can't be written down—'I shall not state what followed.' Two days later the same tremendous thing took place in the covered cab taking her to the station. Edward was beside her, her son on top of the carriage, next to the driver. 'I shall not relate ALL that passed,' she noted, 'suffice it to say I leaned back at last in silent joy in those arms I had so often dreamed of.' Summerscale, disapproving, describes the scene as 'louche': 'Isabella's conduct in the carriage was especially shameless: a child, her son, was sitting on the roof while she and Edward Lane whispered and touched inside.'

That winter and the next Isabella spent with her family in Boulogne, where Henry had rented a house. Things were no longer going well. At their last meeting Edward had effectively told her their relationship was over: 'The Dr. came to my room and sat a long while talking coldly of life, reputation, chances, caution and my partner.' She tried her best, cut off a lock of his hair, told him how much she had always loved him, spoke of his 'fine face and mouth' and his 'love-telling eyes', but 'the interview closed without even a kiss.' The weather in Boulogne was awful, she rowed with Henry; none of the other young men available to flirt with, her sons' tutors principally, had Edward's love-telling eyes. She was miserable. In the spring of 1856, she fell ill, probably with diphtheria, and in her delirium gave herself away. Henry found her diary and vowed to destroy her.

Isabella returned to England alone with her eldest son, the one that wasn't Henry's. Barred from the family home, they rented rooms in Reigate. Everything that had been hers was now Henry's; she wasn't allowed to see the younger children. 'I was careless & thoughtless & so deserved to suffer,' she told Combe. However unhappy she was, however much she missed her children, the argument most often was internal, bump to bump. In the autumn she visited Moor Park to tell Edward what had happened, assuring him that she would do whatever she could to keep his part in the story a secret. The following year Henry was granted a judicial separation in the consistory court.

Isabella, as she'd promised Edward, didn't resist the suit and his name wasn't mentioned.

Extracts from her diary, meanwhile, were doing the rounds among their Edinburgh friends. Edward, aghast at what he read, denied everything. Isabella, he said, was 'a rhapsodical and vaporing fool'. He had never flirted with her; was easily bored in her company; had never written a line to her 'which might not be proclaimed at the market cross'. Everyone agreed that Henry was a beast—'the consummation of human meanness, paltriness, rascality and cruelty'—and to that extent Isabella's friends felt sorry for her, but each of them feared for his own reputation and no one stood by her. 'Mrs. Combe & I never liked her,' Combe asserted, and he didn't think she was brainy either (her 'deficient coronal region gave a cold low tone to her intellectual manifestations, that deprived her of all interest for us'). His only concern now was to save Edward (and extricate himself), which would be most simply achieved by persuading Isabella to plead insanity.

For a short time she angrily (and eloquently) resisted, denouncing first her husband and then all those, 'mere strangers, no ways authorised', who at Henry's behest had 'considered themselves at liberty to pry into, to peruse, to censure, to select from, my private writings, with curious, unchivalrous, ignoble hands'. She could no more have done that, she said, than she could have 'listened meanly to their prayers, their midnight whisperings in sleep, or their accents of delirium'. Then, as before, she gave in. In the last letter she would write to Combe she did as she'd been asked to do, and described the contents of her diary as 'the wildest imaginings of a mind exhausted with the tyranny of long years', effectively disowning what, apart from her children, had mattered most to her.

When it became public knowledge that Henry had applied to the new court for a divorce, Combe lobbied all the newspaper editors in

London on Edward's behalf, though he hardly needed to: everyone had already made up their mind—'Mrs. Robinson was crazy' and Dr. Lane 'entirely innocent'. Or, to put it differently, either Isabella was mad or she was, in the words of the *Times* leader writer, 'as foul and abandoned a creature as ever wore woman's shape'. (For the *Saturday Review* it was a matter of her 'luscious sentimentality'.) All her friends, or former friends, feared for their reputation. The medical press overcame its dislike of the sort of medicine Edward practised and lined up behind him. If Isabella's diary was accepted as evidence, the *British Medical Journal* argued, every doctor with a handsome face—and 'less favoured ones' too—might some day find himself 'plunged . . . into utter ruin'. I'd hoped that George Drysdale, who believed that in women as in men 'strong sexual appetites are a very great virtue,' might have spoken up for her, butI should have remembered how zealously he'd guarded his own secrets. Her lawyer—with little else to say—asserted that she was suffering from 'uterine disease', the catch-all for middle-class women whose behaviour was out of line, especially those women who liked men in the way that men like women.

Parliament took Edward's cause to heart and the Divorce Act was amended on his behalf, allowing him to appear as a mere witness rather than a co-respondent. Technically the issue was still adultery—on her part but, bizarrely, not his. What mattered was Isabella's bad character, her shamelessness, her morbid imagination, her lack of balance, her insanity—and Edward's innocence. (Combe, in London for the start of the trial, was taken ill and died before it was known that Edward wouldn't be implicated. The following day, the undertakers—Messrs. Sloman and Workman—removed his head from his body so that the skull could be subjected to phrenological analysis. His headless body travelled back to Edinburgh accompanied by his wife.)

The court granted its first divorce in May 1858. Henry's case was heard a month later. In September the judges delivered their verdict:

Isabella was not guilty and Henry, enraged, didn't get his divorce. The argument that the diary was not to be trusted, which had been used all along to exonerate Edward, was now used to exonerate Isabella. She wrote to please herself, the chief justice of the court said in his summing up: 'To statements so made it is not open to us to add anything by way of inference.' The verdict changed no one's mind: the journal was still a fiction; Isabella was still insane; and Edward had been vindicated. On the other hand, no one—apart from Henry—seems to have felt the need to punish her any further. She didn't take poison or throw herself under a train. What money she had when she died, she left to her favourite son, and when he died in 1930 he left half of his to German conscripts wounded in the First World War or, if that were to prove difficult, to soldiers injured by British forces in the Boer War. I suppose that should be taken as a message of sorts.

Whether she was an adulteress in reality or only in her own head, who's to say? The trial judge in his summing up described her as a 'woman of more than ordinary intelligence and of no inconsiderable attainments'. She was an intellectual of a kind, interested in the world, in ideas, in what other people were thinking and writing, and in her children. If she found her diary beguiling to write, it is also beguiling to read. Kate Summerscale is a gifted and informative storyteller; her only fault is to have made too much of the resemblance between Isabella and Emma Bovary, as if to pin her down in the hostile gaze of her contemporaries.

Book reviewed:

Mrs. Robinson's Disgrace: The Private Diary of a Victorian Lady by Kate Summerscale

What a Mother

Marianne Moore was born in her mother's childhood bedroom; grown up, she lived with her mother—most often shared her bed—until her mother died. She was then 59 and her mother 85; she lived another 25 years and died in 1972 a happy spinster, a famous poet, and a grande dame.

Mary Warner Moore—the mother in question—had scarcely had a mother, which must be to the point. The one she was born to died two years later and the aunt who replaced her was judged unsatisfactory and dismissed after less than a year—two mothers lost before she was three. The family was Scotch-Irish, stern, devout, and patriotic. Her father, Reverend Warner, was pastor to the Presbyterian church in Gettysburg; he watched the battle from a trapdoor in his roof and when it ended delivered his eyewitness account not only in churches and lecture halls up and down the East Coast, but in the House of Representatives with Lincoln himself in the audience.

It was said that Mary was 'a beauty' with many young men to choose among. That the one she decided on, John Moore, was known only for his sense of humour and love of the theatre is puzzling at first—she has seemed so earnest—but it turns out that performance was something she too enjoyed. Pretending to be someone or something else, preferably a small fluffy animal or a character from *The Wind in the Willows*, suited her well. Speaking in her own voice never got her as far. She married John Moore in 1885 in her father's church and settled down in a Boston suburb where Moore thought he had prospects. Marianne's brother, Warner, was born the following year. The prospects didn't materialise and by the time of Marianne's birth a year after that, John Moore was in an insane asylum. Mary left him to the care of his family and, children in tow, returned to her father.

Marianne never met her father and claimed not to know what he looked like until she was practically middle-aged (had no one told her about the red hair that the two of them shared?); asked what he did, she said she couldn't remember. There were no recriminations. Mary had what she wanted: her children to herself; and if either child gave any sign of minding we're not told of it here. 'We are the happiest people in the world,' the young Warner told his mother, who wasn't in the least surprised. The March sisters could well have said the same: happiness was a duty as well as a right in pre-Freudian America, an acknowledgment that God wished America well. But God, as Mary told her children, wished them and their mother especially well. 'Don't forget that we three are "a peculiar people",' she used to tell them. 'That is, according to the Scriptures, a people *set apart*.' A family, she would also say, whose members were so close to each other that 'we are like people interrupted in love-making the minute any outside persons come in.' It sounds ominous— Helen Vendler refers to 'the dreadful pathology' of the Moore household—but Linda Leavell speaks of a 'family idyll' in her illuminating biography and describes a memoir Marianne began many years afterwards as making 'a utopia of her childhood'. Being 'set apart' had its uses; and while Marianne sometimes chafed, she didn't complain. Her mother, she said many years later, was 'the least possessive of beings'. It's hard to know how she can have meant it but clear that she—sort of—did.

In that utopia nothing was straightforward. Words had their own usages, and ages and genders were never quite settled. Make-believe was pervasive. Early on Marianne decreed that she was Warner's brother not his sister, and in family letters (there are more than 30,000 in the Rosenbach archive in Philadelphia) she is consistently, and at all ages, referred to as 'he'. 'Although they assumed many different personae over the years,' Leavell writes, 'the one constant past childhood was Marianne's insistence that she be Warner's *brother* and hence *he* in the home language.'

Leavell doesn't speculate about these things. Freud and Co. aren't called on: the story tells itself. Warner, the sturdy male, was a less agile shape-shifter, but Mary was interchangeably Bunny and Fawn and on occasion stay-at-home Mole—always a delicate creature who had to be humoured and looked after by her 'two uncles'. 'If you had a family, you might go home, but as you're an orphan fawn I'm obliged to keep you, and do for you,' Marianne wrote in 1904. It's one instance among hundreds. Indulging their mother—making it a rule to put her concerns first—allowed Mary to get her own way and at the same time helped Marianne and her brother to bear it.

Mary didn't worry that her children would one day grow up and leave her: she determined early on that there would be no growing up. In the summer of 1911, she visited Europe for the first time (London and Paris principally), accompanied by Marianne. The high point of the trip, she told Warner, was a visit to Kensington Gardens to pay homage to Peter Pan. 'Since I am very indulgent to my childhood romances, and keep holiday with them almost religiously,' she wrote,

'*I just bowed the knee* and worshipped like the Oriental or the Romanist at the sound of prayer bells.' It was another role she'd assigned herself in the family fairy tale. 'Be a little child again,' she repeatedly advised Marianne, and with that in mind did her best to ensure that neither of her children, though both by now were college students, had interests that weren't communal, friends who weren't 'our kind', likes that weren't hers, thoughts she couldn't share. 'Remember how well Peter Pan flew, till he began to consider the manner of his flying,' she wrote to Warner: 'Oh! don't be introspective!' What she meant, I imagine, was 'don't keep anything from me.' Warner by then was 18.

Marianne enrolled at Bryn Mawr, the high-powered women's college in Pennsylvania, in 1905. When in her second year she developed a crush on her fellow student Peggy James, Mary 'courted' her too ('courted' is Leavell's word): William James's daughter was very much 'our kind', and since Mary expected her family to live together always, she could only assume that Peggy would be joining the household—whether as Marianne's partner or Warner's was immaterial. But Marianne's feelings for Peggy wore off—'I shan't play with Peggy anymore'—and there wouldn't be anyone else, of either sex, in Marianne's life for Mary to court. Not then and not later. Her masculine appearance was commented on, maybe unfairly—she wore big jackets. She had never weighed enough, she would say later, to be 'matrimonially ambitious'.

From Mary's point of view Bryn Mawr was safe; it wasn't far away and the terrain was familiar: she too had taught at women's colleges and had crushes on her fellow teachers and students (see below). Though she was less close to Warner, his departure for Yale in 1904 had been more upsetting. 'It is sad almost to the degree of unbearable to think the old life is gone,' she wrote to him. The rituals of college life—football, dating—were so alien she didn't even have the vocabulary with which to disparage them, and the prevailing secularism only made everything worse. 'O I wish I wish you were not out on the wild wild sea of "this generation",' she wrote a few weeks later.

Punishing Warner for being too much a boy didn't stop there. When he decided to buy a car—he was by now 28 and a clergyman like his grandfather—Marianne wrote to warn him of the danger his getting a car would pose to Mary's health: 'It would seem morbid to you perhaps to think that Mole could get sick again because you thought of getting a car but . . . it isn't so unreasonable, for Mole would wish that without a suggestion from anyone you ought to know just what is unsuitable.' When a little later he decided to marry, Mary wrote to her future daughter-in-law to warn her that she didn't approve of the match. She expected to be listened to but she wasn't. When eventually she came to terms with the new arrangement Warner, by this point on the cusp of middle age, described himself as 'a sick, sick boy, coming to life'.

The rules were different for Mary. Sometime in the course of 1900, before either of her children had left home, she began a relationship with another English teacher, a woman called Mary Norcross, younger than her, a friend of the family, again 'our kind'. Being in love with a woman, sleeping together, sometimes living together: none of it was a big deal, Leavell stresses. There was a lot of that sort of thing around and no one called it 'lesbianism'. For ten years Norcross was like a fourth member of the family; then at the end of 1909 she fell in love with a rich cousin. Mary was distraught and Marianne was trapped: 'You can certainly feel assured that you were never more needed in your life and probably never will be more needed than you are just this winter by the Fawn,' Norcross wrote to her in September 1910. She would live with her mother for a further 37 years, playing 'the role', as Leavell puts it, 'of indulgent Uncle to her adorable Bunny'.

'The Paper Nautilus', Marianne's most nearly autobiographical poem, published in 1940, describes the 'thin glass shell' secreted by the mother for herself and her eggs, a kind of hatchery. It would be a challenge to read it without thinking of Mary recalling Marianne to the shell and the pair crawling inside like two cephalopods recolonising the nursery. The first stanza speaks of entrapment but in the last lines the argonaut clinging to its little edifice suggests that

> love
> is the only fortress
> strong enough to trust to.

Love, it seems, is something Marianne is allowed to experience only in the form Mary wished her to experience it—as her mother's daughter and Warner's sister/brother.

Marianne first published some of her poems in *Tipyn o'Bob*, the Bryn Mawr student magazine; jaunty, decidedly un-introspective poems like this:

> He often expressed
> A curious wish;
> To be interchangeably
> Man and fish;
> To nibble the bait
> Off the hook,
> Said he,
> And then slip away
> Like a ghost
> In the sea.

It was 'impersonal' and to her mind 'unforced'. (The first draft was written in a philosophy class and called 'The Bored Lady'—the eventual title was 'Ennui'.) Though simpler, it wasn't very different from the later poems that would lead Eliot to place her 'among the half-dozen most "exciting" contemporary European and American poets'. Asked about the poem's meaning by one of her teachers, she skirted the question and said 'that it was simply living in the pleasure of the moment'. 'I am governed by the pull of a sentence as the pull of a fabric is governed by gravity,' she would tell the *Paris Review* several decades later—the interviewer was the poet Donald Hall. Her teachers for the most part had more old-fashioned tastes; and the writers they admired tended not to be the same as those—Browning, Yeats, James—she would pick out. She had no time for Edwardian sentiment and shied away from the prevailing pieties. When, a few years on, Mary complained of a lack in her daughter's work of the 'stinging greatness of truth and high principle', Marianne was unfazed: 'spiritual aspiration, love and meditation,' she remarked, 'are themes no puppy can do justice to.' The full-grown dog would have much the same view.

In 1907, while still a student, she was invited by a friend to spend a few days in New York. A letter to her mother more than 150 pages long described in prodigious detail what she'd seen in the city—the layout of the Tiffany shop as well as the jewellery, the design of Carnegie Hall as well as the concert. This interest in things to the side of things, in 'the fringe of the important fact', as Marianne put it, hadn't helped her get good grades (her academic work, one teacher said, was 'like unsettled coffee') but it would in time define her poetry; its movement from one apparently unconnected fact to another, one quotation to another, one image to another, allowing her, Leavell writes, 'to let the rhythm of a poem create the mood even if her readers missed the "meaning".' 'Neatness of finish! Neatness of finish!' she exclaimed in 'An Octopus':

> Relentless accuracy is the nature of this octopus
> with its capacity for fact.

Asked by Donald Hall how she came 'to be an artist', she replied: 'Endless curiosity, observation, research—and a great amount of joy in the thing.'

In place of a diary she kept a notebook—'I salvage anything promising and set it down in a small notebook.' She didn't use it to write about her feelings or about herself. She was interested in the fate of her poems, not in the mood she was in. Her mother had warned against introspection; consciously or unconsciously, she'd taken the lesson to heart. Or perhaps she didn't need a lesson. Ideas, attitudes to this and that were more rewarding, and more fun to think about and make fun of, even her own. But words principally gave her pleasure. Sentences, metaphors, tropes, her own—she worked constantly at them—and other people's, including her mother's, were noted down and reappear in the poems, which borrow many of Mary's mannerisms as well as those of the home language more generally: not its sentimentality but its histrionic tone and nursery décor and its tendency to metonymise and otherwise play with figures of speech. Like Wallace Stevens, whom she much admired, she made jokes, and even more than in Stevens's case, the jokes were sly, hardly perceptible, there for her own pleasure. Yet for all the ironies, visible and invisible, some of the poems even have a moral.

She graduated in 1909 and over the next five years, while working in one clerical job or another, weathered the rejections of every magazine that published poetry other than the Bryn Mawr literary annual. The first editor to recognise her work was Floyd Dell, at the *Masses*; he didn't want to publish her—or not yet—but he saw what she was trying to do and wrote to tell her so. That was in March 1914. It was the first acknowledgment she received, and it augured a change in her—or in modernism's—fortunes. In July, Harriet Monroe, the editor of *Poetry*, accepted five poems; in April 1915 two of her poems appeared in the *Egoist*, the paper Richard Aldington edited ('I am so delighted to have them take me I shouldn't mind if they charged me'); in August, HD invited her to come to London (she didn't take up the invitation); and in October Alfred Kreymborg, the editor of *Others*, took five poems—these were all magazines whose modernist line she approved of and whose contents she'd carefully studied. In November, invited again to spend a few days in New York (Mary was also asked but they claimed not to be able to afford two sets of new clothes), she 'made her modernist debut', as Leavell puts it, meeting artists, poets, editors—people whom she understood and who understood her. Ten days later she returned full of excitement to the small town in Pennsylvania where Mary and she were then living. 'He knows not what he eats nor what he sees at Riverbank,' Mary reported to Warner, 'can think only of the edge of the great sea, where he has sojourned. I look very gravely, not to say sternly, at some of the experiences unfurled—and think I ought to have taken the scull myself . . . after eleven . . . I stuck him into the tub, and he subsided partially until he was taken out and dried when away [his tongue] went fast as ever.' That's how it would be from now on. One minute hobnobbing with the poets and editors in New York, the next minute babbling in the tub with the Bunny.

Mary didn't understand her daughter's poetry. Marianne's 'dogged pursuit of unconventional metre', Leavell explains, 'unsentimental subject matter and cryptic language ran counter to all that her English-teacher mother held dear'. Mary expected poems to have a meaning and as far as she could see there was very little meaning in Marianne's work. Her first collection—*Poems*—came out in 1921. She hadn't wanted a book published (Bryher arranged it behind her back): there were too few poems (24 in all) and the moment wasn't right. Reviewers in the mainstream press who accused her of 'superficial unconventionality' proved her point. Mary, no less perplexed, accounted for her bewilderment by likening the collection to 'a veiled Mohammedan woman', an image that expressed both the distance between the two women and the pleasure in language that they shared. Mary had always been fussy about the way her children spoke ('language was never a trivial matter to the Moores'); and whatever the content of Marianne's poems, her diction at least was as precise and grammatically correct as her English-teacher mother could have wished. Right to the end she showed Mary everything she wrote before any outsider was allowed to see it and would change a word if Mary thought she had used it wrongly. No poem left the house unless she sanctioned it. 'Last evening my hair turned grey, and I took on ten years, when I had to say that poems he has worked on for months,—for days unremittingly and speechlessly—were not just right yet,' Mary wrote to Warner on 18 June 1921. 'I was determined to finish some poems for the *Dial*,' Marianne wrote to him the next day, 'but Mole doesn't commend them for presenting so I have painfully and reluctantly scrapped them.' Yet Leavell is adamant that Marianne didn't want her work to have her mother's approval. She did and she didn't: she did and didn't want to be understood. In 'An Ardent Platonist', an unusually messy poem published in 1918 and never reprinted though often quoted by critics trying to describe Marianne's relationship to her work, and to her mother, she wrote:

> to
> understand
> One is not to find one formidable . . .
>   to be philosophical is to be no
>   longer mysterious; it is to be no
> Longer privileged, to say what one thinks in
>   order to be understood.

The veiled Mohammedan woman stood at the gate.

    Mother and daughter moved to New York in 1918. In the small

towns in New Jersey and Pennsylvania where they'd lived until then Marianne was seen as 'a rather mousy little person' with nothing much to say for herself. In New York a wand was waved; and in the company of her fellow modernists she turned into an 'astonishing' figure 'with Titian hair . . . and a mellifluous flow of polysyllables which held every man in awe' (as Kreymborg described her). After the five lean years during which no editor bothered to acknowledge her poems almost everyone (of her kind) wanted to publish them. Though some found Marianne prim, her devotion to her mother annoying, her opinions too fierce, no one now ignored her. The heroes of modernist poetry each praised her verse for what he himself set most store by. For William Carlos Williams, she had achieved modernism's 'unbridled leap'; for Eliot she was an enduring member of the 'tradition'; for Stevens a romantic; and for Pound someone who had resisted the romantic impulse from the start. Both Pound and Eliot championed her. She was even being paid for her work.

But for all that a wand had been waved there were no pumpkins turned into carriages waiting at the door of the apartment they rented when they got to New York. They lived as if they didn't quite know how to do it, not as bohemians but as characters in a fairy tale who might prefer to have a white marble fireplace than a bed to themselves. The apartment was on a pretty street in Greenwich Village, and that was important, but it was also below ground, had only one room and that barely big enough for a bed, a sofa, and some chairs; there was no kitchen, no fridge, no phone: 'Mary prepared meals on a hotplate in the bathroom throughout the 11 years they lived there,' Leavell reports. They ate the meals sitting on the edge of the bath or in the bath itself. Although Mary constantly worried that Marianne was too thin, too frail, too delicate ('my mother comes in 16 times a day bringing me apples and things to eat'), her attitude to food was all her own: on one occasion she 'planned to serve onions and prunes for lunch. Then she decided to invite a guest and scraped together a menu of cooked apples, canned corn, salad dressing and cocoa.'

The various poetry magazines and their crowds came and went—*Others*, the one to which Marianne had been closest, ceased publication in 1919, so did the *Egoist*, but Scofield Thayer, Marianne's staunchest advocate, took over the *Dial* and in 1925 asked her to be its acting editor while he went to Vienna to be psychoanalysed by Freud. Two years later when his shaky grip on reality obliged him to resign, Marianne took his place. Asked by Donald Hall what had made the *Dial* such a good paper in the years when she was editing it, she said 'lack of fear': 'We didn't care what other people said . . . Everybody liked what he was doing and when we made grievous mistakes we were sorry but we laughed over them.' (How bad were those mistakes, I wonder, and did everyone really laugh?) In *'The Dial*: A Retrospect' Marianne makes out that it was even more fun for everyone when Thayer was in charge: 'there was for us of the staff, whatever the impression outside, a constant atmosphere of excited triumph; and from editor or publisher, inherent fireworks of parenthetic wit too good to print.' Her own editorship was steadier and more modest than Thayer's and sometimes it doesn't get the credit it deserves—especially, Leavell implies, from men. Yet in his autobiography the hyperbolic Williams describes Marianne as 'a rafter holding up the superstructure of our uncompleted building, a caryatid . . . our saint—if we had one—in whom we all felt instinctively our purpose come together to form a stream'.

In 1929 the *Dial* ceased publication. Of the two owners, one was mad and the other, James Sibley Watson, a rich philanthropist, had new interests. Marianne, who wasn't pleased, chose to describe the decision as 'largely chivalry' on their part: 'I didn't have time for work of my own,' she told George Saintsbury, the English man of letters, who'd been one of her contributors. At Warner's insistence, she and her mother left Greenwich Village for a more suitable—'spacious' would be the word—apartment in Brooklyn: they could have had a bed each had they wanted to. Marianne hadn't written any poems since 'The Monkey Puzzle' in 1924 and wouldn't write any now until she gave 'Poetry', or a version of it (as always there were many), to Harriet Monroe in 1931. Time passed; bursitis, bronchitis, laryngitis filled the day as first Mary, then Marianne, and sometimes the two at the same time would take to the bed. For Mary illness offered a further call on Marianne's sympathy; for Marianne it provided a moment of calm in which to write. But as her connection with the world began to fade (there would be a late rebound) the poems were more inclined to speak plainly, or even preach; to come closer, in other words, to something Mary might like.

In 1935 Faber published Marianne's *Selected Poems*. Eliot himself wrote the introduction; and it was there that he spoke of her work forming 'part of the small body of durable poetry written in our time'—the quote reproduced on the cover of every edition of her poems. To begin with Mary 'deplored' the selection: she 'investigated me till my very fleas blushed and I had to do over a great deal of the work,' Marianne told her brother as she got out the 'synonym books and small dictionaries' that she and her mother had used when they were editing her prose—and other people's—for the *Dial*. Marianne had told Thayer at the start of her editorship that she wouldn't have time to see contributors or to write letters. By the end answering letters filled her day: Mary drafted them, Marianne spent hours perfecting them. 'Readers of the *Dial*,' Leavell writes, 'would have been shocked to learn the extent of Mary's involvement,' but readers of her own book would have been surprised had that not been the case. 'Mon dieu! What a mother,' Alyse Gregory, who'd worked at the *Dial* and was, more than anyone, Marianne's friend, wrote to Thayer: 'so large, pale, refined, washed over by the years, but inexorably, permanently, eternally rooted and not to be

overlooked, and remorselessly conversational, sentences with no beginning and no end, and no place left to jump in and stop them'. Mary's
presence is no less insistent in Leavell's book: every time you want
to say something about Marianne, you find yourself confronted with
her mother.

Mary died in 1947; Marianne, worn down by years of anxiety on
Mary's behalf, went to pieces:

> She dropped things, lost things, and broke things. Her hair
> whitened. Her skin sagged. Crying made her eyes puffy. She looked
> exhausted and old beyond her sixty years. In the company of others
> she ate well but at home ate little because she so hated dining alone.

Warner took matters in hand. Not long before she'd been photographed
by Cecil Beaton for *Vogue*. Far from being flattered she thought she
looked terrible. 'Now, now my boy,' Warner wrote to her, 'you and I *can*
do something about "that face".' Bit by bit, massage by massage, facial
by facial, homage by homage she recovered. In September she moved
out of the bedroom she'd shared with her mother.

Fame came in a rush. Leavell dates it to 28 February 1950, when
she addressed a 'large, formally attired' audience at the Museum of
Modern Art, sharing a double bill with Auden. In 1952 her *Collected
Poems* won the National Book Award, the Bollingen Prize, and the
Pulitzer Prize; *Life* magazine published a photo essay in their issue
of 21 September 1953; in 1957 she was profiled (not very flatteringly)
in the *New Yorker*. In 1968 she threw out the ball at the Yankee
stadium to inaugurate the new baseball season (she'd always been a
Dodgers fan) and wrote the liner notes for Cassius Clay's *I Am the
Greatest*. She met Norman Mailer, 'whom she liked immensely', and
George Plimpton and James Baldwin, 'a fine youth'; in 1968 Harry
Belafonte invited her onto *The Tonight Show* along with Petula Clark

and Dionne Warwick; he had been going to ask Robert Kennedy but didn't because she hadn't liked his brother—she was a supporter of Eisenhower and Nixon but also of LBJ, calling herself 'one of his most fervent admirers', Vietnam and all. She was an old lady now, New York State's Senior Citizen of the Year for 1969, both the wrong kind of woman, an insider, and the wrong kind of poet—an elite figure, a poets' poet. Anne Sexton and Adrienne Rich counted for more, as Leavell points out with some displeasure. Her mother had consistently worried that Marianne was too susceptible to other people's attention; that she was too fragile to go out into the world, that it was bad for her health to leave the house, to meet new people, to attend a large gathering. But it seems that few other poets, women poets especially, have enjoyed the world so wholeheartedly or received from it such a ringing endorsement.

Book reviewed:

Holding On Upside Down: The Life and Work of Marianne Moore by Linda Leavell

ACKNOWLEDGMENTS

I'd like to thank everyone who had a hand in giving these pieces a second life: Sue Barrett, Paul Forty, Andrew Franklin, Deborah Friedell, Jeremy Harding, John Lanchester, Jean McNicol, Andrew O'Hagan, and Nicholas Spice. I am also grateful to the editors, including myself, of the publications in which they first appeared.

CREDITS

The pieces reprinted here were first published as follows:

I Was Dilapidated: *Listener*, 4 May 1972

Civis Britannicus Fuit: *New Review*, April 1976

Next to Godliness: *New Yorker*, October 1979

The Language of Novel Reviewing: *The State of the Language*, eds. Leonard Michaels and Christopher Ricks, 1980

Narcissism and Its Discontents: *London Review of Books*, 21 February 1980

Death and the Maiden: *London Review of Books*, 6 August 1981

Divorce Me: *London Review of Books*, 17 December 1981

Patty and Cin: *London Review of Books*, 6 May 1982

Hagiography: *London Review of Books*, 3 March 1983

Vita Longa: *London Review of Books*, 1 December 1983

Sisters' Keepers: *London Review of Books*, 7 June 1984

Fortress Freud: *London Review of Books*, 18 April 1985

Lady Rothermere's Fan: *London Review of Books*, 7 November 1985

Quarrelling: *London Review of Books*, 29 October 1987

Promises: *London Review of Books*, 10 November 1988

Nonchalance: *London Review of Books*, 27 July 1989
Attraction Duty: *London Review of Books*, 10 October 1991
My Distant Relative: *London Review of Books*, 4 August 1994
Brussels: *London Review of Books*, 29 July 1999
What If You Hadn't Been Home: *London Review of Books*, 3 November 2011
Peter Campbell: *London Review of Books*, 17 November 2011
Flirting Is Nice: *London Review of Books*, 11 October 2012
What a Mother: *London Review of Books*, 3 December 2015

Mary-Kay Wilmers cofounded the *London Review of Books* in 1979 and has been its sole editor since 1992. After a childhood spent in the United States, Belgium, and England, Wilmers went to Oxford to read French and Russian. Initially planning on a career as an interpreter, she instead found work as a secretary at Faber & Faber in the time of T. S. Eliot, then moved on to *The Listener* and *The Times Literary Supplement*, and contributed to the *New Statesman*, before cofounding the *LRB*. She is the author of *The Eitingons: A Twentieth-Century Family*, a book about her family and their Cold War deeds and misdeeds, which *The Telegraph* called "transfixingly readable."